HOW TO LOCK-IN A PERFECT GOLF SWING

The Introduction of Thirty-Two Unique and Revolutionary Techniques to Lock-In

- A Perfect Grip
- A Perfect Alignment
- A Perfect Swing

GORDON JACKSON

Author of *HOW TO HIT A GOLF BALL AS STRAIGHT-AS-AN-ARROW* and *HOW GOLF WORKS*

HOW TO LOCK-IN
A PERFECT GOLF SWING

All inquiries should be to:
LOCKED-IN GOLF, INC.
3443 Pinebrake Cove
Memphis, Tennessee 38125

Cover design and layout: Ad Graphics, Inc. – www.TheBookProducer.com
Photos: James Stewart
Printed in the United States of America

ISBN: 978-0-9673304-1-9

DEDICATION

This book is dedicated to my grandchildren whom I hope will enjoy the game of golf as passionately as I have through my lifetime: Alex Suddoth, Peyton Schelp, Carson Schelp, Josh Autry, Chandler Schelp, Bryce Autry, Jackson Isham and Charles Isham.

CONTENTS

PREFACE

Unbeknownst to golfers and instructors alike, the basic flaw relating to golf is the instant you complete a conventional style of grip, your forearms will rotate your elbows to the inside of your shoulder line and your wrists and clubface to an open alignment – assuming there is no clubface rotation during the gripping process.

In other words, whether you prefer an original Vardon overlap, a modified Vardon overlap, traditional interlock or regular (ten-fingers) baseball style of grip, the instant your grip is completed, your forearms will rotate your wrists, clubface and elbows to establish a slice ball flight alignment when there is no clubface rotation during the gripping proceedings.

Once a conventional style of grip is completed (absent any clubface rotation during the gripping process), almost any body movement thereafter, such as widening or narrowing your stance, flexing your knees up or down, raising or lowering your shoulders or arms, or hinging, rotating, arching or cupping your wrists, will cause your forearms to rotate your wrists, clubface and elbows to some extent.

Depending on the type and extent of body movement in such instance, your forearms could rotate your wrists, clubface and elbows to establish either a hook, pull, push, pulled hook, pushed slice, a possible straight or even a more pronounced slice ball flight alignment.

This unbeknownst phenomenon that your forearms will rotate your wrists, clubface and elbows to a variety of ball flight alignments in response to various body movements after a conventional style of grip is formed on a club is what has led to an epidemic of frustration and inconsistency among golfers since the inception of the sport.

It is the very reason why more than ninety percent of golfers are unable to break "90" on a championship course if all strokes are counted, even if their very lives depended on it. It is the reason why average golfers never improve after three years of play.

However, when you understand specifically how and how much to move certain body parts to cause your forearms to rotate your wrists, clubface and elbows to establish and lock-in a straight ball flight alignment you no longer will be frustrated. Your shot making will no longer be inconsistent.

This book instructs you how to move specific body parts to cause your forearms to rotate your wrists, clubface and elbows from a slice ball flight alignment (established the instant a conventional style of grip is assembled on a club) to a straight ball flight alignment during your pre-swing routine.

Not only does this book instruct you how to convert a slice ball flight alignment to a straight ball flight alignment, it will teach you how to secure and lock-in a straight ball flight alignment, once established. This will prevent your forearms from rotating your wrists, clubface and elbows to a different ball flight alignment during the remainder of your pre-swing routine and your backswing.

This Book Introduces and Explains Thirty-Two Techniques to Rotate Your Forearms, Wrists, Clubface and Elbows to Establish and Lock-in a Straight Ball Flight Alignment

Ben Hogan, among many other legendary golfers, was known to remark that the golf swing is ninety percent completed before it even begins.

This particularly is the case when you have established and locked-in a straight ball flight alignment at the completion of your pre-shot routine. In order to lock-in a straight ball flight alignment, however, you must do more than move some body part in a specific manner after a conventional style of grip is formed on a club.

Once you have moved some body part in a precise manner to cause your forearms to rotate your wrists, clubface and elbows from a slice ball flight alignment to establish a straight ball flight alignment during your address proceedings, you must then unlock the lifeline portion of your trail hand from your lead thumb (without completely ungripping your club) and then relock the lifeline portion of your trail hand on your lead thumb a precise number of times to secure and lock-in the straight ball flight alignment established at that point.

The Magic of the Locked-In Techniques™

The LOCKED-IN TECHNIQUES™ addressed in this book re-align the forearm bones, elbow bones and wrist bones to a straight ball flight alignment during the pre-swing proceedings.

Proper bone alignment is what establishes a straight ball flight alignment whether such alignment occurs <u>before</u> or <u>during</u> a golf swing.

It is much easier and far more reliable to align your forearms and in turn, your wrists, clubface and elbows, to establish and lock-in a straight ball flight alignment before your golf swing begins rather than during your golf swing.

The techniques introduced and explained in this book rely on proper bone alignment at final address, not on some "muscle-memory" in an attempt to compensate for a misaligned clubface and an off-line swing path during the golf swing.

When the forearms, wrists, clubface and elbows are rotated to establish and lock-in a straight ball flight alignment at final address, any such compensating movement of the clubface during the downswing will serve only to destroy the straight ball flight alignment established at final address.

The Shoulders Must Be Aligned Squarely Parallel with the Target Line When Using the Locked-In Techniques™

More is required than to establish and lock-in a straight ball flight alignment at final address in order to produce a straight ball flight to a specific target.

In addition, the shoulders must be aligned squarely parallel with the target line and, simultaneously, the sweet spot of the clubface must be centered as near the back of the ball as possible at final address, followed by the execution of a non-manipulative golf swing.

Centering the sweet spot of a clubface as near the back of the ball as possible without allowing it to move in the process is not a difficult task. Aligning the shoulders squarely parallel with the target line is much more complex.

The conventional method of aligning the shoulders parallel with the target line involves far too much guesswork for the average recreational and weekend golfer.

This book presents an easier and far more reliable means to accomplish one of the most critical and essential alignments during the pre-swing proceedings: aligning the shoulders squarely parallel with the intended target line. This unique and innovative method is characterized as the ARROW ALIGNMENT TECHNIQUE™.

You should find the ARROW ALIGNMENT TECHNIQUE™ as fascinating as I did when first discovering it. It is addressed in detail in Chapter Three.

As noted earlier, this book presents thirty-two ways to cause the forearms to rotate the wrists, clubface and elbows from a slice ball flight alignment (the instant a conventional grip is assembled absent any clubface rotation during the gripping process) to establish and lock-in a straight ball flight alignment. When a straight ball flight alignment is not established and locked-in at the completion of the pre-swing routine, the clubface then must be manipulated in some way before or during the golf swing to deliver a square clubface to the ball on an on-line swing path to produce a straight ball golf shot.

Although professional golfers have learned how to use certain compensating movements during their golf swings to re-route their clubfaces to a square alignment and an on-line swing path by the time of impact, such an approach is far too difficult for the average recreational and weekend golfer.

What Happens When There Is Some Clubface Rotation During the Gripping Proceedings?

Typically when there is rotation of the clubface during the gripping process, it will cause the forearms to rotate the wrists, clubface and elbows to a more severe slice ball flight alignment or perhaps to a hook, push, pull, pushed slice or pulled hook ball flight alignment and prevent the forearms to rotate the wrists, clubface and elbows to establish a straight ball flight alignment by some specific movement of a body part after the grip is completed. Moreover, the clubface alignment and swing path will be subject to rotating to other ball flight alignments thereafter in response to additional body movements.

However, when there is no clubface rotation during the time the lead hand and trail hand are assembled on a club but there is some specific body movement between the time the lead hand and trail hand are gripped on a club, the forearms will rotate the wrists, clubface and elbows to establish a straight ball flight alignment.

A companion book, HOW TO HIT A GOLF BALL AS STRAIGHT-AS-AN-ARROW, introduces and teaches thirty ways to move certain body parts in a specific way between the time the lead and trail hands are gripped on a club to align the wrists and in turn, the clubface, squarely and the elbows parallel with the shoulders to establish a straight ball flight alignment during the pre-shot proceedings.

Specifically, in each of the thirty techniques addressed in HOW TO HIT A GOLF BALL AS STRAIGHT-AS-AN-ARROW, there purposely is some clubface rotation between the time the lead hand and trail hand are gripped on a club.

The techniques addressed in this book are different in that some specific body part purposely is moved and the clubface is rotated in a certain way after a conventional style of grip is assembled on a club by both hands.

In determining whether a straight ball flight alignment is established and locked-in as a result of one of the thirty-two techniques discussed in this book or one of the thirty techniques addressed in HOW TO HIT A GOLF BALL AS STRAIGHT-AS-AN-ARROW, there must be some way to test whether a straight ball flight alignment truly is established and locked-in at the conclusion of the proceedings. Considering only one misstep during the procedure can compromise an otherwise straight ball flight alignment and change it into another and typically less desirable alignment, some type of test is imperative.

Chapter Two explains several tests that can be conducted at the completion of each of the thirty-two techniques addressed in this book to determine whether a straight ball flight alignment truly has been established and locked-in at the completion of the proceedings. Such confirmation tests as the SHOULDERS ONLY TEST™, ARMS-LIFT TEST™ and STRAIGHT-UP TEST™ also are explained in the companion books, HOW TO HIT A GOLF BALL AS STRAIGHT-AS-AN-ARROW and HOW GOLF WORKS.

Locked-In Terminology

There are specific terms I prefer to use when teaching the unique and revolutionary techniques introduced in this book.

For example, instead of stating "left hand for right-handers and right hand for left-handers" throughout the book, I prefer to use the term "lead" when describing parts of the body nearest the target and the term "trail" when referring to parts of the body farthest from the target.

Although it may take a short time for readers to adjust to such terms, it provides a less cumbersome way to instruct the many concepts, techniques and tests addressed in this book.

I nonetheless prefer to use more conventional terminology to describe various mechanics of the game.

For example, I prefer to use the term "downswing" instead of "throughswing." If you prefer "throughswing" to "downswing," just transpose the terms in your own mind as you read the text. I prefer the term "backswing" instead of "upswing." If you prefer the latter, merely transpose the terms in your own mind when you read them in the book.

I do not subscribe to such new terms as a "pulled slice." A slice is a slice. I do not understand why it is necessary to confuse a slice with a pull when a pull designs a different pattern of ball flight. There are but seven types of ball flight as John Jacobs describes in the book, THE GOLF SWING SIMPLIFIED: a straight, slice, hook, pull, push, pulled hook or pushed slice ball flight. All other terms relating to ball flight merely are variations of one of the seven. For example, a fade is a slight slice and a draw is a slight hook.

Attempting to give equal treatment to the male and female genders also can be cumbersome, such as he and she, him or her, she and him and her and him. I attempt to provide equal treatment to such terms by using them alternatively but much prefer to use the plural of both, such as they, them or theirs.

This Book Will Change Your Golfing Life and Lower Your Golf Scores

Wouldn't it be fascinating and refreshing to know why you produce an incredible golf shot at times and also to know how to repeat it.

This book will teach you how to do just that: how to establish and lock-in a straight ball flight alignment during your pre-shot routine, then center your clubface correctly behind your ball and, simultaneously, align your shoulders squarely parallel with your target line, at final address. All that will remain will be to allow the clubface to swing on its established path without any forced manipulation during the golf swing and your ball will fly on a straight path to your target, discounting wind conditions and elevation differentials.

This book will remove the frustration, anxiety and stress most golfers encounter on a continuing basis: repeating the same mechanics that produce wayward golf shots and expecting a different result – typically referred to as the "Golfer's Insanity."

When you are able to stand on the first tee in a round of golf, knowing precisely how to assemble and execute your favorite LOCKED-IN TECHNIQUE™, understanding how to test it, how to center your clubface properly behind your ball, how to align your shoulders squarely parallel with your target line and then how to allow your clubface to swing naturally on its established path without any compensating or manipulative movements during your golf swing, your golfing days will never be the same.

You will free yourself forever from the "Golfer's Insanity."

Gordon Jackson

CHAPTER 1

THE VARDON CURSE

A vast majority of golfers, worldwide, prefer to use the Vardon overlap style of golf grip; either that of the original or modified Vardon overlap.

A minority of golfers prefer either the traditional interlock or regular baseball (ten-fingers) style of grip.

I refer to the original Vardon overlap, modified Vardon overlap, traditional interlock and regular baseball (ten-fingers) styles of grip as "conventional" golf grips.

The original and modified Vardon, traditional interlock and regular baseball (ten-fingers) styles of golf grips have a common denominator. The instant they are formed on a golf club they misalign the clubface and its swing path.

Conventional Styles of Golf Grip Establish a Slice Ball Flight Alignment

Whether you prefer an original Vardon overlap, modified Vardon overlap, traditional interlock or regular baseball (ten-fingers) style of grip, the instant each is assembled your forearms will rotate your wrists and in turn, your clubface, to an open alignment and your elbows to an outside-to-inside swing path across your shoulders to establish a slice ball flight alignment, assuming there is no clubface rotation during the gripping process.

If your wrists and elbows are not thereafter rotated to establish a different alignment and swing path before your clubface contacts the ball, you will slice your golf shot. The problem is almost any body movement after a conventional golf grip is assembled on a club will cause the forearms to rotate the wrists, clubface and elbows either to a hook, push, pull, pushed slice, pulled hook or a more severe slice ball flight alignment, assuming once again there is no clubface rotation from the beginning to the end of the gripping proceedings. There also is a remote possibility the wrists, clubface and elbows will rotate to establish a straight ball flight alignment as a result of some body movement once a conventional style of grip is assembled on a club – as experienced occasionally by recreational and weekend golfers – but the odds are greatly against it.

Irrespective of how many instructors may have taught you to grip a golf club in a certain manner or how many instructional books and magazines you have read on how to grip a golf club, if you have adopted a conventional style of grip, you are a victim of what I characterize as the "Vardon Curse." The instant you assemble a conventional style of golf grip on a golf club when there is no clubface rotation during the gripping proceedings, your forearms will rotate your wrists and in turn, your clubface, to an open alignment and your elbows to an outside-to-inside swing path across your shoulders to establish a slice ball flight alignment.

Your Grip Determines Your Initial Clubface Alignment as Well as Its Swing Path

Ball flight is determined by how the clubface is aligned and the path on which it travels when it contacts the ball, at impact.

A slice ball flight occurs when an open clubface contacts the ball on an outside-to-inside swing path across the shoulders at impact. A slice ball flight is one in which the ball initially flies to the inside of the shoulders line and, if sufficient sidespin, then curves to the opposite side of the shoulder line – sometimes referred to as a "banana ball" due to the curvature of the ball in flight. If there is insufficient sidespin the ball will fly only to the inside of the shoulder line and resemble a pulled golf shot.

A hook ball flight alignment occurs when a closed clubface contacts the ball on an inside-to-outside swing path across the shoulders at impact. A hook flights the ball to the outside of the shoulder line initially and then curves it to the inside of the shoulder line. If there is insufficient sidespin the ball will fly only to the outside of the shoulder line.

A pull ball flight alignment is one in which the ball flies on a relatively straight path to the inside of the shoulder line. A pull ball flight occurs when a closed clubface contacts the ball on an outside-to-inside swing path across the shoulders at impact.

A push ball flight alignment is one in which the ball flies on a relatively straight path to the outside of the shoulder line. A push ball flight occurs when an open clubface contacts the ball on an inside-to-outside swing path across the shoulder line at impact.

A pulled hook ball flight is one in which the ball curves extremely to the inside of the shoulder line. It occurs when a severely closed clubface contacts a ball on a pronounced outside-to-inside swing path across the shoulders at impact.

A pushed slice ball flight is one in which the ball curves extremely to the outside of the shoulder line. It occurs when a severely open clubface contacts the ball on a pronounced inside-to-outside swing path across the shoulders, at impact.

A straight ball flight is one in which the ball flies on a straight path that parallels the shoulder line. It occurs when a square clubface contacts the ball on a swing path that parallels the shoulder line at impact.

A fade ball flight is a slight slice. The ball typically curves only slightly to the outside of the shoulder line. A draw is a slight hook. The ball typically curves only minimally to the inside of the shoulder line.

Cause and Effect of Specific Ball Flights

The fact that a slice golf shot typically flies the ball to the inside of the shoulder line initially and then curves it to the outside of the shoulder line is an effect, not a cause. What causes a ball to fly in such a pattern is the alignment of the forearms at impact. The forearms will have rotated the wrists and in turn, the clubface, to an open alignment and the elbows to an outside-to-inside swing at impact when a slice golf shot is produced.

The phenomenon that a hook golf shot typically flies the ball to the outside of the shoulder line initially and then curves it to the inside of the shoulder line is an effect, not a cause. What causes the ball to fly in such a pattern is the alignment of the forearms at impact. The forearms will have rotated the wrists and in turn, the clubface, to a closed alignment and the elbows to an inside-to-outside swing path across the shoulders at impact when a hook golf shot is produced.

The reality that a pull golf shot flies the ball on a relatively straight path to the inside of the shoulder line is an effect, not a cause. What causes the ball to fly in such a pattern is the alignment of the forearms at impact. The forearms will have rotated the wrists and in turn, the clubface, to a closed alignment and the elbows to an outside-to-inside swing path across the shoulders at impact when a pull golf shot is produced.

The proposition that a push golf shot flies the ball on a relatively straight path to the outside of the shoulder line is an effect, not a cause. What causes the ball to fly in such a pattern is the alignment of the forearms at impact. The forearms will have rotated the wrists and in turn, the clubface, to an open alignment and the elbows to an inside-to-outside swing path across the shoulders at impact when a push golf shot is produced.

The same phenomenon applies with respect to a pushed slice and pulled hook ball flight. How the forearms have rotated the wrist and in turn, the clubface, and also how the forearms have rotated the elbows at impact will determine whether a pushed slice, pulled hook or some other ball flight will be produced.

The fact that a straight ball flight results when the clubface contacts the ball squarely on a swing path that parallels the shoulder line is an effect, not a cause. What causes a ball to fly on a straight path parallel with the shoulders is how the forearms are rotated at impact. The forearms will have rotated the wrists and in turn, the clubface, to a square alignment and the elbows to an on-line swing path at impact when a straight golf shot is produced.

How the Forearms Have Rotated the Wrists at Impact Will Determine Clubface Alignment

How the wrists are aligned to hinge and unhinge the clubface during the backswing and downswing will determine whether the clubface is open, closed or square at any point during the pre-shot proceedings or the golf swing.

An open clubface means the heel of the clubface is forward of its toe in relation to its path. A closed clubface means the toe of the clubface is forward of its heel in relation to its path. A square clubface means that neither the heel nor the toe of the clubface is forward of the other in relation to its path.

When a conventional style of grip is formed on a club, whether an original or modified Vardon overlap, traditional interlock or regular baseball (ten-fingers), the forearms will rotate the wrists to hinge the clubface to an open alignment.

When the wrists are aligned to hinge the club squarely perpendicular to the tip-end of the right shoulder for right-handers or, to the tip-end of the left shoulder for left-handers, a square clubface will be indicated. However, how the wrists appear to be aligned in relation to the tip-end of the trail shoulder during the pre-shot proceedings is not what determines clubface alignment.

Instead, how the wrists actually hinge the clubface in relation to the tip-end of the trail shoulder is what determines true clubface alignment.

The instant either an original or modified Vardon overlap, modified Vardon overlap, traditional interlock or regular baseball (ten-fingers) style of golf grip is formed on a golf club, the forearms will rotate the wrists to hinge the clubshaft slightly to the outside of the tip-end of the trail shoulder and in turn to an open alignment, assuming there is no clubface rotation during the gripping proceedings.

The Appearance of the Clubface Behind the Ball at the Completion of the Pre-Shot Routine Does Not Determine "True" Clubface Alignment

True clubface alignment is determined by how your forearms have rotated your wrists to hinge during your backswing, not by how your clubface appears to be aligned behind your ball at final address.

In order to establish a truly square clubface alignment at the completion of your pre-shot routine, your forearms must have rotated your wrists to hinge your clubshaft squarely perpendicular to the tip-end of your trail shoulder irrespective of how your clubface appears to be aligned.

The <u>instant</u> you grip a golf club with either an original Vardon overlap, modified Vardon overlap, traditional interlock or regular baseball (ten-fingers) style of grip – absent any clubface rotation during the gripping stage – your forearms will rotate your wrists and in turn, your clubface, to an open alignment whether your clubface appears to be square, closed or open.

If you purposely turn your clubface to what may appear to be a closed alignment before you assemble a conventional style of grip, your clubface nonetheless will be open in relation to the tip-end of your trail shoulder the instant you assume such grip, absent any clubface rotation during the gripping process.

How your wrists are aligned to hinge your clubshaft in relation to your trail shoulder joint (the tip-end of your trail shoulder) is what determines true and effective clubface alignment, not how your clubface appears to be aligned during your pre-shot routine.

Even if you purposely turn your clubface to what may appear to be a square alignment (at 90 degrees) to the ball before you assume your grip, the instant you assume either an original Vardon overlap, modified Vardon overlap, traditional interlock or regular baseball (ten fingers) style of grip absent any clubface rotation, your forearms nevertheless will rotate your wrists and in turn, your clubface, to an open alignment in relation to the tip-end of your trail shoulder (right shoulder for right-handers; left shoulder for left-handers).

The Number of Knuckles You Observe on Your Lead Hand Will Not Determine Clubface Alignment

Whether you are able to observe one, two, three or four knuckles (or fractions thereof) on your lead hand when you grip a club, your forearms nonetheless will rotate your wrists to an open alignment the instant you assemble a conventional style of grip, assuming no clubface rotation during the gripping process.

If you have been taught a stronger type of conventional grip, such as being able to observe three or more knuckles on your lead hand, will square your clubface and "cure your slice," you have been ill-advised.

A stronger type of conventional grip will not change the alignment of your wrists in relation to the tip-end of your trail shoulder. Your wrists and your clubface nonetheless will be aligned to hinge slightly to the outside of the tip-end of your trail shoulder and in turn, create an open alignment regardless of how many knuckles can be observed after forming either an original Vardon overlap, modified Vardon overlap, traditional interlock or regular baseball (ten-fingers) style of grip when there is no clubface rotation during the gripping process.

A stronger grip may cause you to align your shoulders to the outside of your intended target line and, as a result of such alignment, cause you to swing along the target line and produce a different ball flight. However, if you align your shoulders squarely parallel with your intended target line and execute a non-manipulative golf swing, you nonetheless will produce a slice golf shot.

The Direction of Your "v's" When Gripping a Club Will Not "Square" Your Clubface

Some instructors insist if the "v's" (formed between the index finger and thumb of each hand when a grip is assembled on a golf club) point in a specific direction, a square clubface alignment will be established.

It doesn't matter whether both "v's" point in the same direction or in different directions, the instant a conventional style of grip is formed on a golf club, the forearms will rotate the wrists and in turn, the clubface, to an open alignment in relation to the tip-end of the trail shoulder, when there is no clubface rotation during the gripping process. It makes no difference whether one or both "v's" point more to the tip-end of the trail shoulder or elsewhere. It is not how the "v's" appear to be aligned in relation to the tip-end of the trail shoulder that determines whether a square clubface is established. Instead, it is how the wrists and in turn, the clubface, are aligned to hinge in relation to the tip-end of the trail shoulder that determines "true" clubface alignment.

If you observe professional tour players, you should note in most cases at the completion of their backswings, their clubshafts either point to the tip-end of their trail shoulders and/or hover directly over them. This indicates at such point in their swing the clubface is "square." Indeed, this is the best indication of whether a clubface is square or not.

One of the greatest myths associated with golf is the notion that the alignment of the "v's" in some way determines whether a square clubface alignment is established. It doesn't.

If you assume either an original Vardon overlap, modified Vardon overlap, traditional interlock or regular baseball (ten-fingers) style of golf grip, the moment it is assembled on a club your clubface will be aligned to hinge to the outside of the tip-end of your trail shoulder irrespective of how many knuckles you can observe on your lead hand or in which direction your "v's" point.

How Your Forearms Have Rotated Your Elbows in Relation to Your Shoulders Determines the Swing Path of Your Clubface at Impact

Many golfers believe it is the relationship between the shoulders and the intended target line that determines the swing path of the clubface. The conventional theory is the swing path of the clubface, whether inside-to-outside, outside-to-inside or straight, is referenced to the intended target line. This is not what determines the swing path of the clubface.

Instead, what determines the swing path of the clubface is how the elbows are aligned in relation to the shoulders.

It should not take much discussion to realize the relationship between the shoulders and the intended target line is not what determines the swing path of the clubface.

For instance, assume a golfer aligns his or her shoulders at a 90 degree (right) angle to the intended target line. No matter how he or she swings the club, one of the seven aforementioned ball flights will result. If the ball slices, it will not slice in relation to the intended target line when the shoulders are aligned at a 90 degree angle to the target line. It will slice only in relation to the shoulder line. If the ball hooks, it will not hook in relation to the intended target line when the shoulders are aligned at a right angle to the target line. It will hook only in relation to the shoulder line.

If the ball flies in a straight direction, it will do so in relation to the shoulder line, not in relation to a target line that is aligned at a 90 degree angle to the shoulder line.

If the elbows are aligned on an inside-to-outside swing path in relation to the shoulders at impact, the ball will either hook, push or push slice, depending on whether the clubface is closed, open or extremely open. The ball will hook, push or push slice, respectively, in relation to the intended target line only if the intended target line correspondingly is aligned squarely parallel with the shoulder line.

If the elbows are aligned on an outside-to-inside path in relation to the shoulders at impact, the ball will either slice, pull or pull hook, depending on whether the clubface is open, closed or extremely closed. The ball will slice, pull or pull hook, respectively, in relation to the intended target line only if the intended target line correspondingly is aligned squarely parallel with the shoulder line.

If the elbows are aligned squarely parallel with the shoulders at impact, the ball will fly on a parallel path with the shoulders, not necessarily on a parallel path with the intended target line unless it too is aligned squarely parallel with the shoulders and the elbows.

One easy and simple way to demonstrate how the elbows rotate to an outside-to-inside swing path across the shoulder line the <u>instant</u> a conventional style of grip is assembled on a golf club when there is no clubface rotation during the gripping process is to conduct the

Locked-In Elbows Test™

Place a ball on some surface, whether the surface is a practice mat or grass. Grasp a clubshaft in a horizontal manner with your hands about one or two feet apart. Then extend your arms and lock your elbows. Raise or lower your extended arms up or down until the clubshaft overlays (bisects) the ball from your line of vision. Observe the direction in which the clubshaft points.

Next, maintain your spine angle, ungrasp the club from its horizontal alignment, ground the sole of the clubface and assume either an original Vardon overlap, modified Vardon overlap, traditional interlock or regular baseball style of grip. Then while maintaining the same spine angle, grasp the club shaft once again in a horizontal manner with your hands about one or two feet apart and then, once again, extend your arms and lock your elbows.

Raise or lower your extended arms up or down until your clubshaft once again overlays (bisects) the ball from your line of vision.

You should observe your clubshaft no longer points in the same direction as before. You should observe, instead, it points to the inside of your shoulder line, indicating that while your shoulders remained aligned squarely parallel with the imaginary reference line, your elbows rotated to the inside of your shoulder line. It did so the instant you assumed a conventional grip on your club.

One of the most fascinating phenomena in golf is when your elbows are aligned squarely parallel with your shoulders, your wrists and clubface correspondingly will be aligned to hinge squarely perpendicular to the tip-end of your trail shoulder; meaning a square clubface alignment will be established in such instance. Likewise, when your wrists and clubface are aligned to hinge squarely perpendicular to the tip-end of your trail shoulder, your elbows correspondingly will be aligned squarely parallel with your shoulders.

Remember, however, your shoulder line is your "effective" target line. Your intended target line only becomes an "effective" target line when also aligned parallel with your shoulder line.

You may not yet be convinced the <u>instant</u> a conventional style of grip is assembled on a club – absent any clubface rotation during the gripping process – your forearms will rotate your wrists and clubface to an open alignment and your elbows to an outside-to-inside swing path across your shoulders to establish a slice ball flight alignment. You may not yet be convinced the validity of the "Vardon Curse."

If not, I invite you to conduct some other tests in addition to the LOCKED-IN ELBOWS TEST™.

For example, I invite you to conduct

The Wrist Swing Test™

One such test is what I characterize as the WRIST SWING TEST™. The WRIST SWING TEST™ consists of centering the clubface as near the back of the ball as possible without causing the ball to move, then forming a grip on the handle of the club, after which the club is swung only with the wrists. All other parts of the body are frozen when the club is swung.

Were you to conduct the WRIST SWING TEST™ after gripping a club with either an original or modified Vardon overlap, traditional interlock or regular baseball (ten-fingers) style of grip, you would observe the ball to roll or fly slightly to the outside of your shoulder line, indicative of an open clubface.

When conducting the WRIST SWING TEST™ and the ball rolls or flies on a straight line that is parallel with the shoulder line, it indicates a square clubface has been established.

Once any of the thirty-two techniques discussed in this book are used to establish and lock-in a straight ball flight alignment, the sweet spot of the clubface is then centered as near the back of the ball as possible and then the WRIST SWING TEST™ is conducted, the ball will roll or fly on a straight path that is parallel with the shoulder line. This will indicate that a square clubface was established and, correspondingly, the elbows were aligned parallel with the shoulders in such an instance.

The Straight-Up Test™

Another test that can be conducted to determine whether the wrists have rotated the clubface to a square alignment and the elbows to an on-line swing path to establish a straight ball flight alignment is the STRAIGHT-UP TEST™.

The STRAIGHT-UP TEST™ consists of identifying a straight line on which the leading edge of the clubface should be placed, such as a straight line atop a practice mat or a tiled floor, or a straight line indented into the surface by the leading edge of the clubface.

When conducting the STRAIGHT-UP TEST™, the leading edge of the clubface should be placed squarely on the referenced straight line when the grip is formed on the club. Then, when the clubface is raised about one foot above the surface with the shoulders only and the clubface rotates counterclockwise, an outside-to-inside swing path will be indicated.

If there is no clubface rotation in such instance, an on-line swing path will be indicated.

If you were to conduct the STRAIGHT-UP TEST™ after an original or modified Vardon overlap, traditional interlock or regular baseball (ten fingers) style of grip is formed on a club (assuming no clubface rotation during the gripping process), you would observe when your shoulders are raised to lift the clubface about a foot above the surface, your clubface would rotate counterclockwise, indicative of an outside-to-inside swing path across your shoulders.

On the other hand, when the leading edge of the clubface remains aligned with the referenced or straight line on the surface when raised about a foot above the surface, an on-line swing path will be indicated and, correspondingly, also a square clubface alignment.

When each of the thirty-two techniques discussed in this book is assembled and executed correctly and then the STRAIGHT-UP TEST™ is conducted, there will be no counterclockwise rotation of the clubface, indicating a straight ball flight alignment has been established and locked-in.

The Shoulders Only Test™

Another test that can be used to determine whether the wrists have rotated the clubface to a square alignment and whether the elbows have rotated to a parallel alignment with the shoulders to create an on-line swing path of the clubface is the SHOULDERS ONLY TEST™.

Once you have gripped a club, straightened your legs to the maximum extent, locked your knee joints and then raise your shoulders only (without lifting your clubface from the surface) and the sole of your clubface slides freely in your direction, it will indicate a square clubface alignment and also an on-line swing path.

However, once you have gripped a club, straightened your legs, locked your knee joints and then raise your shoulders only (without lifting the clubface from the surface) and your clubface rotates counterclockwise or clockwise, it will indicate a square clubface and an on-line swing path have not been established.

For example, if you were to place the sole of your clubface on some surface such as a practice mat, then assume either an original or modified Vardon overlap, traditional interlock or regular baseball (ten-fingers) style of grip on the handle of your club, straighten your legs and lock your knee joints after which you very, very slowly raise your shoulders (while keeping your clubface grounded), you would observe instead of the sole of the clubface sliding freely in your direction, there would be some resistance of the clubface and it would rotate counterclockwise or clockwise instead, indicating a non-square clubface and an off-line swing path.

When conducting the SHOULDERS ONLY TEST™, the clubface must remain grounded throughout the procedure. Also, the legs must be straightened and the knee joints locked (and remained locked) during the test. The arms, wrists and hands should remain inactive and passive and move only in response to raising the shoulders.

Keep in mind also when your shoulders are raised while your knee joints are locked and your clubface is grounded to conduct the SHOULDERS ONLY TEST™, your clubface may rotate vertically (up and down) instead of rotating counterclockwise or clockwise. When the clubface rotates vertically (up and down) it also indicates a straight ball flight alignment has been established.

The shoulders may be lowered instead of raised, while keeping the clubface grounded, as an alternative means of conducting the SHOULDERS ONLY TEST™. The same disciplines apply. The knee joints must be locked and the arms, wrists and hands must remain inactive and passive and only move in response to raising or lowering the shoulders.

If there ever is any doubt in my mind as to whether I have established and locked-in a straight ball flight alignment, I rely as much or more on lowering my shoulders with my knee joints locked in place when conducting the SHOULDERS ONLY TEST™ to see if the clubface rotates counterclockwise or clockwise as I do in raising my shoulders with my knee joints locked in place to see if the clubface slides freely in my direction.

The Arms-Lift Test™

Another test that can be conducted to determine whether a straight ball flight alignment has been established and locked-in is the ARMS-LIFT TEST™.

This test consists of immobilizing the shoulders and knees and, while keeping the clubface grounded, lifting the arms upward as far as possible.

If the clubface rotates counterclockwise or clockwise, a locked-in straight ball flight alignment will not be indicated. However, if instead, the clubface does not rotate counterclockwise or clockwise when the arms are lifted with the clubface grounded, it will indicate a locked-in straight ball flight alignment has been established.

Were you to conduct the ARMS-LIFT TEST™ after assuming a conventional grip, your clubface would rotate counterclockwise or clockwise when lifting your arms upward while keeping the clubface grounded, indicating an open clubface and an outside-to-inside swing path.

On the other hand when the STRAIGHT-UP TEST™ is conducted after one of the thirty-two techniques addressed in this book properly is assembled, the clubface will not rotate counterclockwise or clockwise. Instead, the clubface will rotate vertically – either up or down. The same result will occur when the STRAIGHT-UP TEST™ is conducted on any of the thirty properly assembled techniques addressed in the companion book, HOW TO HIT A GOLF BALL AS STRAIGHT-AS-AN-ARROW, all of which will indicate a straight ball flight alignment is established and locked-in.

The STRAIGHT-UP TEST™, SHOULDERS ONLY TEST™ and ARMS-LIFT TEST™ are referred to as confirmation tests and should be conducted at the completion of each of the thirty-two unique and revolutionary techniques that will be discussed in subsequent chapters of this book.

Harry Vardon Never Claimed His Overlap Grip to Be a Panacea

It probably is unfair to Harry Vardon, the legendary golfer who originated the overlap grip, to characterize the conventional styles of grip as the "Vardon Curse."

Vardon was never known to make any claims that his grip was the perfect or the "be all/end all" to the gripping challenge. It merely worked for him at the time. It worked for him because, according to some reports, he opened his lifeline/thumb connection during his backswing to square his clubface.

However, for millions of golfers since such time, it has been a curse- because the instant such a grip is assumed a slice ball flight alignment will be established.

I do not expect you to accept what I have discussed so far at face value even after conducting some of the tests addressed in this chapter.

However, once you assemble and execute one or more of the thirty-two LOCKED-IN TECHNIQUES™ introduced and addressed later in this book, you should have no doubt about the anatomical reality that the <u>instant</u> you assume a conventional style of grip on a club – absent any clubface rotation – your forearms will rotate your wrists, clubface and elbows to establish a slice ball flight alignment. You should have no doubt about the validity of the "Vardon Curse."

SUMMARY POINTS

1. When either an original or modified Vardon overlap, traditional interlock or regular baseball (ten-fingers) style of golf grip is formed on a club – when there is no clubface rotation during the gripping proceedings – the forearms will rotate the wrists, clubface and elbows to establish a slice ball flight alignment.

2. I characterize the rotation of the forearms, wrists and clubface to establish a slice alignment when a conventional style of golf grip is formed on a club as the "Vardon Curse."

3. Once a conventional style of grip is formed on a club, unless the forearms, wrists and elbows are rotated to a different alignment before the clubface contacts the ball, a slice golf shot will result.

4. Almost any body movement after assuming a conventional style of grip will rotate the wrists, clubface and elbows to establish a different alignment.

5. How the wrists are aligned to hinge in relation to the tip-end of the trail shoulder determines the alignment of the clubface: whether open, closed or square.

6. A conventional style of golf grip – whether an original or modified Vardon overlap, traditional interlock or regular baseball (ten- fingers) style of grip – rotates the wrists to hinge the clubface to an open alignment the instant it is assembled when there is no clubface rotation during the gripping process.

7. **Regardless of how many knuckles may be visible on the lead hand after a conventional grip is formed on a golf club, the wrists and clubface nonetheless will be rotated to an open alignment – assuming no clubface rotation during the gripping process.**

8. **Irrespective of how the "v's" between the index finger and thumb of each hand are aligned once a conventional grip is formed on a golf club, the wrists and clubface nonetheless will be rotated to an open alignment – assuming no clubface rotation during the gripping process.**

9. **The instant either an original or modified Vardon overlap, traditional interlock or regular baseball (ten-fingers) style of grip is formed on a club, the elbows will be rotated to an outside-to-inside swing path across the shoulders, assuming no clubface rotation during the gripping process.**

10. **When an open clubface on an outside-to-inside swing path across the shoulders exists at impact, a slice golf shot will result.**

11. **The shoulder line constitutes the "true" reference line in terms of determining ball flight, not the intended target line.**

12. **Therefore, the shoulder line is the "effective" target line. The intended target line only becomes an "effective" target line when aligned squarely parallel with the shoulder line.**

13. **The appearance of the clubface behind a ball does not determine "true" clubface alignment. Instead, how the wrists are aligned to hinge and unhinge in relation to the trail shoulder joint determines "true" clubface alignment.**

14. When an open clubface strikes the ball on an outside-to-inside swing path to produce a slice ball flight, it is an "effect," not the "cause," of the ball flight.

15. The "cause" of a slice ball flight is the alignment of the wrists and elbows at impact. The same proposition applies to all other ball flights. How the wrists and elbows are aligned at impact is what determines each type of ball flight.

16. The WRIST SWING TEST™ can illustrate how a conventional golf grip rotates the clubface to an open alignment the instant it is assembled.

17. The LOCKED-IN ELBOWS TEST™ can validate how a conventional golf grip rotates the elbows to an outside-to-inside swing path across the shoulders the instant it is assembled on a golf club.

18. The STRAIGHT-UP TEST™ as well as the ARMS-LIFT TEST™ also can demonstrate how a conventional golf grip rotates the wrists and clubface to an open alignment and the elbows to an outside-to-inside swing path across the shoulders the moment it is formed on a club.

19. The SHOULDERS ONLY TEST™ is an easy and simple one to conduct to determine whether a straight ball flight alignment has been established.

CHAPTER 2

HOW TO CURE THE VARDON CURSE

As mentioned in the previous chapter, the instant either an original Vardon overlap, modified Vardon overlap, traditional interlock or regular baseball (ten-fingers) style of grip is assembled on a golf club, the forearms will rotate the wrists and in turn, the clubface, to an open alignment and the elbows to an outside-to-inside swing path across the shoulders to establish a slice ball flight, assuming no clubface rotation during the gripping process. I characterized this phenomenon as the "Vardon Curse."

Each of the conventional styles of grip is formed in the same manner with the lead hand. The trail hand is formed differently on the club with respect to the four conventional types of grip.

A conventional style of grip is formed on the lead hand by placing the club handle diagonally across the palm and fingers, with the club running from the mid-point of the index finger back to and beneath the fatty pad of the palm, and then by wrapping the fingers around the club. (Figure 2-1).

An original Vardon overlap grip is assembled on a golf club by overlapping the little finger of the trail hand on top of the index finger of the lead hand in a piggyback manner and then by wrapping the fingers around the club and locking the lifeline of the trail hand squarely and securely on the thumb of the lead hand to complete the grip. (Figure 2-2).

A modified Vardon overlap grip is formed on a club by overlapping the little finger of the trail hand on the groove atop the index and middle fingers of the lead hand while simultaneously wedging the tip-end of the lead index finger into the web formed between the little and ring fingers of the trail hand. It is completed by wrapping the fingers around the club and then locking the lifeline of the trail hand squarely and securely on the lead thumb. (Figure 2-3).

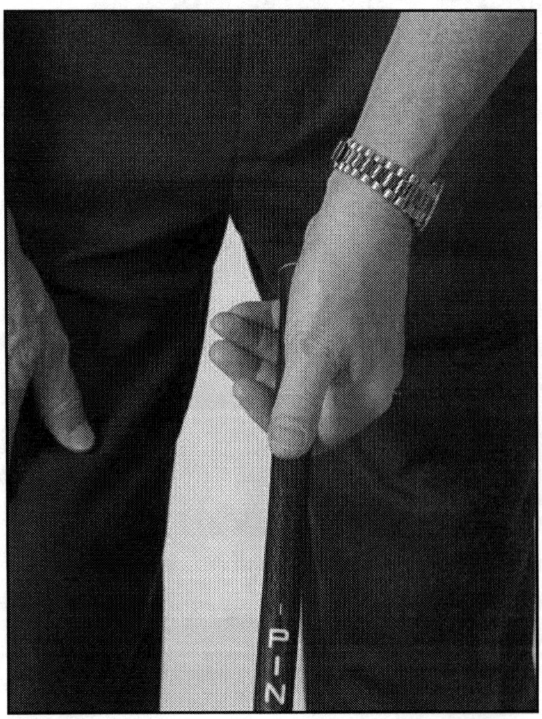

Figure 2-1

Each conventional style of grip is formed on the lead hand in the same manner. The club handle is placed diagonally across the palm and fingers, running from the mid-point of the index finger back to and beneath the fatty pad of the palm. The fingers then are wrapped around the club handle to complete the lead hand grip.

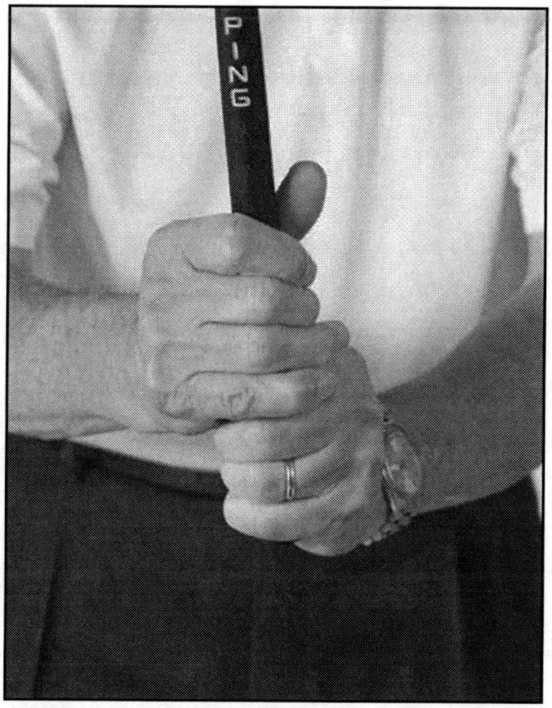

Figure 2-2

The original Vardon overlap style of grip is formed on a club by overlapping the tip end of the little finger of the trail hand on top of the middle knuckle of the index finger of the lead hand in a piggyback manner and then by wrapping the fingers around the club handle and locking the lifeline portion of the trail hand squarely and securely on the lead thumb to complete the grip.

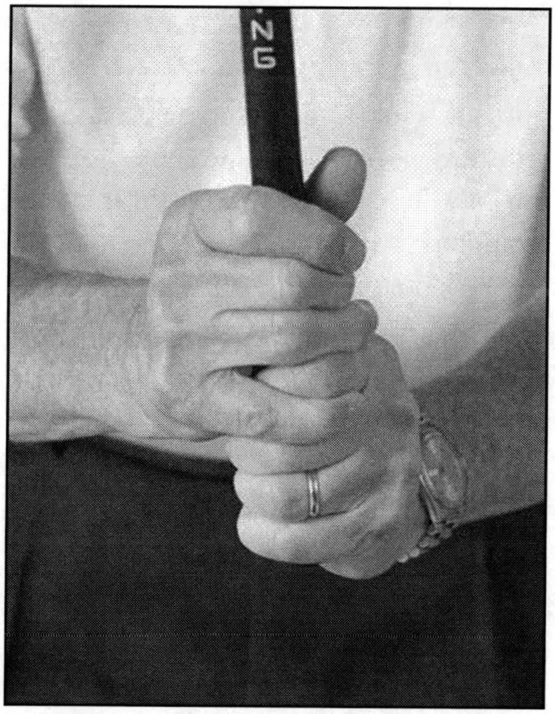

Figure 2-3

The modified Vardon overlap style of grip is formed on a club by overlapping the little finger of the trail hand atop the groove between the index and middle fingers of the lead hand while simultaneously wedging the tip-end of the lead index finger into the web between the little and ring fingers of the trail hand. The grip is completed by wrapping the fingers around the club and then locking the lifeline portion of the trail hand squarely and securely on the lead thumb.

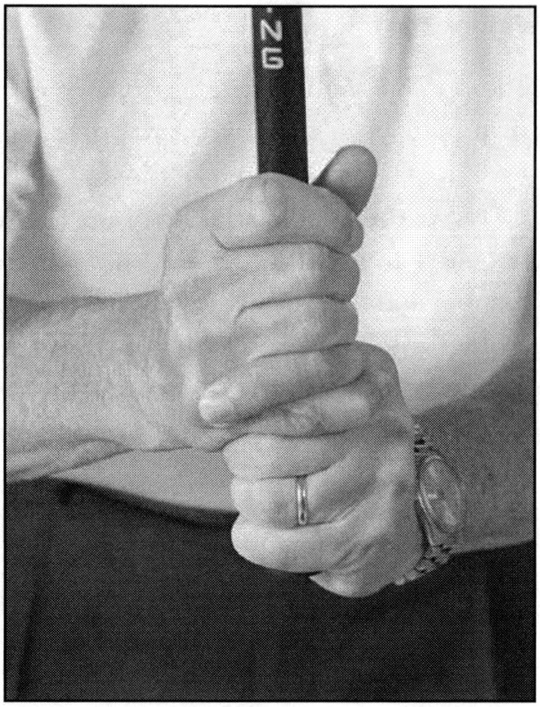

Figure 2-4

A traditional interlock style of grip is assembled on a club by slotting the little finger of the trail hand firmly into the web between the index and middle fingers of the lead hand and then by wrapping the fingers around the club and locking the lifeline portion of the trail hand squarely and securely on the lead thumb to complete the grip.

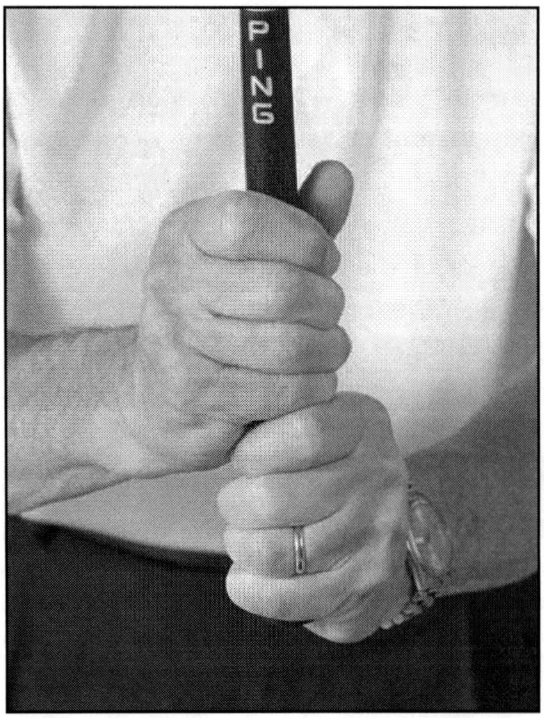

Figure 2-5

A regular baseball (ten-fingers) style of grip is assembled on a club by placing the little finger of the trail hand snugly against the index finger of the lead hand and then wrapping the trail fingers around the club and locking the lifeline portion of the trail hand squarely and securely on the lead thumb to complete the grip.

A traditional interlock style of grip is formed by slotting the little finger of the trail hand firmly into the web between the index and middle fingers of the lead hand and then by wrapping the fingers around the club and locking the lifeline of the trail hand squarely and securely on the lead thumb to complete the grip. (Figure 2-4).

A regular baseball (ten-fingers) style of grip is assembled by placing the trail hand on the club so its little finger snugly fits against the index finger of the lead hand and then by wrapping the fingers around the club and locking the lifeline of the trail hand squarely and securely on the lead thumb to complete the grip. (Figure 2-5).

There Are a Variety of Ways to Cure the "Vardon Curse"

One way to cure the "Vardon Curse" is to move some part of the body after a conventional grip is assumed to cause the forearms to rotate the wrists, clubface and elbows from the slice alignment – established the instant a conventional style of grip is formed – to a straight ball flight alignment during the pre-shot proceedings and then lock-in such alignment.

In subsequent chapters I will share with you thirty-two different ways to move certain body parts in a specific manner after your grip is formed to cause your forearms to rotate your wrists, clubface and elbows from the slice alignment – established the instant a conventional style of grip is assembled – to establish a straight ball flight alignment and then how to lock-in such an alignment.

Another way to cure the "Vardon Curse" is to adjust the conventional styles of golf grip so the forearms, wrists, clubface and elbows will be aligned to establish a straight ball flight alignment instead of a slice ball flight alignment the instant the grip is completed – and then lock-in such alignment.

In the companion book, HOW TO HIT A GOLF BALL AS STRAIGHT-AS-AN-ARROW, I introduce thirty new and innovative techniques to align the forearms, wrists, clubface and elbows to establish a straight ball flight alignment the instant the grip is completed and then how to lock-in such alignment during the pre-shot routine.

As mentioned in the previous chapter, in each of the thirty new techniques addressed in HOW TO HIT A GOLF BALL AS STRAIGHT-AS- AN-ARROW, there is a purposeful and specific body movement between the time the lead hand is formed on the club in a conventional (diagonal) manner and the time the trail hand is assembled on the club.

In addition, I introduce and instruct twenty-eight new and different techniques to establish and lock-in a straight ball flight alignment during the pre-swing proceedings in another companion book, HOW GOLF WORKS.

A less reliable way to convert a slice ball flight alignment – established the instant a conventional grip is assembled – to a straight ball flight alignment is to manipulate the clubface in some way during the golf swing. This is the least effective means to cause such a conversion. It typically involves a lot of guesswork and so-called "muscle-memory."

When using the "muscle-memory" method to convert a slice ball flight alignment – established the instant a conventional style of grip is formed on a club in which there is no clubface rotation during the gripping proceedings – to a straight ball flight alignment by the point of impact, the clubface must be swung either to the inside or to the outside of its established swing path in a very precise manner during the golf swing. Given the reality that the elbows will rotate to a parallel alignment with the shoulders for only a fraction of a degree during the golf swing, such a conversion is most difficult.

Although a slice ball flight alignment will be established the instant either an original Vardon overlap, modified Vardon overlap, traditional interlock or regular baseball style of grip is formed on a golf club when there is no clubface rotation during the gripping process, almost any body movement thereafter will rotate the forearms, wrists, clubface and elbows either counterclockwise or clockwise to some extent.

However, unless you know which body parts to move, in which direction they must be moved and to what extent they must be moved after a conventional style of grip is formed on a club any such movement typically is a recipe for disaster.

The solution to this dilemma is to know which body parts to move, the direction they must be moved and to what extent they must be moved after a conventional style of grip is formed on a club in which there is no clubface rotation during the gripping process.

The thirty-two LOCKED-IN TECHNIQUES™ addressed in this book will instruct you which body parts to move, the direction they must be moved and the extent they must be moved after a conventional style of grip is assembled. The thirty-two LOCKED-IN TECHNIQUES™ addressed in this book will cure the "Vardon Curse."

If a conventional golf grip establishes a slice alignment the instant it is formed on a golf club, how then have professional tour players and low handicap amateurs been able to play golf so effectively and successfully through the years without having had any knowledge of the various techniques discussed in this book or the techniques addressed in the aforementioned companion books?

The answer is despite the lack of knowledge about these various techniques or an understanding of the "Vardon Curse," they have been able to groove an effective golf swing out of instinct, trial and error and "muscle-memory."

Many of the best golfers in the world instinctively have learned to rotate their forearms to square the clubface and achieve an on-line swing path by manipulating the clubface in some specific and unique manner <u>during their pre-shot routines</u>.

Other better players have learned to re-route the club to an on-line swing path and square alignment by manipulating the clubface <u>during their golf swings</u>.

Although some professional tour players and low handicap amateurs instinctively have learned to manipulate their clubface in some manner during their pre-shot routines to square their clubface and establish an on-line swing path, few if any have been able to understand the mechanics about how to lock-in such a straight ball flight alignment during their pre-swing proceedings.

One of their favorite means of manipulating the clubface in some way to establish a straight ball flight alignment during their pre-swing proceedings is to "offset" the face of the club in relation to the ball. Then when the sweet spot of the clubface is centered directly behind the ball, the clubface supposedly will square itself and rotate to an on-line swing path.

The difficulty for the recreational and weekend golfer in attempting to use this "offsetting" approach to establish a straight ball flight alignment is the lack of understanding as to the manner and the extent to which the clubface must be "offset" to accomplish such objective. In other words, the "offsetting" technique involves far too much guesswork for the average recreational and weekend golfer.

Another way numerous professional and low amateur golfers have been able to produce effective golf shots is the use of what is known as "muscle-memory" as noted earlier: forcing the muscles during the golf swing to re-route the clubface to a square alignment and an on-line swing path by the point of contact with the ball.

Irrespective of what means or method is used to convert a slice ball flight alignment to a straight ball flight alignment – whether before or during the golf swing – the forearm bones, elbow bones, wrist bones and shoulder bones must be aligned in a specific way at impact. Therefore,

Bone Alignment Is the Key to Establishing a Straight Ball Flight Alignment

Your bones must be aligned precisely in the following manner when your clubface contacts your ball in order to hit a golf shot on a straight path in the direction of your target and on a path that parallels your shoulder line.

- **Your elbow bones must be aligned squarely parallel with your shoulder bones.**
- **Your wrist bones must be aligned to unhinge squarely to the ball at impact.**
- **Your shoulder bones must be aligned squarely parallel with your intended target line.**
- **The mid-point of your shoulder line must be aligned squarely perpendicular to the back of your ball.**

In the companion books, HOW TO HIT A GOLF BALL AS STRAIGHT-AS-AN-ARROW and HOW GOLF WORKS, as well as in the subsequent chapters of this book, you will be instructed how to rotate your bones to establish and lock-in a straight ball flight alignment during your pre-shot routine. Then, all that will remain will be to center the sweet spot of your clubface as near the back of the ball as possible (if not already so centered), align your shoulders parallel with your intended target line and execute a non-manipulative golf swing so the impact position of your clubface will duplicate its address position. There should be no intentional or inadvertent manipulation of the clubface during the golf swing.

The four bone alignments mentioned above must exist at the completion of the pre-shot routine if a natural, non-manipulative golf swing is to produce a straight ball flight on-line with the intended target and on a straight path that parallels the shoulder line. That is, the elbow bones must be aligned squarely parallel with the shoulders, the wrist bones must be aligned to hinge and unhinge a square clubface, the shoulder bones must be aligned squarely parallel with the intended target line and the mid-point of the shoulder line must be aligned squarely perpendicular to the back of the ball – all at the completion of the pre-shot proceedings – in order for a non-manipulative golf swing to flight a ball on a straight path in the direction of a specific target.

If the four bone alignments do not exist at the completion of the pre-shot routine, the clubface must be manipulated in some manner to re-route the clubface during the golf swing to a straight ball flight alignment by the time the clubface contacts the ball in order to hit a golf ball on a straight path in the direction of a specific target.

"Muscle-Memory" Is Not a Reliable Solution to the "Vardon Curse"

Those who rely on the "muscle-memory" approach in an attempt to re-route their clubface to a square alignment and an on-line swing path during their backswing must do so by either swinging the clubface to the outside or to the inside of its established path.

Even assuming the shoulders are aligned squarely parallel with the intended target line, there are no reference points to help a golfer determine precisely how much the clubface should be swung to the outside or inside of its established path to rotate the wrists to a square alignment and the elbows to an on-line swing path by the time the clubface contacts the ball at impact.

Keep in mind if the sweet spot of the clubface is centered as near the back of the ball as possible and the shoulders are aligned parallel with the intended target line but the forearms, wrists, clubface and elbows have been rotated to establish a slice ball flight alignment when the swing begins, by swinging the clubface either to the inside or to the outside of its established swing path during the golf swing the clubface could possibly, although unlikely, rotate the clubface to a square alignment and the elbows to an on-line swing path by the time of impact.

However, the clubface would rotate to establish a straight ball flight alignment in such an instance only for an infinitesimal fraction of a degree, as explained in the companion book, HOW GOLF WORKS. The odds against establishing a straight ball flight alignment by swinging the clubface either to the inside or to the outside of its established swing path during the golf swing therefore are extraordinarily high.

What most likely will happen in such a case is the following:

ONE: If the clubface is swung only slightly to the outside of its established swing path, the clubface may not even rotate out of its established swing path by the time the backswing is completed. In such case, a non-manipulative downswing would then deliver an open clubface to the ball on an outside-to-inside swing path across the shoulders to produce a slice ball flight alignment.

TWO: If the clubface is swung more than slightly to the outside of its established swing path in such case, the wrists and clubface most likely would rotate to

a closed alignment and the elbows most likely would rotate to an inside-to-outside swing path across the shoulders. A non-manipulative downswing would then deliver a closed clubface to the ball on an inside-to-outside swing path across the shoulders at impact to produce a hook ball flight.

THREE: If the clubface is swung even more to the outside of its established path, the wrists and clubface most likely would rotate to an open alignment and the elbows most likely would rotate to an inside-to-outside swing path across the shoulders. In such case, a non-manipulative downswing would then deliver an open clubface to the ball on an inside-to-outside swing path across the shoulders at impact to produce a push ball flight.

FOUR: If the clubface is swung appreciably to the outside of its established path, the wrists and clubface most likely would rotate to an extremely open alignment and the elbows would most likely rotate to a pronounced inside-to-outside swing path across the shoulders. In such case, a non-manipulative downswing would then deliver an extremely open clubface to the ball on a pronounced inside-to-outside swing path at impact to produce a pushed slice ball flight.

On the other hand, assuming again the sweet spot of the clubface is centered as near the back of the ball as possible and the shoulders are aligned squarely parallel with the target line but the forearms, wrists, clubface and elbows are rotated to a slice alignment at final address (as they are the instant a conventional style of grip is assembled), the following is likely to happen when the clubface is swung to the inside of its established path during the backswing.

FIVE: If the clubface is swung only slightly to the inside of its established swing path, it may not even rotate out of its established slice ball flight alignment. In such case, a non-manipulative downswing would then deliver an open clubface to the ball on an outside-to-inside swing path across the shoulders at impact to produce a slice ball flight.

SIX: If the clubface is swung slightly more to the inside of its established swing path, the wrists and clubface most likely would rotate to a closed alignment and the elbows most likely would rotate to an outside-to-inside swing path across the shoulders. In such case, a non-manipulative downswing would then deliver a closed clubface to the ball on an outside-to-inside swing path across the shoulders at impact to produce a pull ball flight.

SEVEN: If the clubface is swung appreciably more to the inside of its established swing path, the wrists and clubface most

likely would rotate to an extremely closed alignment and the elbows most likely would rotate to a pronounced outside-to-inside swing path across the shoulders. In such case, a non-manipulative downswing would then deliver an extremely closed clubface to the ball on a pronounced outside-to-inside swing path across the shoulders at impact to produce a <u>pulled hook</u> ball flight.

The above examples are based on the forearms, wrists, clubface and elbows being rotated to a slice ball flight alignment at the "starting point" of the golf swing. This naturally occurs if first the shoulders are aligned squarely parallel with the intended target line and, simultaneously, the sweet spot of the clubface is centered as near the back of the ball as possible after which a conventional grip is assembled on a club – assuming no clubface rotation during the gripping process.

However, if a conventional grip is first assembled on the club and then there is some body movement before the shoulders are aligned squarely parallel with the intended target line and, simultaneously, the sweet spot of the clubface is centered as near the back of the ball, the forearms could rotate the wrists, clubface and elbows to establish various ball flight alignments, depending on how much the clubface is swung to the outside or to the inside of its established swing path.

Aligning the Shoulders to the Left or Right of the Intended Target Line and Attempting to Swing the Clubface Along the Target Line During the Takeaway Stage of the Backswing Will Not Cure the "Vardon Curse"

Another "muscle-memory" approach used by many golfers is to align their shoulders either to the inside or to the outside of the intended target line and then attempt to swing the clubface along the target line during the takeaway stage of the backswing in an effort to square the clubface and establish an on-line swing path before impact.

Depending on how much the shoulders purposely are aligned to the inside or outside of the intended target line in such instance, a variety of ball flight alignments may exist by the time of impact.

If the shoulders purposely are aligned to the inside of the intended target line in such instance and the clubface is swung along the target line during the backswing, the forearms could rotate the wrists, clubface and elbows to establish either a slice, pull or pull hook ball flight at impact, depending once again on how much the shoulders were aligned to the inside of the intended target line at final address.

If the shoulders purposely are aligned to the outside of the target line in such instance and the clubface is swung along the target line during the backswing, the forearms could rotate the wrists, clubface and elbows to establish either a slice, hook, push or pushed slice at impact, depending on the degree the shoulders were aligned to the inside of the intended target line at final address.

This "muscle-memory" approach also involves far too much guesswork and is equally unreliable as that discussed above.

Another muscle-memory approach is to cup or arch the wrists during the backswing in an effort to square the clubface and establish an on-line swing path before impact.

Cupping the Wrists During the Backswing in an Effort to Rotate the Wrists, Clubface and Elbows to Establish a Straight Ball Flight Alignment Also Is Not an Effective Remedy for the "Vardon Curse"

Ben Hogan's so-called "secret" was believed by some to be nothing more than the act of cupping his wrists during his backswing.

Although cupping your wrists during your backswing may rotate your wrists and clubface from an open alignment to a square alignment and your elbows from an outside-to-inside swing path to an on-line swing path, all of which will establish a straight ball flight alignment, it nonetheless requires a manipulation of the clubface during the golf swing.

More significant is the requirement that the wrists and the clubface must be rotated to an open alignment and the elbows must be rotated to an outside-to-inside swing path across the shoulders at the completion of the pre-swing proceedings in order for a cupping of the wrists to establish a straight ball flight alignment during the backswing. This means the forearms, wrists, clubface and elbows must be rotated to a slice ball flight alignment at final address to serve as a "starting point" in order for a cupping of the wrists during the backswing to establish a straight ball flight alignment.

Even though an original Vardon overlap, modified Vardon overlap, traditional interlock or regular baseball (ten-fingers) style of grip will rotate the wrists and clubface to an open alignment and the elbows to an outside-to-inside swing path across the shoulders to establish a slice ball flight alignment the instant they are assembled, absent any clubface rotation during the gripping proceedings, any body movement thereafter will rotate the wrists, clubface and elbows to a different alignment or, a more severe slice alignment, depending on the type and degree of body movement. As a result, cupping the wrists during the backswing is a risky proposition if the forearms, wrists, clubface and elbows have rotated out of their inherent alignment by the time the pre-shot routine is completed.

Attempting to become a modern-day Ben Hogan by cupping your wrists during your backswing typically is a recipe for disaster for the average recreational or weekend golfer.

Arching the Wrists During the Backswing in an Effort to Square the Clubface and Establish an On-Line Swing Path Likewise Is Not an Effective Answer to the "Vardon Curse"

Another "muscle-memory" technique employed by some excellent golfers is to arch (bow) their wrists during their backswing in an effort to rotate their wrists, clubface and elbows to a straight ball flight alignment. The same challenges await those who attempt this technique as for those who attempt to cup their wrists, as discussed earlier.

If the wrists, clubface and elbows are not rotated to a slice ball flight alignment at the conclusion of the pre-shot routine, they will rotate to establish some ball flight alignment other than a straight one if the wrists are arched during the golf swing.

Only if the wrists, clubface and elbows are rotated to establish a slice ball flight alignment at the completion of the pre-swing routine will arching the wrists during the backswing establish a straight ball flight alignment.

Arching the wrists during a golf swing in an attempt to square the clubface and establish an on-line swing path by the time the clubface contacts the ball likewise involves far too much guesswork for the average weekend and recreational player.

Bone Alignment Is a More Reliable Means to Establish a Straight Ball Flight Alignment and Remedy the "Vardon Curse"

Given the many potentially disastrous results associated with the "muscle-memory" approach in an effort to convert a slice alignment into a straight alignment during the golf swing, as discussed above, there must be a safer and more reliable means to achieve such objective. Locking-in the elbow bones, wrist bones and shoulder bones in a precise manner in relation to the ball and the intended target line during the pre-swing proceedings and then executing a non-manipulative golf swing provides for a far more reliable means to cause such a conversion.

In subsequent chapters, you will experience how easy it is to rotate your wrists, clubface and elbows from a slice alignment that is created the instant a conventional grip is assembled on a golf club to a straight ball flight alignment simply by a movement of various body parts in a precise manner. You also will learn how to lock-in a straight ball flight alignment once it is established.

Rotating your wrists, clubface and elbows from their inherent slice alignment to a straight alignment satisfies only a part of the necessary bone alignment requirements during the pre-shot proceedings to produce a straight golf shot to a given target.

Also required is the sweet spot of the clubface must be centered as near the back of the ball as possible and, simultaneously, the shoulders must be aligned squarely parallel with the intended target line at the completion of the pre-shot routine, followed by a non-manipulative golf swing – all of which will be discussed in the next chapter.

SUMMARY POINTS

1. **How your bones are aligned at impact will determine your ball flight.**

2. **Four bone alignments must exist at impact to produce a straight ball flight on a straight path in the direction of a specific target.**

3. **The wrists must be aligned to unhinge squarely to the ball.**

4. **The elbows must be aligned squarely parallel with the shoulders.**

5. **The shoulders must be aligned squarely parallel with the intended target line.**

6. **The mid-point of the shoulder line must be aligned squarely perpendicular to the back of the ball.**

7. **The "offsetting" approach in an attempt to convert a slice alignment to a straight alignment <u>is unreliable</u>.**

8. **The "muscle-memory" approach in an attempt to convert a slice alignment to a straight alignment likewise <u>is unreliable</u>.**

9. **Attempting to rely on "muscle-memory" to swing the clubface either to the outside or to the inside of its established swing path during the backswing in an effort to rotate the wrists, clubface and elbows to a straight ball flight alignment entails too much guesswork.**

10. Aligning the shoulders either to the inside or to the outside of the intended target line and then swinging the clubface along the target line during the takeaway in an attempt to convert a slice alignment into a straight alignment likewise involves far too much guesswork.

11. Cupping the wrists during the backswing in an effort to convert a slice (or other) alignment to a straight alignment is a recipe for disaster for the typical recreational and weekend golfer.

12. Arching the wrists during the backswing also is an unreliable "muscle-memory" technique to convert a slice (or other) alignment to a straight alignment.

13. Rotating the wrists, clubface and elbows from their inherent slice alignment to establish and lock-in a straight ball flight alignment satisfies only part of the essential bone alignments necessary to hit a golf shot on a straight path to a specific target.

14. Centering the sweet spot of the clubface as near the back of the ball as possible and aligning the shoulders squarely parallel with the intended target line at final address are the other essential bone alignments that are necessary to produce a straight golf shot to a specific target. They will be addressed in the next chapter.

CHAPTER 3

NEVER AGAIN SKULL OR CHUNK A GOLF SHOT

To hit a golf ball in the direction of a specific target and on a straight path that parallels the shoulder line, the forearms, wrists, clubface and elbows must be rotated to establish a square clubface and an on-line swing path at impact. In addition, the shoulders must be aligned squarely parallel with the intended target line and the clubface must reach its lowest arc (bottom-out) when it contacts the ball.

If these four alignments exist at final address as discussed in the preceding chapter, followed by a non-manipulative golf swing so there is no intentional or inadvertent re-routing of the clubface during the golf swing, the ball will fly on a straight path in the direction of the intended target and also on a straight path that parallels the shoulder line.

This book will share with you thirty-two ways to re-route your forearms, wrists, clubface and elbows from their inherent slight slice alignment to establish a straight ball flight alignment during your pre-shot routine. None of these thirty-two techniques however will produce a straight ball flight in the direction of a specific target and on a straight path that parallels the shoulder line unless also and, simultaneously, the shoulders are aligned squarely parallel with the intended target line and the sweet spot of the clubface is centered as near the back of the ball as possible at the completion of the pre-shot routine, followed by a non-manipulative golf swing.

This chapter is devoted to the last two of the four essential bone alignments necessary to produce a straight ball flight to a specific target:

- **The shoulder bones must be aligned squarely parallel with the intended target line**

  And

- **The mid-point of the shoulder line must be aligned squarely perpendicular to the back of the ball**

When all four bone alignments as discussed in the preceding chapter exist at final address, followed by a non-manipulative golf swing, the sweet spot of the clubface will "bottom out" squarely at the point of contact with the ball and on a swing path that parallels the shoulder line to produce a straight ball flight in line with the intended target.

Golf shots are skulled or chunked when the four bone alignments to produce a straight golf shot to a specific target do not exist at impact. A skulled or "thinned" golf shot occurs when the leading edge (sole) rather than the sweet spot of the clubface first contacts the ball. It generally produces a "thin" golf shot with a very low trajectory. A chunked golf shot occurs when the leading edge of the clubface "bottoms-out" before the sweet spot of the clubface contacts the ball. It typically produces a "fat" golf shot.

The First Order of Business to Prevent a Chunked or Skulled Golf Shot Is to Align Your Shoulders Squarely Parallel with Your Intended Target Line at Final Address

The conventional means of aligning the shoulders squarely parallel with the intended target line during the pre-swing proceedings is unreliable for the average recreational and weekend golfer. It is much like relying on "muscle-memory" to square the clubface and establish an on-line swing path during the golf swing. There is too much guesswork involved in the process.

The conventional approach of aligning the shoulders squarely parallel with the intended target line entails several steps.

First, the golfer is to identify the intended target line by standing behind the ball, while facing the target. Then he or she is to identify some object such as a discolored blade of grass, divot or twig that lies on the intended target line a few feet in front of the ball. The line between the ball and the chosen object then is to serve as an intermediate target line. So far, there are no problems.

The golfer then is to center his or her clubface squarely behind the ball at a 90 degree angle to the intermediate target line. Next, while he or she moves from the back of the ball to the address position, the clubface must continue to be centered at a 90 degree angle on the intermediate target line behind the ball. The golfer then is to move and adjust his or her feet and posture until the shoulders are at a 90 degree angle to the clubface.

This routine supposedly will align the shoulders squarely parallel with the intended target line. I don't think it will for the average recreational and weekend golfer.

Why the Conventional Approach of Aligning the Shoulders Squarely Parallel with the Intended Target Line Is Unreliable

In the description above about how golfers typically attempt to align their shoulders squarely parallel with their intended target line, there are several potential problems.

First, unless one is very careful and experienced, it is risky to rely on the clubface remaining centered behind the ball at a 90 degree angle while moving from the back of the ball to the address position, assuming the clubface is centered at a 90 degree angle when the movement begins.

Second, it is also difficult to continue holding the clubface at a 90 degree angle to the intended target line behind the ball when adjusting the stance and posture to the ball.

Assuming, however, that the clubface initially was centered behind the ball at a 90 degree angle to the intended target line and remained at a 90 degree angle to the clubface while addressing the ball, the instant a conventional style of grip is then formed on the golf club, the wrists and clubface will rotate to an open alignment and the elbows will rotate to an outside-to-inside swing path across the shoulder line to establish a slice ball flight alignment. This means even if the shoulders are aligned squarely parallel with the intended target line at final address, a non-manipulative golf swing nonetheless will produce a slice ball flight.

I believe there is a more reliable way to align your shoulders squarely parallel with your intended target line during your pre-swing proceedings. I call it the

Arrow Alignment Technique™

The ARROW ALIGNMENT TECHNIQUE™ does not rely on aligning the clubface to the target at a 90 degree angle behind the ball.

When you close your lead eye (left eye for right-handers, right eye for left-handers), turn your head and open (trail) eye as far as possible in the direction of a specific target and the tip-end of the "arrow" formed at the top of your nose and the upper inside corner of your open eye points to a specific target, your shoulders should be aligned squarely parallel with your intended target line.

If after turning your head and open trail eye in the direction of your target as far as possible and your "arrow" does not point directly at your intended target, you must adjust your stance until it does.

A Quick Way to Locate Your Arrow Alignment

Identify some straight line that runs a considerable distance such as at the edge of a walkway, sidewalk or driveway. Assume the end of the line is your target. Then place a golf ball or, a facsimile of a golf ball such as a piece of paper, on the straight line so identified. Center the face of your golf club as near the back of the ball (or facsimile of your ball) as possible. Align your shoulders squarely parallel with the straight-lined edge of the walkway, sidewalk or driveway while gripping your club in a conventional manner. Then, while immobilizing all other body parts and maintaining your spine angle to the ball (or to a facsimile of a ball), close your lead eye, focus your open trail eye on the tip-end of the "arrow" formed at the top of your nose and the upper inside corner of your open eye and turn your head counterclockwise as far as possible without crimping your neck. You should then observe the tip-end of the "arrow" will point directly at your imaginary target at the end of the referenced line. This will confirm your shoulders correspondingly will be aligned squarely parallel with your referenced straight line.

The reason why the ARROW ALIGNMENT TECHNIQUE™ is so reliable is the alignment of your target line and your arrow line is the same when your open trail eye and head are turned as far as possible in the direction of the target while maintaining the same angle of your spine. As a result, when you conduct the ARROW ALIGNMENT TECHNIQUE™ correctly, your shoulders should be aligned squarely parallel with your target line.

Not only is the ARROW ALIGNMENT TECHNIQUE™ much more reliable in aligning your shoulders squarely parallel with your intended target line than the conventional method, it is much easier and quicker.

Obviously, if there is some vision or neck impairment, the ARROW ALIGNMENT TECHNIQUE™ would not be beneficial in such an alignment procedure. Otherwise, it should become the alignment technique of choice for those who want to be assured their shoulders truly are aligned squarely parallel with their intended target line at final address.

It Is Impossible to Produce a Straight Ball Flight to an Intended Target When the Shoulders Are Misaligned with the Intended Target Line and a Non-Manipulative Golf Swing Is Executed

When the sweet spot of the clubface is centered as near the back of the ball as possible but the shoulders are misaligned with the intended target line at final address, it is impossible to produce a straight golf shot in the direction of an intended target on a path that parallels the shoulder line when a non-manipulative golf swing is executed.

Assume the forearms have rotated the wrists, clubface and elbows to establish a straight ball flight alignment and the sweet spot of the clubface is centered as near the back of the ball as possible. If the shoulders are aligned to the inside of the intended target line and a non-manipulative golf swing is executed, the ball will fly to the inside of the intended target line instead of on a straight path in the direction of the intended target – because the shoulder line is the "effective" target line.

If in the same example, assume the shoulders are aligned to the outside of the intended target line and a non-manipulative golf shot is executed, the ball will fly on a straight path but only in a direction to the outside of the intended target line – because the shoulder line is the "effective" target line.

However, the tendency in either case will be to steer the clubface down the target line during the downswing to compensate for the shoulders misalignment. In doing so, the "ball position" will change and a skulled or chunked golf shot most likely will occur.

To avoid a skulled or chunked golf shot, your shoulders must be aligned squarely parallel with your intended target line when your clubface contacts the ball. To help ensure your shoulders are aligned squarely parallel with your intended target line when your clubface contacts a ball, you must center the sweet spot of your clubface as near the back of your ball as possible and align your shoulders squarely parallel with your intended target line at final address. Then assuming you also have established and locked-in a straight ball flight alignment and then execute a non-manipulative golf swing, your clubface will "bottom-out" when the sweet spot of your clubface contacts the ball at impact and produce a straight ball flight in the direction of your target.

The Second Order of Business to Avoid a Chunked or Skulled Golf Shot Is to Position Your Clubface Correctly in Relation to Your Ball and Your Shoulders

The fourth bone alignment as discussed in Chapter Two relates to "ball position." In order to achieve an ideal "ball position," the mid-point of your shoulder line must be aligned squarely perpendicular to the back of your ball.

This naturally occurs when the sweet spot of your clubface is centered as near the back of your ball as possible and, simultaneously, your shoulders are aligned squarely parallel with your intended target line; assuming also you have established and locked-in a straight ball flight alignment at such point.

The concept of so-called "ball position" is confusing to many golfers because it suggests the ball is moved in some way. Quite the contrary. In most situations if the ball is in play, a penalty is assessed if the ball is moved.

Many golfers attempt to adjust their stance in some way to achieve an ideal "ball position." This approach in an attempt to establish an ideal "ball position" is somewhat flawed, however.

What determines when, where and how the clubface reaches the lowest point of its swing arc is how the shoulders are aligned in relation to the ball when the clubface contacts the ball. It is the relationship between the shoulders and the ball rather than the relationship between the stance and the ball that determines when, where and how the clubface will "bottom-out" during the downswing. An adjustment of the stance nonetheless may be necessary to align the shoulders squarely parallel with the intended target line.

When the Wrists, Clubface and Elbows Are Rotated to Establish a Straight Ball Flight Alignment and, Simultaneously, the Shoulders Are Aligned Squarely Parallel with the Intended Target Line and the Sweet Spot of the Clubface Is Centered as Near the Back of the Ball as Possible, an Ideal "Ball Position" Will Exist

Professional tour players as well as low handicap amateurs engage in all sorts of exercises in an attempt to find the correct "ball position" for a specific golf shot. Many will move several inches back from their normal stance and engage in a few practice swings to observe at what point the clubface will "bottom-out," then move nearer the ball and attempt to duplicate the practice swing during their actual swing.

Some contend the "bottom-out" point of the clubface merely is in line with the chin which may come as a surprise to those who turn their chin away from the ball during their pre-shot routine.

The sweet spot of the clubface will bottom-out at the point the clubface contacts the ball and avoid a skulled or chunked golf shot if the four pre-shot alignments exist at final address and remain at impact. They are, once again:

- **The sweet spot of the clubface must be centered as near the back of the ball as possible (so the mid-point of the shoulders will be aligned perpendicular to the back of the ball).**
- **The shoulders must be aligned squarely parallel with the intended target line.**
- **The wrists and clubface must be rotated to a square alignment so they will hinge perpendicular to the tip-end of the trail shoulder during the backswing and unhinge squarely to the ball at impact.**
- **The elbows must be aligned squarely parallel with the shoulders.**

These four pre-shot alignments must exist at the completion of each pre-shot routine, followed by a non-manipulative golf swing, in order to produce a straight ball flight.

In order for the clubface to "bottom-out" when the sweet spot of the clubface contacts the ball, the shoulder-to-target alignment must correspond with the mid-point of the shoulders-to-the back of ball alignment after a straight ball flight alignment has been established and locked-in. If not, the following most likely will occur:

- When the shoulders are aligned to the outside of the intended target line at final address in such instance, the clubface "effectively" will be centered at some point behind the ball even when centered as near the back of the ball as possible. Likewise, when the clubface is centered at some point behind the ball instead of as near the back of the ball as possible, the shoulders "effectively" will be aligned to the outside of the intended target line even though aligned parallel with the intended target line. In either case, a skulled or chunked golf shot is likely to result if a non-manipulative golf swing is executed.
- When the shoulders are aligned to the inside of the intended target line in such instance at final address, the clubface "effectively" will be centered ahead (in front) of the back of the ball

even when centered as near the back of the ball as possible. Likewise, when the clubface is centered (in front) of the back of the ball in such instance at final address, the shoulders "effectively" will be aligned to the inside of the intended target line even though aligned parallel with the intended target line. In either case, a skulled or chunked golf shot is likely to result.

In the subsequent chapters, you will be instructed precisely how to rotate your wrists, clubface and elbows from their inherent slight slice alignment – established the instant a conventional style of grip is assembled – to a straight ball flight alignment and then how to lock-in such an alignment. Moreover, you will be instructed how to center the sweet spot of your clubface as near the back of your ball as possible.

You then will be instructed how to use the ARROW ALIGNMENT TECHNIQUE™ to align your shoulders squarely parallel with your intended target line. When all such alignments exist at final address, a non-manipulative golf swing will produce a golf shot on a straight path in the direction of your target and on a parallel path with your shoulders.

If you follow my instructions precisely, you will never again chunk or skull a golf shot.

SUMMARY POINTS

1. To avoid a chunked or skulled golf shot, four essential alignments must exist at impact as discussed in the previous chapter.

2. The techniques to rotate the wrists and clubface from an open alignment to a square alignment and the elbows from an outside-to-inside swing path across the shoulders to an on-line swing path will be addressed in subsequent chapters.

3. However, the focus of this chapter is about how to align the shoulders squarely parallel with the intended target line and also how to align the mid-point of the shoulders squarely perpendicular to the back of the ball to establish an ideal "bottom-out" position.

4. The conventional approach to align the shoulders squarely parallel with the intended target line involves too much guesswork and is far too unreliable.

5. A more reliable means to align the shoulders squarely parallel with the intended target line is to utilize the ARROW ALIGNMENT TECHNIQUE™.

6. When the lead eye is closed and the trail eye is focused on its inside corner an "arrow" configuration will appear between the top of the nose and the bottom of the eye socket of the trail eye. If then the spine is stabilized and the head and trail eye are turned as far as possible in the direction of the target and the arrow points directly at the target, the shoulders will be aligned squarely parallel with the intended target line.

7. If necessary, the stance can be adjusted until the tip-end of the "arrow" points directly at the target. This is all that is required to align the shoulders squarely parallel with the intended target line.

8. If the sweet spot of the clubface is centered as near the back of the ball as possible but the shoulders are misaligned with the intended target line at final address, it is impossible to hit a golf ball on a straight path in the direction of the target and on a straight path that parallels the shoulder line if a non-manipulative golf swing is executed.

9. If a straight ball flight alignment is established and locked-in, the sweet spot of the clubface is centered as near the back of the ball as possible and, simultaneously, the shoulders are aligned squarely parallel with the intended target line at final address, the clubface will "bottom-out" at the point the sweet spot of the clubface contacts the ball if a non-manipulative golf swing is executed.

10. If the shoulders are aligned to the outside of the intended target line, even though the sweet spot of the clubface is centered as near the back of the ball as possible, the clubface "effectively" will be centered at some other point behind the ball in terms of ball position – and a chunked or skulled golf shot will likely result if a non-manipulative golf swing is executed.

11. If the shoulders are aligned to the inside of the intended target line, even though the sweet spot of the clubface is centered as near the back of the ball as possible, the clubface "effectively" will be centered at some other point in front of the back of the ball in terms of ball position – and a skulled or chunked golf shot will likely result if a non-manipulative golf swing is executed.

12. Whether you will be able to produce a straight ball flight to a specific target when applying the techniques to be discussed in the following chapters will depend in large part on how well you align your shoulders parallel with your intended target line and center the sweet spot of your clubface as near the back of the ball as possible and, also, how well you are able to execute a non-manipulative golf shot.

CHAPTER 4

INTRODUCTION OF THE PUSH OUT-N-LOCK TECHNIQUE™

The PUSH OUT-N-LOCK TECHNIQUE™ is the first of the thirty-two techniques that will be introduced and discussed in this and subsequent chapters.

In each of these thirty-two techniques, the proceedings begin with one of the four conventional styles of grip – either with an original Vardon overlap, a modified Vardon overlap, a traditional interlock or regular baseball (ten-fingers) style of golf grip. Each of these styles of grip establishes a slice ball flight alignment the instant they are formed on a club, assuming there is no clubface rotation during the gripping process.

Each of the Thirty-Two Techniques Requires a Precise Number of "Locks" of the Lifeline/Thumb Connection

A conventional golf grip is not a completed grip until the lifeline portion of the trail hand is locked on the lead thumb. I refer to this procedure as locking the "lifeline/thumb connection."

As I explain in HOW TO HIT A GOLF BALL AS STRAIGHT-AS-AN-ARROW, when the lifeline of the trail hand is locked on the lead thumb to complete either an original or modified Vardon overlap, traditional interlock or regular baseball (ten-fingers) style of grip, a new form of bone joint effectively results, not unlike that of an elbow, wrist or shoulder joint..

The lifeline of the trail hand is the crease that runs down the center of the hand – between the base of the thumb and the fatty pad of the palm. (Figure 4-1).

The ulna and radius bones of the lead forearm effectively are joined with the ulna and radius bones of the trail forearm when the lifeline of the trail hand is locked on the lead thumb. Once joined, almost any body movement thereafter will cause the forearms to

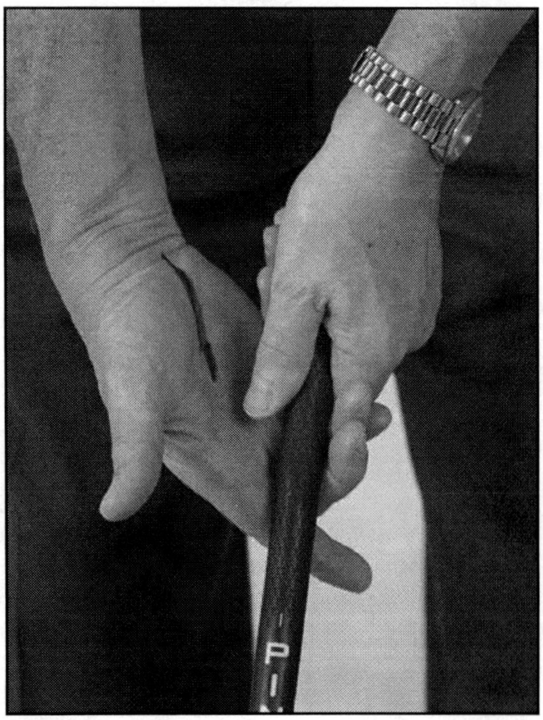

Figure 4-1

The lifeline of the trail hand is the crease that runs down the center of the palm – between the base of the thumb and the fatty pad of the palm as shown.

rotate the wrists, clubface and elbows either counterclockwise or clockwise unless such bones are locked-in to a specific alignment.

When the lifeline portion of the trail hand is locked on the lead thumb it must fit squarely and snugly against the thumb. This procedure cannot be compromised when assembling the thirty-two techniques addressed in this book.

In addition, when the lifeline portion (simply referred to as the "lifeline") of the trail hand is unlocked from the lead thumb and then relocked on the lead thumb in order to lock-in a specific alignment, it must be unlocked from the lead thumb by at least an inch or more without completely ungripping the club and then relocked on the lead thumb. The grip must remain in tact during this procedure except for the unlocking and relocking of the lifeline/thumb connection.

When the lifeline of the trail hand is relocked on the lead thumb it once again must fit squarely and snugly on the lead thumb.

The thirty-two techniques discussed in this and the subsequent chapters involve some specific and precise body movement to cause the forearms to rotate the wrists, clubface and elbows from a slice alignment to a straight alignment between the time a conventional style of grip is completed and the unlocking and relocking of the lifeline/thumb connection a precise number of times. Once the wrists, clubface and elbows are rotated to establish a straight ball flight alignment, the lifeline/thumb connection typically must be unlocked and relocked either once or twice – depending on the specific body movement – to secure and lock-in the alignment and prevent the forearms, wrists, clubface and elbows from rotating to a different alignment during the remainder of the pre–shot routine and the backswing.

How to Assemble and Execute the Push Out-N-Lock Technique™

The PUSH OUT-N-LOCK TECHNIQUE™ is compatible with either an original Vardon overlap, modified Vardon overlap, traditional interlock or regular baseball (ten-fingers) style of grip.

The ***first step*** in assembling and executing the PUSH OUT-N-LOCK TECHNIQUE™ is to ground the sole of your clubface in the middle of your stance and then assume your preferred conventional style of grip on a club.

This means the lead hand must be gripped on the club in a diagonal manner as described in Chapter Two and then the trail hand must be assembled on the club either in the form of an original or modified Vardon overlap, traditional interlock or regular baseball (ten-fingers) style of grip. The grip then must be completed by locking the lifeline of the trail hand squarely and securely on the lead thumb.

The ***second step*** in completing the PUSH OUT-N-LOCK TECHNIQUE™ is to immobilize your shoulders and knees, keep your wrists relaxed and use your arms only to push your clubface outward and away from your body as far as possible. This will cause the sole of your clubface to slide on the surface away from your body as far as possible. The clubface needs to slide outward by at least two lengths of the clubface.

Pushing your clubface outward and away from your body as far as possible after assuming a conventional grip and, while keeping your shoulders and knees immobilized, is the body movement that will cause your forearms to rotate your wrists, clubface and elbows from a slice alignment to establish a straight alignment at the completion of the proceedings.

The shoulders and clubface must be held in their respective positions until the proceedings are completed.

The ***third step*** in completing the PUSH OUT-N-LOCK TECHNIQUE™ is to unlock the lifeline of your trail hand from your lead thumb by at least an inch without completely ungripping the club and then relock the lifeline of your trail hand on your lead thumb. This single unlocking and relocking of the lifeline/thumb connection as soon as the sole of the clubface has slid away from your body as far as possible is what secures and locks-in the straight ball flight alignment and prevents your forearms, wrists, clubface and elbows from rotating to a different ball flight alignment during the remainder of your pre-shot routine and backswing. (Figure 4-2).

The PUSH OUT-N-LOCK TECHNIQUE™ does not need to be assembled and completed with the sweet spot of the clubface centered as near the back of the ball as possible. As long as the lifeline/thumb connection remains locked once the proceedings are completed it can be assembled and completed elsewhere and then later centered as near the back of the ball as possible.

Once the proceedings are completed, the SHOULDERS ONLY TEST™, ARMS-LIFT TEST™ and STRAIGHT-UP TEST™ must be conducted to determine whether the PUSH OUT-N-LOCK TECHNIQUE™ has been assembled and executed correctly and, in turn, whether a straight ball flight has been established and locked-in.

If there is any clockwise or counterclockwise rotation of the clubface during any of the three tests, the grip should be disassembled and the steps outlined above should be repeated until there is no clubface rotation during the three tests.

Figure 4-2

STEP 1: The first essential step to assemble and execute the PUSH OUT-N-LOCK TECHNIQUE™ is to grip both hands on the club in a conventional manner with the clubface grounded in the middle of the stance.

STEP 2: The second essential step is to then keep the clubface grounded, immobilize the shoulders and knees, keep the wrists, hands and forearms relaxed and push the club outward and away from the body as far as possible until the clubface stops rotating clockwise.

STEP 3: Next, the clubface must be held in such position until the lifeline of the trail hand is unlocked from the lead thumb by at least an inch without completely ungripping the club.

STEP 4: The clubface must continue to be held in such position until the lifeline of the trail hand is relocked squarely and securely on the lead thumb.

Why the Push Out-N-Lock Technique™ Works

The reason why the PUSH OUT-N-LOCK TECHNIQUE™ works is when the sole of the clubface slides away from the body as far as possible (by at least two lengths of the clubface) while immobilizing the shoulders and knees and, keeping the sole of the clubface grounded, the forearms will rotate the elbows to a parallel alignment with the shoulders to establish an on-line swing path of the clubface.

When the elbows are aligned parallel with the shoulders the wrists correspondingly will rotate the clubface to a square alignment, all of which will establish a straight ball flight alignment. Such an alignment however will not be locked-in at this point.

In order to lock-in the straight ball flight alignment, the lifeline/thumb connection then must be unlocked and relocked once and no more thereafter.

Altogether, the PUSH OUT-N-LOCK TECHNIQUE™ requires two "locks" of the lifeline/thumb connection.

The first of the two "locks" of the lifeline/thumb connection that is required to assemble and execute the PUSH OUT-N-LOCK TECHNIQUE™ occurs when the lifeline of the trail hand is locked squarely and securely on the lead thumb to complete the grip.

The second of the two "locks" occurs after the clubface is pushed away from the body as far as possible while immobilizing the shoulders and knees when then the lifeline of the trail hand is unlocked from the lead thumb by at least an inch without completely ungripping the club and then relocked on the lead thumb.

Disciplines Required to Assemble and Execute the Push Out-N-Lock Technique™

The PUSH OUT-N-LOCK TECHNIQUE™ requires precision.

The first discipline is to ground the leading edge (sole) of the clubface in the middle of the stance and keep it grounded during the entire procedure. It must continue to be grounded even when the sole of the clubface slides away from the body; that is, it cannot be lifted from the surface during such time.

The second discipline is critical. There absolutely can be no movement or rotation of the clubface during the gripping of the lead and trail hand on the club or between the time the lead and trail hands are assembled on the handle of the club. If the clubface is moved or rotated in any manner during such times the PUSH OUT-N-LOCK TECHNIQUE™ will not establish a straight ball flight alignment.

If the clubface accidentally moves forward, backwards or sideways during the gripping process, you should disassemble your grip completely and begin the proceedings anew.

One way to help prevent the clubface from rotating during the gripping proceedings is to press the sole of the clubface into the surface before assembling a grip on the club.

The third discipline associated with assembling and executing the PUSH OUT-N-LOCK TECHNIQUE™ is the clubface cannot be allowed to move or rotate after the grip is formed except for the rotation caused by the hands being pushed away from the body as far as possible which will cause the sole of the clubface to slide outward and away from the body. Any other rotation or movement of the clubface will cause the forearms, wrists, clubface and elbows to rotate to a different ball flight alignment. The wrists, hands and arms must be relaxed when the club is pushed away from the body to allow the clubface to rotate fully clockwise.

A fourth discipline is the shoulders and knees must be immobilized while the clubface is pushed away from the body as far as possible and while the sole of the clubface remains grounded. In doing so, the sole of the clubface should slide at least two lengths of the clubface away from the body.

When the clubface is pushed away from the body as far as possible while immobilizing the shoulders and knees, the forearms will rotate the elbows to a parallel alignment with the shoulders to create an on-line swing path and the wrists and clubface to a square alignment, all of which will establish a straight ball flight alignment. If the clubface is not pushed out and away from the body as far as possible in such instance, a straight ball flight alignment will not be established. Once the clubface is pushed out as far as possible, it must be held in such position until the completion of the proceedings.

Another discipline associated with the gripping proceedings is the lead hand cannot be loosened and tightened or partially ungripped and regripped once initially gripped on the club. Any such loosening or tightening or partial ungripping or regripping of the lead hand after it initially is gripped on a club will cause the forearms to rotate the wrists, clubface and elbows to a different ball flight alignment.

A conventional style of grip means a correctly assembled conventional style of grip. None of the thirty-two LOCKED-IN TECHNIQUES™ addressed in this book will cause the forearms to rotate the wrists, clubface and elbows to establish and lock-in a straight ball flight alignment at the completion of the proceedings unless a properly assembled conventional style of grip is assumed prior to any required body movement thereafter.

If a modified Vardon overlap is preferred, the tip-end of the lead index finger must fit snugly into the web between the little and ring fingers of the trail hand as explained in Chapter Two. If you have difficulty in doing such without rotating your clubface in the process, you may want to change your grip to another conventional type of grip.

If the original Vardon overlap style of grip is used, the tip end of the little finger of the trail hand must be overlapped on top of the middle knuckle of the lead hand.

An additional discipline is the body must be positioned squarely to the clubface when the PUSH OUT-N-LOCK TECHNIQUE™ is performed. That is, the shoulders and stance should be at a 90 degree angle to the clubface during the proceedings. If the shoulders and stance are aligned diagonally in relation to the clubface during the procedure, the forearms, wrists, clubface and elbows may rotate to a different ball flight alignment when the club is pushed forward and away from the body.

This means also you must push your arms and, in turn, your clubface evenly away from your body. One arm cannot be involved more or less than the other when the hands are pushed away from the body.

Your elbows must be disconnected completely from your rib cage throughout the proceedings when performing the PUSH OUT-N-LOCK TECHNIQUE™. If either or both elbows are connected to the rib cage at any stage of the proceedings, your forearms will rotate your wrists, clubface and elbows to a different ball flight alignment at the completion of the procedure.

Another significant discipline is the lifeline of the trail hand must be squarely and firmly locked on the lead hand to complete the grip – which constitutes the first "lock" of the lifeline/thumb connection. However, there can be no further unlocking or relocking of the lifeline/thumb connection until the sole of the clubface is pushed away from the body as far as possible while immobilizing the shoulders and the knees.

At the very instant the clubface stops sliding away from your body, the lifeline of your trail hand must be unlocked by at least an inch from your lead thumb without ungripping the club and then relocked on your lead thumb. This is the only time the lifeline/thumb connection may be unlocked and relocked. If unlocked and relocked once more thereafter, your forearms will rotate your wrists, clubface and elbows to establish some alignment other than a straight ball flight alignment.

Once you have assembled and executed the PUSH OUT-N-LOCK TECHNIQUE™ you must conduct the three confirmation tests addressed in Chapter One to determine whether you assembled and executed it correctly.

For example,

You Should Conduct the Shoulders Only Test™ at the Completion of the Push Out-N-Lock Technique™

The SHOULDERS ONLY TEST™ should be conducted at the completion of the PUSH OUT-N-LOCK TECHNIQUE™. Merely straighten your legs to the maximum extent and lock your knee joints while keeping your arms, wrists and hands relaxed and your clubface grounded. Then very, very slowly raise your shoulders and head upward while continuing to keep your clubface grounded and observing your clubface closely. If your clubface slides freely in your direction, it will indicate the PUSH OUT-N-LOCK TECHNIQUE™ was assembled and executed correctly and a straight ball flight alignment has been established and locked-in. However, if there is any resistance to the clubface sliding freely in your direction but, instead, the clubface rotates even minutely clockwise or counterclockwise, it will indicate it was not assembled and executed correctly. The clubface will slide freely in your direction when conducting the SHOULDERS ONLY TEST™ only if a straight ball flight alignment has been established and locked-in.

You may also lower your shoulders while locking your knee joints and relaxing your arms and wrists as an alternative means of conducting the SHOULDERS ONLY TEST™. If your clubface does not rotate counterclockwise or clockwise in response to lowering your shoulders appreciably, it will indicate the PUSH OUT-N-LOCK TECHNIQUE™ was assembled and completed correctly. However, if there is even a fraction of a degree of clockwise or counterclockwise rotation of the clubface when you lower your shoulders in conducting the SHOULDERS ONLY TEST™, it will indicate the technique was not assembled and executed correctly.

Another important discipline associated with the SHOULDERS ONLY TEST™ is the knees may not be allowed to rock back and forth when the shoulders are raised. The knee joints must remain locked and the knees must remain still when the test is conducted.

If there is any counterclockwise or clockwise rotation of the clubface when conducting the SHOULDERS ONLY TEST™ you should disassemble your grip and begin the procedure anew.

You also should

Conduct the Arms-Lift Test™ at the Completion of the Push Out-N-Lock Technique™

The ARMS-LIFT TEST™ entails immobilizing the shoulders and knees, relaxing the arms, wrists and hands and then lifting the arms upward as far as possible while keeping the clubface grounded. If the clubface rotates even slightly counterclockwise or clockwise instead of vertically (up and down), it will indicate the PUSH OUT-N-LOCK TECHNIQUE™ was not performed correctly and a straight ball flight alignment has not been established and locked-in.

In such case, you should disassemble your grip and repeat the procedure.

You must lift your arms as high as possible, however, when conducting the ARMS-LIFT TEST™ in order to observe if there is any counterclockwise or clockwise rotation of the clubface. You only will be able to observe whether the clubface rotates counterclockwise or clockwise when conducting the ARMS-LIFT TEST™ near the completion stage of lifting your arms upward as far as possible rather than during the initial stage of doing so.

Also, I recommend you

Conduct the Straight-Up Test™ at the Completion of the Push Out-N-Lock Technique™

The STRAIGHT-UP TEST™ may be the most reliable of all the confirmation tests introduced and discussed in Chapter One.

When the sole of the clubface is grounded, as it should be when assembling and executing each of the thirty-two techniques discussed in this book, it should make a very slight indentation into the surface. This indentation should serve as your reference line when the clubface is lifted from the surface when conducting the STRAIGHT-UP TEST™. If there is no clear indentation line, you can identify where it should be and then use it as a reference line.

Remember when conducting this test, the knees must remain stabilized and the arms, wrists and hands must remain relaxed and passive as the shoulders are lifted upward until the clubface is raised to about a foot above the surface. If the clubface rotates counterclockwise or clockwise from its reference line – the indentation line on the surface – when raised about a foot above the surface, it will indicate the PUSH OUT-N-LOCK TECHNIQUE™ was not assembled and executed correctly and that a straight ball flight alignment has not been established and locked-in.

However, if there is no counterclockwise or clockwise clubface rotation from the reference line when the clubface is raised above the surface it will indicate that the PUSH OUT-N-LOCK TECHNIQUE™ was assembled and executed correctly and a straight ball flight alignment has been established and locked-in.

Once the Push Out-N-Lock Technique™ Is Confirmed the Other Pre-Shot Requirements Then Must Be Completed

The PUSH OUT-N-LOCK TECHNIQUE™ only establishes and locks-in a straight ball flight alignment in reference to the shoulder line.

If then the sweet spot of the clubface is centered as near the back of the ball as possible and a non-manipulative golf swing is executed, the ball will fly on a straight path that parallels the shoulder line. However, the ball will fly on a straight path in the direction of the intended target only if, simultaneously, the shoulders are aligned squarely parallel with the intended target line.

Therefore, in addition to establishing and locking-in a straight ball flight, the sweet spot of your clubface must be centered as near the back of your ball as possible and, simultaneously, your shoulders must be aligned squarely parallel with your intended target line at the completion of your pre-swing proceedings in order for a non-manipulative golf swing to produce a straight ball flight in the direction of your intended target.

It is a rather simple matter to center the sweet spot of your clubface as near the back of your ball as possible. However, much more is involved in attempting to align your shoulders squarely parallel with your intended target line.

The ARROW ALIGNMENT TECHNIQUE™ should be used not only to align your shoulders squarely parallel with your intended target line when using the PUSH OUT-N-LOCK TECHNIQUE™ but when using any of the other thirty-one techniques discussed in this book as well.

Remember in conducting the ARROW ALIGNMENT TECHNIQUE™, the only parts of the body that move are the turning of the trail eye and head in the direction of the target as far as possible while observing the tip-end of the alignment arrow formed at the inside corner of the trail eye. The shoulders and head do not move up, down or sideways. The spine angle must remain in tact. Neither do the feet or the knees move.

When the trail eye and head are turned in the direction of the target as far as possible while the sweet spot of the clubface remains centered as near the back of the ball as possible, all that then is required is to adjust your feet, if necessary, until the tip-end of the alignment arrow points directly at the target. Once the ARROW ALIGNMENT TECHNIQUE™ confirms your shoulders are aligned squarely parallel with your intended target line, merely turn your head and eyes back to the ball, ensure the sweet spot of your clubface has remained centered as near the back of your ball as possible and then execute a non-manipulative golf swing.

Recommended Practice Routines When Using the Push Out-N-Lock Technique™ in Combination with the Arrow Alignment Technique™

When practicing while using the PUSH OUT-N-LOCK TECHNIQUE™ in combination with the ARROW ALIGNMENT TECHNIQUE™, you should begin with a wedge and then progress through your set with each next most lofted club thereafter until all are used. With each club you should begin merely with a wrist swing, then with a ½ swing, on to a ¾ swing and conclude with a full swing. The steps below should be followed in each practice session:

STEP 1: **Select a safe and relatively flat hitting surface. Place a ball on the surface. Identify your target as well as your intended target line.**

STEP 2: **Then select a short club to begin your practice, such as a wedge. Assemble and complete the PUSH OUT-N-LOCK TECHNIQUE™ by following the steps and adhering to the disciplines discussed in this chapter. Ground the sole of your clubface when assembling and completing the PUSH OUT-N-LOCK TECHNIQUE™ but it is not necessary to complete the procedure with the clubface centered behind your ball. You can center the sweet spot of the clubface behind your ball after assembling and executing the PUSH OUT-N-LOCK TECHNIQUE™ as long as you do not unlock your lifeline/thumb connection in the process.**

STEP 3: **Once you have assembled and completed the PUSH OUT-N-LOCK TECHNIQUE™, you should conduct the SHOULDERS ONLY TEST™, ARMS-LIFT TEST™ and the STRAIGHT-UP TEST™ to determine whether the technique was performed correctly and whether a straight ball flight has been established and locked-in. If not, repeat the first two steps until the procedure is confirmed by these tests.**

STEP 4: **Once confirmed, center the sweet spot of your clubface as near the back of your ball as possible (if not already so centered) without allowing the clubface to move the ball in the process. Assume a comfortable posture and stance to the ball and then align your shoulders parallel with your intended target line to the best of your ability.**

STEP 5: **Conduct the ARROW ALIGNMENT TECHNIQUE™ and adjust your feet, if necessary, until your alignment arrow**

points directly at your target when you turn your trail eye and head in the direction of your target as far as possible while immobilizing all other parts of your body.

STEP 6: Once the ARROW ALIGNMENT TECHNIQUE™ confirms your shoulders are aligned squarely parallel with your intended target line, ensure the sweet spot of your clubface has remained centered as near the back of your ball as possible and then execute a natural, non-manipulative golf swing.

When you execute a non-manipulative golf swing, your downswing should deliver a square clubface to your ball on a path that matches your shoulders and target line and, in turn, produce a straight golf shot in the direction of your target.

When the thirty-two techniques addressed in this book are assembled and completed correctly, a straight ball flight alignment will be established and locked-in. When the other pre-shot requirements are met, the straight ball flight alignment will remain in tact even if the clubface is swung to the inside or to the outside of its established swing path during the backswing.

However, if during the downswing the clubface is "steered" or forced out of its established path, the straight ball flight alignment will not remain in tact. When the clubface is "steered" out of its established path on the downswing, it effectively will change the "ball position" in relation to the shoulders as well as the shoulder alignment in relation to the target line. As a result, the forearms will rotate the wrists, clubface and elbows to establish a different ball flight alignment by the time the clubface contacts the ball.

When the clubface is swung either to the inside or to the outside of its established swing path during the backswing it typically is caused by the shoulders being misaligned with the intended target line at final address. The outside or inside movement of the clubface during the backswing typically is a subconscious attempt to realign the shoulders with the intended target line before the downswing begins. In turn, the tendency during the downswing will be to attempt to "steer" the clubface down and along the intended target line instead of along its established swing path and cause the clubface to mis-hit the ball.

Therefore, it is imperative you align your shoulders squarely parallel with your intended target line at the completion of your pre-swing proceedings while the sweet spot of your clubface remains centered as near the back of the ball as possible. As a result, there should be no subconscious tendency to swing the clubface to the inside or outside of its established path either during the backswing or the downswing.

SUMMARY POINTS

1. **The first order of business in each of the thirty-two techniques addressed in this book is to form a conventional style of grip on a club and lock the lifeline of the trail hand firmly on the lead thumb to complete the grip.**

2. **The forearms, wrists, clubface and elbows must then be rotated by some body movement from the initial slice alignment to a straight ball flight alignment.**

3. **When the lifeline of the trail hand is locked on the lead thumb to complete a conventional golf grip, the ulna and the radius bones of the lead forearm are joined with the ulna and radius bones of the trail forearm to create an "effective" new bone joint not unlike that of a wrist, elbow or shoulder joint.**

4. **Once the lifeline of the trail hand initially is locked on the lead thumb to create an "effective" new bone joint, almost any body movement thereafter will cause the forearms to rotate the wrists, clubface and elbows to some extent unless a specific ball flight alignment is locked-in.**

5. **The thirty-two techniques discussed in this book are designed to rotate the forearms, wrists, clubface and elbows from a slice alignment to a straight ball flight alignment.**

6. **The first step in assembling and executing the PUSH OUT-N-LOCK TECHNIQUE™ is to ground the sole of the clubface in the middle of the stance.**

7. **The second step is to form a conventional style of golf grip on a club and lock the lifeline of the trail hand firmly on the lead thumb to complete the grip.**

8. **The shoulders and knees then must be immobilized and the wrists should be relaxed, as the hands are pushed outward and away from the body as far as possible. The sole of the clubface should slide correspondingly outward and away from the body by at least two lengths of the clubface.**

9. **Once the hands cease to push the clubface away from the body as far as possible, the lifeline of the trail hand must be unlocked from the lead thumb and then relocked on the lead thumb.**

10. **However, the lifeline/thumb connection may only be unlocked and relocked once at this point. If unlocked and relocked once more thereafter, the forearms, wrists, clubface and elbows will rotate to establish a different ball flight alignment.**

11. **Once the PUSH OUT-N-LOCK TECHNIQUE™ is completed, such confirmation tests as the SHOULDERS ONLY TEST™, ARMS-LIFT TEST™ and STRAIGHT-UP TEST™ should be conducted to determine if assembled correctly.**

12. **Once the PUSH OUT-N-LOCK TECHNIQUE™ is confirmed, the sweet spot of the clubface should be centered as near the back of the ball as possible (if not already so centered) and the ARROW ALIGNMENT TECHNIQUE™ should be conducted to align the shoulders squarely parallel with the intended target line.**

13. **Once the shoulders are aligned squarely parallel with the intended target line and the sweet spot of the clubface remains centered as near the back of the ball as possible, a non-manipulative golf swing should be executed.**

14. **There should be several meaningful practice sessions with the PUSH OUT-N-LOCK TECHNIQUE™ before using it in actual play.**

CHAPTER 5

INTRODUCTION OF THE PULL IN-N-LOCK TECHNIQUE™

The PULL IN-N-LOCK TECHNIQUE™ requires the sole of the clubface to slide in toward the body by at least two lengths of the clubface after a conventional style of grip is formed on a club.

The clubface should be grounded, the shoulders and knees should be immobilized and the wrists should remain passive and inactive and only move in response to the hands being pulled in toward the body after a conventional style of grip is formed on a club.

The PULL IN-N-LOCK TECHNIQUE™ is compatible with all four conventional styles of grip whether that of an original Vardon overlap, modified Vardon overlap, traditional interlock or regular baseball (ten-fingers) type of grip.

Once the clubface has slid inward toward the body by at least two lengths of the clubface after a conventional style of grip has been assembled on a club, the lifeline/thumb connection must be unlocked and relocked twice but no more thereafter.

How to Assemble and Execute the Pull In-N-Lock Technique™

First, ground the sole of your clubface in the middle of your stance. It does not necessarily need to be grounded directly behind your ball. You can ground it in the near vicinity of your ball and once the proceedings are completed, then transfer and center the sweet spot of your clubface as near the back of your ball as possible.

Second, grip your lead hand on your club in a conventional (diagonal) manner. You must not allow any clubface rotation when gripping your lead hand on your club.

Third, then grip your trail hand on your club in a conventional manner without allowing any clockwise or counterclockwise rotation of your clubface. Complete your grip by locking the lifeline of your trail hand firmly on your lead thumb.

Fourth, immobilize your shoulders and knees and keep your wrists passive as you pull the handle of your club in toward your body which, in turn, will slide your clubface in toward your body. You must stand far enough away from your ball when gripping your hands on the club to allow your clubface to slide in your direction as far as possible but by at least two lengths of your clubface.

Fifth, once you have slid your clubface in towards your body as far as possible, you then must unlock the lifeline of your trail hand by at least an inch from your lead thumb without completely ungripping your club and then relock your lifeline on your lead thumb.

Sixth, then once again you must unlock the lifeline of your trail hand from your lead thumb by at least an inch without completely ungripping your club and then, once again, relock the lifeline of your trail hand on your lead thumb.

Your lifeline/thumb connection may not be unlocked and relocked thereafter. (Figure 5-1).

Seventh, conduct the SHOULDERS ONLY TEST™, ARMS-LIFT TEST™ and STRAIGHT-UP TEST™ at the completion of the proceedings. If the clubface rotates counterclockwise

Figure 5-1

STEP 1: The first essential step to assemble and execute the PULL IN-N-LOCK™ is to grip both hands on the club in a conventional manner with the clubface grounded in the middle of the stance.

STEP 2: The second essential step is to then keep the clubface grounded, immobilize the shoulders and knees, keep the wrists, hands and forearms relaxed and pull the club inward toward the body as far as possible – until the clubface stops rotating counterclockwise.

STEP 3: Next, the clubface must be held in such position until the lifeline of the trail hand is unlocked from the lead hand by at least an inch without completely ungripping the club.

STEP 4: The clubface must continue to be held in such position until the lifeline of the trail hand is relocked squarely and firmly on the lead thumb.

STEP 5: The clubface must be held in the same position until once again, the lifeline of the trail hand is unlocked from the lead thumb by at least an inch without completely ungripping the club.

STEP 6: The clubface must be held in such position until, once again, the lifeline of the trail hand is relocked squarely on the lead thumb.

or clockwise during any of the three tests, you must disassemble your grip and repeat the procedure until there is no clubface rotation when the three tests are conducted.

Why the Pull In-N-Lock Technique™ Works

When the clubface is pulled in toward the body as far as possible after a conventional style of grip is formed on a club and while immobilizing the shoulders and knees, the forearms will rotate the elbows to a parallel alignment with the shoulders to create an on-line swing path of the clubface.

When the forearms rotate the elbows to a parallel alignment with the shoulders the wrists correspondingly will rotate the clubface to a square alignment, all of which will establish a straight ball flight alignment.

Although a straight ball flight alignment will be established at this point, it will not be locked-in. In order to lock-in the straight ball flight alignment, the lifeline/thumb connection then must be unlocked and relocked twice but no more thereafter.

Altogether, the PULL IN-N-LOCK TECHNIQUE™ requires three "locks" of the lifeline/thumb connection. The first of the three "locks" occurs when the lifeline of the trail hand is locked squarely and securely on the lead thumb to complete the grip. The second of the three "locks" occurs after the clubface is slid in towards the body when then the lifeline of the trail hand is unlocked by at least an inch from the lead thumb without completely ungripping the club and then relocked on the lead thumb.

The third of the three "locks" occurs when then, once again, the lifeline of the trail hand must be unlocked from the lead thumb by at least an inch without completely ungripping the club and then, once again, the lifeline must be relocked on the lead thumb.

Disciplines Required to Assemble and Execute the Pull In-N-Lock Technique™

The most critical discipline associated with the assemblage and execution of the PULL IN-N-LOCK TECHNIQUE™ is the pulling in of the club handle towards the body as far as possible after assuming a conventional style of grip.

The shoulders and knees must be immobilized during this pulling-in maneuver. Also, as with the case of the PUSH OUT-N-LOCK TECHNIQUE™, the clubface must be grounded when the grip is assumed. It should be grounded in the middle of the stance and the club handle should be pulled in towards the body in a straight manner, rather than in a diagonal manner. In turn, the clubface should slide in towards the body in a straight rather than in a diagonal manner.

An additional discipline is the elbows must be disconnected from the rib cage during the proceedings. If either or both elbows are connected to the rib cage during the proceedings, the forearms will rotate the wrists, clubface and elbows to a different ball flight alignment at the completion of the proceedings.

Another discipline is the clubface cannot be allowed to rotate counterclockwise or clockwise during the proceedings except for the rotation caused by the clubface being pulled in toward the body after a conventional grip is assembled on the club.

Remember the clubface must be pulled in toward the body by at least two lengths of the clubface while immobilizing the shoulders and knees. Therefore, the stance line must be positioned far enough away from the target line when the grip is assumed to allow room enough for such movement. The hands, wrists and arms must be relaxed to allow the clubface to rotate fully clockwise when the club is pulled in toward the body as far as possible.

Each of the thirty-two LOCKED-IN TECHNIQUES™ addressed in this book requires a properly assembled conventional style of grip. As mentioned in the preceding chapter, if you have difficulty assuming your preferred conventional style of grip without allowing any clubface rotation, you should change to one of the other conventional types of grip.

The SHOULDERS ONLY TEST™, ARMS-LIFT TEST™ and STRAIGHT- UP TEST™ must be conducted at the completion of the proceedings to determine whether the technique has been assembled and executed correctly and, as a result, whether a straight ball flight alignment has been established and locked-in. If not, the procedure should be repeated until all three tests confirm that it has.

Once the proceedings are completed, the sweet spot of your clubface must be centered as near the back of your ball as possible (if not already so centered) and, simultaneously, your shoulders must be aligned squarely parallel with your intended target line at final address, followed by a non-manipulative golf swing, if your objective is to hit a ball on a straight path in the direction of your target.

Recommended Practice Routines When Using the Pull In-N-Lock Technique™ in Combination with the Arrow Alignment Technique™

Your should engage in some meaningful practice sessions before using the PULL IN-N-LOCK TECHNIQUE™ in actual play.

In each of your practice sessions you should locate a safe and relatively flat practice area. You should also conduct the ARROW ALIGNMENT TECHNIQUE™ to align your shoulders parallel with your intended target line.

You also should follow these steps when using the PULL IN-N-LOCK TECHNIQUE™ in your practice sessions:

STEP 1: Place a ball on the surface of your practice area. Identify a very narrow and specific target. Also, identify your intended target line.

STEP 2: Ground the sole of your clubface in the middle of your stance either directly behind your ball or in its near vicinity. Keep it grounded throughout the proceedings even though it will slide on the surface in your direction when you pull the club handle in towards your body.

STEP 3: Assemble and execute the PULL IN-N-LOCK TECHNIQUE™, as instructed throughout this chapter. Remember to immobilize your shoulders and knees as you pull your hands in toward your body as far as possible after assuming a conventional grip. The lifeline/thumb connection must be unlocked and relocked twice after sliding the clubface in towards your body by at least two lengths of the clubface.

STEP 4: Once you have completed the proceedings, conduct the SHOULDERS ONLY TEST™, ARMS-LIFT TEST™ and STRAIGHT-UP TEST™. Repeat the proceedings, if necessary, until the three tests confirm the technique has been completed correctly and a straight ball flight alignment has been established and locked-in.

STEP 5: Center the sweet spot of your clubface as near the back of your ball as possible (if not already so centered) and assume a comfortable posture and stance to your ball. Align your shoulders parallel with your intended target line to the best of your ability.

STEP 6: Conduct the ARROW ALIGNMENT TECHNIQUE™ and adjust your stance, if necessary, until your alignment arrow points directly at your target when you turn your head and trail eye in the direction of your target as far as possible while immobilizing all other parts of your body.

STEP 7: Ensure the sweet spot of your clubface has remained centered as near the back of the ball as possible and then execute a non-manipulative golf swing.

You should begin each practice session with your most lofted club and then practice with each next most lofted club in succession thereafter. With each club, you should begin with simply a wrist swing, then with a ½ swing, then with a ¾ swing and conclude with a full swing.

SUMMARY POINTS

1. The PULL IN-N-LOCK TECHNIQUE™ requires a sliding of the clubface in toward the body as far as possible – by at least two lengths of the clubface – after a conventional grip is formed on a club.

2. The sole of the clubface must be grounded in the middle of the stance during the proceedings even though the clubface will slide on the surface when the hands pull the club handle in toward the body.

3. The shoulders and knees must be immobilized and the wrists should remain relaxed and passive when the hands pull the clubface in toward the body.

4. The lead hand must be gripped on the club in a conventional (diagonal) manner and there may be no clockwise or counterclockwise rotation of the clubface while the lead hand is being gripped on the club.

5. The PULL IN-N-LOCK TECHNIQUE™ is compatible with all four conventional styles of grip.

6. Therefore, the trail hand may be assembled on the club either in the form of an original Vardon overlap, modified Vardon overlap, traditional interlock or regular baseball (ten-fingers) style of grip.

7. There cannot be any clockwise or counterclockwise rotation of the clubface during the time the trail hand is gripped on the club or between the time the lead and trail hands are gripped on the club.

8. **The grip is completed by locking the lifeline of the trail hand firmly on the lead thumb.**

9. **Once the clubface is slid in toward the body by at least two lengths of the clubface and the clubface rotates fully clockwise, the lifeline/thumb connection must be unlocked and relocked twice but no more thereafter.**

10. **The SHOULDERS ONLY TEST™, ARMS-LIFT TEST™ and STRAIGHT-UP TEST™ must be conducted at the completion of the proceedings to determine whether the technique was assembled and executed correctly and whether a straight ball flight alignment has been established and locked-in. If not, the grip should be disassembled and the procedure repeated until the PULL IN-N-LOCK TECHNIQUE™ is confirmed as properly completed.**

11. **The ARROW ALIGNMENT TECHNIQUE™ should be conducted to align the shoulders parallel with the intended target line when using the PULL IN-N-LOCK TECHNIQUE™.**

CHAPTER 6

INTRODUCTION OF THE DOUBLE CONNECT-N-LOCK TECHNIQUE™

The DOUBLE CONNECT-N-LOCK TECHNIQUE™ may become one of the most preferred of all the LOCKED-IN TECHNIQUES™ discussed in this book.

The objective in assembling and executing the DOUBLE CONNECT-N-LOCK TECHNIQUE™ is to make some adjustment after the grip is completed to cause the forearms to rotate the wrists, clubface and elbows to establish a straight ball flight alignment.

The adjustment in this technique is to connect both elbows to the rib cage without allowing the clubface to rotate after assuming a conventional style of grip on the club and then unlock and relock the lifeline/thumb connection once but no more thereafter.

When performed precisely, it will cause the forearms to rotate the elbows to a parallel alignment with the shoulders and cause the wrists to rotate the clubface to a square alignment.

It is an easy, fast and simple technique to perform.

How to Assemble and Execute the Double Connect-N-Lock Technique™

First, ground the sole of your clubface in the middle of your stance.

Second, ensure your elbows are disconnected from your rib cage and then assemble either an original Vardon overlap, modified Vardon overlap, traditional interlock or regular baseball (ten-fingers) style of grip. The lead hand must be assembled on the club in a diagonal manner as discussed in Chapter Two.

Third, complete your grip by locking the lifeline of your trail hand squarely and firmly on your lead thumb.

Fourth, then press both of your elbows firmly against your rib cage. Keep your elbows pressed against your rib cage and then unlock the lifeline of your trail hand from your lead thumb at least by an inch without completely ungripping your club and then relock the lifeline of your trail hand on your lead thumb.

Fifth, then relax your elbows and allow them to disconnect from your rib cage. (Figure 6-1).

Sixth, conduct the SHOULDERS ONLY TEST™, ARMS-LIFT TEST™ and STRAIGHT-UP TEST™ to determine whether you assembled and executed the technique correctly.

Why the Double Connect-N-Lock Technique™ Works

Once a conventional style of grip is assembled and the elbows then are pressed against the rib cage, the forearms will rotate the elbows to a parallel alignment with the shoulders to create an on-line swing path of the clubface.

As discussed previously, when the elbows are aligned squarely parallel with the shoulders to create an on-line swing path of the clubface the wrists correspondingly will rotate the clubface to a square alignment and in turn, a straight ball flight alignment will be established.

Figure 6-1

STEP 1: The first essential step to assemble and execute the DOUBLE CONNECT-N-LOCK TECHNIQUE™ is to grip both hands on the club in a conventional manner with the clubface grounded in the middle of the stance and the elbows disconnected from the rib cage.

STEP 2: The second essential step is to then connect both elbows firmly against the rib cage and hold them against the rib cage until the completion of the proceedings.

STEP 3: While continuing to hold the elbows against the rib cage, the next step is to unlock the lifeline of the trail hand from the lead thumb by at least an inch without completely ungripping the club.

STEP 4: Then, while continuing to hold the elbows against the rib cage in the same manner, relock the lifeline of the trail hand squarely and securely on the lead thumb. *(The elbows then may be disconnected from the rib cage.)*

Although a straight ball flight alignment will be established at such point, it will not be locked-in.

In order to lock-in the straight ball flight alignment, the lifeline/thumb connection then must be unlocked and relocked once but no more thereafter.

Once a straight ball flight alignment is locked-in, the elbows then must be disconnected from the rib cage and allowed to return to a comfortable position.

Disciplines Required to Assemble and Execute the Double Connect-N-Lock Technique™

It is not necessary to lift the clubface from the surface when pressing the elbows against the rib cage after assuming a conventional style of grip on a club. Merely fold or pull your elbows against your rib cage.

A most important discipline is there can be no clubface rotation during the gripping process. This means you cannot loosen and tighten or partially ungrip and then regrip your lead hand once it has been gripped on your club. It means also the clubface cannot be allowed to rotate during the time your lead or trail hand is gripped on a club or between the time your lead hand and your trail hand are assembled on your club.

One way to help prevent the clubface from rotating during the gripping proceedings is to press the sole of the clubface into the surface before commencing the grip of the club.

If you do not properly assume a conventional style of grip on your clubface – whether that of an original Vardon overlap, modified Vardon overlap, traditional interlock or regular baseball (ten-fingers) – neither this nor any other of the LOCKED-IN TECHNIQUES™ will establish and lock-in a straight ball flight alignment.

For example, if you do not fit the tip-end of your lead index finger snugly into the web between the little and ring fingers of your trail hand when forming a modified Vardon overlap grip on your club, the proceedings to assemble and execute the DOUBLE-CONNECT-N-LOCK TECHNIQUE™ will not establish and lock-in a straight ball flight alignment.

If you suffer from arthritis, you may find it difficult to form a modified Vardon overlap or a traditional interlock style of grip on your club. If so, you should not hesitate to change to an original Vardon overlap style of grip or even to a regular baseball (ten-fingers) type of grip.

However, if you use an original Vardon overlap grip, the tip end of the little finger of the trail hand (just beneath the fingernail) must be overlapped on top of the middle knuckle of the lead index finger.

An additional discipline is the lifeline/thumb connection cannot be unlocked and relocked before pressing your elbows against your rib cage. A straight ball flight is not established and locked-in until after you have unlocked and relocked your lifeline/thumb connection once after pressing your elbows against your rib cage.

The DOUBLE CONNECT-N-LOCK TECHNIQUE™ requires a total of two "locks" of the lifeline/thumb connection. The first of the two "locks" of the lifeline/thumb connection necessary to assemble and execute the DOUBLE CONNECT-N-LOCK TECHNIQUE™ occurs when the lifeline of the trail hand is locked squarely and securely on the lead thumb to complete the grip.

The second of the two "locks" of the lifeline/thumb connection occurs after the elbows are pressed against the rib cage when then the lifeline of the trail hand is unlocked by at least an inch from the lead thumb without completely ungripping the club and then relocked on the lead thumb.

The lifeline/thumb connection may not be unlocked and relocked thereafter. If unlocked and relocked once more thereafter, the forearms will rotate the wrists, clubface and elbows to a different ball flight alignment.

The final discipline associated with assembling and executing the DOUBLE CONNECT-N-LOCK TECHNIQUE™ is to relax the elbows and allow them to disconnect from the rib cage once the proceedings are completed.

Always Conduct the Shoulders Only Test™, Arms-Lift Test™ and the Straight-Up Test™ at the Completion of the Double Connect-N-Lock Technique™

Whether practicing or playing, always conduct the SHOULDERS ONLY TEST™ at the completion of the DOUBLE CONNECT-N-LOCK TECHNIQUE™.

You should remember when your shoulders are raised or lowered while your clubface remains grounded and your knee joints locked and, your clubface rotates instead of sliding freely in your direction, it will indicate the technique was not assembled and executed correctly. If the clubface rotates or is resistant to sliding freely in your direction, you should disassemble your grip and repeat the procedure precisely as instructed until the clubface does slide freely when the SHOULDERS ONLY TECHNIQUE™ is conducted.

Also, the ARMS-LIFT TEST™ should be conducted once the DOUBLE CONNECT-N-LOCK TECHNIQUE™ is completed. When conducting the ARMS-LIFT TEST™, you should recall that the clubface must remain grounded and all body parts other than the arms should be immobilized. The shoulders should not be allowed to move during the test; neither should the knees. The wrists and hands do move but only should move in response to the arms being lifted while the clubface remains grounded on the surface.

If the clubface rotates counterclockwise or clockwise when the arms are lifted when conducting the ARMS-LIFT TEST™, it will indicate the technique was not assembled and executed correctly. In such instance you should disassemble the grip and repeat the procedure precisely as instructed.

The STRAIGHT-UP TEST™ requires the clubface to be raised at least a foot above the surface by lifting the shoulders upward at the completion of the DOUBLE CONNECT-N-LOCK TECHNIQUE™. If the clubface rotates counterclockwise or clockwise when the clubface is lifted at least a foot above the surface it will indicate an incorrectly assembled technique. In such a case, you should disassemble the grip and repeat the procedure precisely as instructed until there is no rotation of the clubface when it is lifted from the surface.

Once the three confirmation tests validate the procedure was completed correctly and a straight ball flight alignment has been established and locked-in, you must then center the sweet spot of your clubface as near the back of the ball as possible (if not already so centered) and simultaneously align your shoulders squarely parallel with your intended target line. All that will remain will be to execute a non-manipulative golf swing and the ball should fly on a straight path in the direction of your target.

Recommended Practice Routines When Using the Double Connect-N-Lock Technique™ in Combination with the Arrow Alignment Technique™

Select a safe and relatively flat hitting area and begin each session with your most lofted club; then with each next most lofted club thereafter, in succession, until you have practiced with each club in your set.

With each club, begin with a wrist swing, then with a ½ swing, on to a ¾ swing and finish with a full swing.

The following steps should be helpful in each of your practice sessions.

STEP 1: Place a ball on the surface of your hitting area. Identify your target as well as your intended target line.

STEP 2: Ground your clubface in the middle of your stance, ensure your elbows

are disconnected from your rib cage and assemble either an original Vardon overlap, modified Vardon overlap, traditional interlock or regular baseball (ten-fingers) style of grip without allowing any clubface rotation during the gripping proceedings.

STEP 3: Complete the grip by locking the lifeline of your trail hand squarely and firmly on your lead thumb.

STEP 4: Press your elbows against your rib cage and continue to keep them pressed against your rib cage. Then unlock the lifeline of your trail hand at least by an inch from your lead thumb without completely ungripping your club and then relock your trail lifeline on your lead thumb. Relax your elbows and allow them to disconnect from your rib cage.

STEP 5: Conduct the SHOULDERS ONLY TEST™, ARMS-LIFT TEST and THE STRAIGHT-UP TEST™ to determine whether the technique was assembled and executed correctly and whether a straight ball flight alignment has been established and locked-in. If not, repeat the procedure until the three tests confirm such.

STEP 6: Once confirmed, center the sweet spot of your clubface as near the back of the ball as possible (if not already so centered), assume a comfortable posture and stance to the ball and then align your shoulders parallel with your intended target line to the best of your ability.

STEP 7: Then conduct the ARROW ALIGNMENT TECHNIQUE™ and adjust your stance, if necessary, until your alignment arrow points directly at your target when you turn your head and trail eye in the direction of your target as far as possible while immobilizing all other parts of your body.

STEP 8: Ensure the sweet spot of your clubface has remained centered as near the back of your ball as possible and then execute a non-manipulative golf swing.

The elbows do not need to be pressed against the rib cage too tightly when executing the DOUBLE CONNECT-N-LOCK TECHNIQUE™, only enough to connect them to the rib cage. Each elbow should be pressed against the rib cage in the same manner. If one is pressed more tightly than the other, it could compromise the proceedings.

SUMMARY POINTS

1. **The DOUBLE CONNECT-N-LOCK TECHNIQUE™ requires a conventional style of grip to be assembled on a club while the clubface is grounded.**

2. **The grip is completed by locking the lifeline of the trail hand squarely and firmly on the lead thumb.**

3. **The clubface cannot be allowed to rotate during the gripping proceedings.**

4. **Once the grip is completed, both elbows must be pressed against the rib cage.**

5. **The elbows must remain pressed against the rib cage while the lifeline/thumb connection is unlocked and relocked.**

6. **The elbows then must be relaxed and allowed to disconnect from the rib cage.**

7. **The sole of the clubface must be grounded in the middle of the stance during the proceedings.**

8. **Once the proceedings are completed and the elbows are disconnected from the rib cage , the SHOULDERS ONLY TEST™, ARMS-LIFT TEST™ and the STRAIGHT-UP TEST™ must be conducted to determine whether the technique has been**

properly assembled and executed. If not confirmed, the grip should be disassembled and the procedure repeated precisely as instructed until the tests do confirm the DOUBLE CONNECT-N-LOCK TECHNIQUE™ has been assembled and executed correctly.

9. **Whether practicing or playing, the ARROW ALIGNMENT TECHNIQUE™ should be used to align the shoulders squarely parallel with the intended target line.**

CHAPTER 7

INTRODUCTION OF THE ARMS LIFT-N-LOCK TECHNIQUE™

The ARMS LIFT-N-LOCK TECHNIQUE™ also should be one of the easiest LOCKED-IN TECHNIQUES™ to assemble and execute because it essentially involves the same maneuver as that of the ARMS-LIFT TEST™. It, however, cannot be assembled and executed in a lackadaisical manner.

It first requires the sole of the clubface to be grounded and remain grounded during the proceedings. It then requires the shoulders and knees to be immobilized and the wrists to remain passive and inactive as the arms are lifted upward as far as possible after a conventional style of grip is assembled on a club. When the arms are lifted upward in such a manner, the clubface should rotate counterclockwise, stop and then slide in the direction of the body. Then the lifeline/thumb connection must be unlocked and relocked once.

The ARMS-LIFT TECHNIQUE™ is compatible with all four conventional styles of grip whether that of an original Vardon overlap, modified Vardon overlap, traditional interlock or regular baseball (ten-fingers) style of grip.

How to Assemble and Execute the Arms Lift-N-Lock Technique™

The ***first step*** in completing the ARMS LIFT-N-LOCK TECHNIQUE™ is to ground the sole of the clubface in the middle of the stance. It can be grounded in the near vicinity of the ball and once the proceedings are completed, the sweet spot of the clubface then can be centered as near the back of the ball as possible.

The ***second step*** is to assume a conventional (diagonal) style of grip with the lead hand. The clubface may not be allowed to rotate clockwise or counterclockwise during the time the lead hand is being gripped on the club.

The ***third step*** is to grip the trail hand on the club either in the form of an original Vardon overlap, modified Vardon overlap, traditional interlock or regular baseball (ten-fingers) style of grip. There cannot be any clockwise or counterclockwise rotation of the clubface during the time the trail hand is gripped on the club or between the time the lead and trail hands are gripped on the club.

The grip is completed by locking the lifeline of the trail hand squarely and securely on the lead thumb.

The ***fourth step*** of the procedure is most critical. Once a conventional style of grip is formed on the club, the shoulders and knees must be immobilized, the wrists must remain passive and inactive and the clubface must remain grounded as the arms are lifted upward as far as possible. This arms-lifting maneuver is the body movement that causes the forearms to rotate the wrists, clubface and elbows to establish a straight ball flight alignment at the completion of the proceedings. The arms must be lifted upward until the clubface rotates fully counterclockwise and begins to slide in toward the body. The arms must be held in such position until the completion of the proceedings.

The ***fifth step*** is then to unlock the lifeline of the trail hand from the lead thumb by at least an inch without completely ungripping the club and then relock the lifeline on the lead thumb. The lifeline/thumb connection may not be unlocked or relocked thereafter. If unlocked and relocked once more thereafter, the forearms, wrists, clubface and elbows will rotate to establish a different ball flight alignment. (Figure 7-1).

Figure 7-1

STEP 1: The first essential step to assemble and execute the ARMS LIFT-N-LOCK TECHNIQUE™ is to grip the club with both hands in a conventional manner with the clubface grounded in the middle of the stance.

STEP 2: Next, keep the clubface grounded, immobilize the shoulders and knees, and then lift the arms upward as far as possible – until the clubface stops rotating counterclockwise and begins to slide in toward the body. Hold the clubface in such position until the proceedings are completed.

STEP 3: While continuing to hold the arms upward as far as possible, unlock the lifeline of the trail hand from the lead thumb by at least an inch without completely ungripping the club.

STEP 4: Then, while continuing to hold the arms upward as far as possible, relock the lifeline of the trail hand squarely and securely on the lead thumb.

Why the Arms Lift-N-Lock Technique™ Works

When the arms are lifted upward as far as possible (until the clubface stops rotating fully counterclockwise) after a conventional style of grip is assumed and, while the shoulders and knees are immobilized and the clubface grounded, the forearms will rotate the elbows to a parallel alignment with the shoulders to create an on-line swing path of the clubface.

When the elbows are rotated to a parallel alignment with the shoulders the wrists correspondingly will rotate the clubface to a square alignment, all of which will establish a straight ball flight alignment.

However, to lock-in the straight ball flight alignment the lifeline/thumb connection then must be unlocked and relocked once – but no more thereafter.

The ARMS-LIFT-N-LOCK TECHNIQUE™ requires a total of two "locks" of the lifeline/thumb connection: <u>once</u> when the lifeline of the trail hand is locked on the lead thumb to complete the grip; <u>twice</u> when the lifeline/thumb connection is unlocked and relocked after the arms are lifted upward as far as possible.

Disciplines Required When Assembling and Executing the Arms Lift-N-Lock Technique™

The clubface must be grounded in the middle of the stance throughout the procedure. The only time the clubface should move is in response to the arms being lifted upward until the clubface stops rotating counterclockwise and begins to slide in toward the body.

One of the most critical disciplines relating to this technique is there can be no clubface rotation or movement during the gripping proceedings. There can be no rotation or movement of the clubface between the time the lead hand and the trail hand are assembled on the club or during the time each is gripped on the club. If there accidentally is some rotation or movement of the clubface during the gripping process, you should disassemble the grip and begin the procedure anew.

One way to help prevent the clubface from rotating during the gripping proceedings is to press the sole of the clubface into the surface before assembling the grip.

Once the lead hand is gripped on the club, it thereafter may not be loosened and tightened or partially ungripped and regripped. Any such movement will cause the forearms to rotate the wrists, clubface and elbows to a different ball flight alignment at the completion of the proceedings.

An additional discipline associated with the assemblage and execution of the ARMS LIFT-N-LOCK TECHNIQUE™ is a correctly assembled conventional style of grip must be formed on a club. This means the lead hand must be assembled on a club in a diagonal manner and the trail hand must be gripped on the club in the form of an original or modified Vardon overlap, traditional interlock or regular baseball (ten-fingers) type of grip.

Another critical discipline is to ensure only the arms are involved in rotating the clubface counterclockwise. No other part of the body may be involved. The shoulders and knees must be immobilized and the wrists should remain relaxed and passive when the arms are lifted upward as far as possible with the clubface remaining grounded.

An additional discipline is the elbows must be disconnected from the rib cage during the entire proceedings. If either or both elbows are connected to the rib cage during any stage of the proceedings, the forearms will rotate the wrists, clubface and elbows to establish a different ball flight alignment at the completion of the proceedings.

When practicing or playing while using the ARMS LIFT-N-LOCK TECHNIQUE™ the three confirmation tests must be conducted at the completion of the proceedings to determine whether the ARMS LIFT-N-LOCK TECHNIQUE™ has been assembled and executed correctly. Perhaps the best confirmation test to determine whether the ARMS LIFT-N-LOCK TECHNIQUE™ has been assembled and executed correctly is the ARMS-LIFT TEST™.

Once the proceedings are completed to assemble and execute the ARMS LIFT-N-LOCK TECHNIQUE™, simply stabilize your shoulders and knees once again, relax your wrists and hands and then lift your arms and, only your arms, upward as far as possible while continuing to keep the sole of your clubface grounded.

If the clubface rotates counterclockwise or clockwise you will know the ARMS LIFT-N-LOCK TECHNIQUE™ was not assembled and executed correctly. However, if the clubface remains aligned to its original alignment a correctly assembled and executed ARMS LIFT-N-LOCK TECHNIQUE™ will be indicated.

Once the three tests confirm the technique was assembled and executed correctly and a straight ball flight alignment has been established and locked-in, you should center the sweet spot of your clubface as near the back of the ball as possible (if not already so centered), simultaneously align your shoulders parallel with your intended target line and then execute a non-manipulative golf swing.

When practicing with the ARMS LIFT-N-LOCK TECHNIQUE™ you should conduct the ARROW ALIGNMENT TECHNIQUE™ to align your shoulders squarely parallel with your intended target line.

Recommended Practice Routines When Using the Arms Lift-N-Lock Technique™ in Combination with the Arrow Alignment Technique™

You should begin each practice session with your most lofted club and then proceed through your set, practicing with each next most lofted club thereafter in succession. With each club, begin with a wrist swing, then with a ½ swing, on to a ¾ swing and conclude with a full swing.

The following are the steps recommend in each practice session:

STEP 1: Select a safe and relatively flat hitting area. Place a ball on the surface. Then identify your target and your intended target line.

STEP 2: Ground the sole of your clubface in the middle of the stance during the proceedings, either behind the ball or in the near vicinity of your ball. Then form a conventional style of golf grip on your club without allowing your clubface to rotate or move at any point in the gripping proceedings. The lifeline of your trail hand must be squarely and securely locked on your lead thumb to complete your grip.

STEP 3: Immobilize your shoulders and knees, keep your wrists passive and inactive and your clubface grounded as you lift only your arms upward as far as possible – until your clubface stops rotating counterclockwise and then begins to slide in your direction.

STEP 4: You must then unlock the lifeline of your trail hand from your lead thumb by at least an inch without completely ungripping your club and then relock your lifeline on your lead thumb.

STEP 5: At the completion of the ARMS LIFT-N-LOCK TECHNIQUE™, you should conduct the SHOULDERS ONLY TEST™, STRAIGHT-UPTEST™ and ARMS-LIFTTEST™. Once the three tests confirm the ARMS LIFT-N-LOCK TECHNIQUE™ was assembled and executed correctly and a straight ball flight alignment has been established and locked-in, proceed to the next step.

STEP 6: Center the sweet spot of your clubface as near the back of your ball as possible (unless already so centered), without moving your ball in the process.

Assume a comfortable posture and stance to your ball and then align your shoulders parallel with your intended target line to the best of your ability.

STEP 7: Conduct the ARROW ALIGNMENT TECHNIQUE™ and adjust your feet, if necessary, until your alignment arrow points directly at your intended target when you turn your head and trail eye in the direction of your target as far as possible while immobilizing all other parts of your body.

STEP 8: Ensure the sweet spot of your clubface has remained centered as near the back of your ball as possible and then execute a non-manipulative golf swing.

If all these steps properly are followed, your ball should fly on a straight path in the direction of your intended target. If a correct club is chosen and sufficient clubhead speed is supplied, the ball should fly not only on a straight path in the direction of your target but on a straight path to your intended target.

SUMMARY POINTS

1. **The ARMS LIFT-N-LOCK TECHNIQUE™ involves the same body maneuver as the ARMS-LIFT TEST™ in that the shoulders and knees must be immobilized and the arms must be lifted upward as far as possible (until the clubface stops rotating counterclockwise and begins to slide in toward the body), without raising the clubface from the surface.**

2. **The ARMS LIFT-N-LOCK TECHNIQUE™ is compatible with all four conventional styles of grip.**

3. **There can be no clubface rotation or movement during the gripping proceedings.**

4. **The sole of the clubface must be grounded in the middle of the stance and remain grounded during the entire proceedings when assembling and executing the ARMS LIFT-N-LOCK TECHNIQUE™.**

5. **The lifeline of the trail hand must be locked on the lead thumb to complete the grip. This is the first of the two "locks" of the lifeline/thumb connection that is necessary to assemble and execute the ARMS LIFT-N-LOCK TECHNIQUE™.**

6. **The body movement that is required to cause the forearms to rotate the wrists, clubface and elbows to establish a straight ball flight alignment is to then immobilize the shoulders and knees, keep the wrists passive and inactive and the clubface grounded, and then lift the arms upward until the clubface stops rotating counterclockwise and the clubface begins to slide in toward the body.**

7. **The lifeline of the trail hand then must be unlocked from the lead thumb by at least an inch without completely ungripping the club and then relocked on the lead thumb. This is the second of the two "locks" of the lifeline/thumb connection that is necessary to assemble and execute the ARMS LIFT-N-LOCK TECHNIQUE™.**

8. **Once the ARMS LIFT-N-LOCK TECHNIQUE™ is completed, the SHOULDERS ONLY TEST™, STRAIGHT-UP TEST™ and ARMS-LIFT TEST™ should be conducted to determine whether the technique has been assembled and executed correctly. If not confirmed, the procedure should be repeated until confirmed.**

9. **Each practice session should combine the ARMS LIFT-N-LOCK TECHNIQUE™ and the ARROW ALIGNMENT TECHNIQUE™ to ensure a straight ball flight alignment is established and the shoulders are aligned squarely parallel with the intended target line at the completion of the pre-shot routine.**

CHAPTER 8

INTRODUCTION OF THE ARMS DROP-N-LOCK TECHNIQUE™

The ARMS DROP-N-LOCK TECHNIQUE™ is different from the ARMS-LIFT TECHNIQUE™ in that the arms are dropped and pushed downward as far as possible instead of being lifted upward after a conventional grip is formed on a club.

Also in contrast to the ARMS-LIFT TECHNIQUE™, once a conventional style of grip is assumed on a club and the arms are dropped and pushed downward as far as possible they must be held in such position until the lifeline/thumb connection is unlocked and relocked twice instead of only once.

Both techniques are similar however in that the sole of the clubface must be grounded and remain grounded throughout the entire proceedings. The shoulders and knees must be immobilized throughout the entire proceedings.

The ARMS DROP-N-LOCK TECHNIQUE™ is compatible with all four conventional styles of grip, whether an original Vardon overlap, modified Vardon overlap, traditional interlock or regular baseball (ten-fingers) style of grip is preferred.

How to Assemble and Execute the Arms Drop-N-Lock Technique™

First, the sole of the clubface should be grounded in the middle of the stance and remain grounded throughout the proceedings. It does not need to be grounded directly behind the ball, necessarily. It can be grounded near the vicinity of the ball and once the proceedings are completed, the sweet spot of the clubface then can be centered as near the back of the ball as possible.

Second, the club must be gripped with the lead hand in a conventional (diagonal) manner. The clubface should not be allowed to rotate during this gripping process.

Third, the trail hand must be gripped on the club in either the form of an original Vardon overlap, modified Vardon overlap, traditional interlock or regular baseball (ten-fingers) style of grip. There may not be any clubface rotation allowed during the time the trail hand is gripped on the club or between the time the lead hand and trail hands are gripped on the club. The grip is completed by locking the lifeline of the trail hand squarely and securely on the lead hand.

Fourth, the shoulders and knees should be immobilized and the wrists should remain passive and inactive as the arms are lowered or pushed downward as far as possible and until the clubface stops rotating clockwise.

The arms must be pushed downward as far as possible only after a conventional grip is assumed and prior to unlocking and relocking the lifeline/thumb connection. If the arms are lowered before a conventional grip is assumed, it will not cause the forearms to rotate the wrists, clubface and elbows to establish a straight ball flight alignment at the completion of the proceedings. If the arms are lowered only after the lifeline/thumb connection is unlocked and relocked, it will not cause the forearms to rotate the wrists, clubface and elbows to establish a straight ball flight alignment.

Fifth, once the arms are lowered until the clubface stops rotating clockwise, the lifeline of the trail thumb must be unlocked from the lead thumb by at least an inch without completely ungripping the club and then re-locked on the lead thumb. Then, once again, the lifeline/thumb connection must be unlocked and relocked in the same manner. (Figure 8-1).

Sixth, the SHOULDERS ONLY TEST™, ARMS-LIFT TEST™ and STRAIGHT-UP TEST™ must then be conducted to determine whether the technique has been performed correctly. If there is any clubface rotation during any of the three tests, it will indicate the technique was not assembled and executed correctly and that a straight ball flight alignment has not been established and locked-in. If not, the grip should be disassembled and the steps repeated until the ARMS DROP-N-LOCK TECHNIQUE™ is confirmed as properly assembled and executed.

Why the Arms Drop-N-Lock Technique™ Works

When the arms are lowered as far as possible after a conventional grip is formed on a club and, while the shoulders and knees are immobilized, the forearms will rotate the elbows to a parallel alignment with the shoulders to create an on-line swing path of the clubface.

When the elbows are aligned squarely parallel with the shoulders the wrists correspondingly will rotate the clubface to a square alignment, all of which will establish a straight ball flight alignment.

However, the alignment will not be locked-in at such point. The lifeline/thumb connection then must be unlocked and relocked twice in order to lock-in the straight ball flight alignment.

If the arms are not lowered enough to rotate the clubface fully clockwise, the forearms will not rotate the elbows to a parallel alignment with the shoulders to create an on-line swing path of the clubface nor will the wrists rotate the clubface to a square alignment – meaning a straight ball flight alignment will not be established in such instance.

Disciplines Required to Assemble and Execute the Arms Drop-N-Lock Technique™

The first discipline associated with the assemblage and execution of the ARMS DROP-N-LOCK TECHNIQUE™ is the shoulders and knees must be immobilized and the clubface must remain grounded when the arms are pushed downward as far as possible and until the clubface stops rotating clockwise. In addition, the wrists should remain passive and inactive when the arms are pushed downward to the maximum extent.

Figure 8-1

STEP 1: The first essential step in assembling and executing the ARMS DROP-N-LOCK TECHNIQUE™ is to assemble a conventional grip on the club with both hands with the clubface grounded in the middle of the stance.

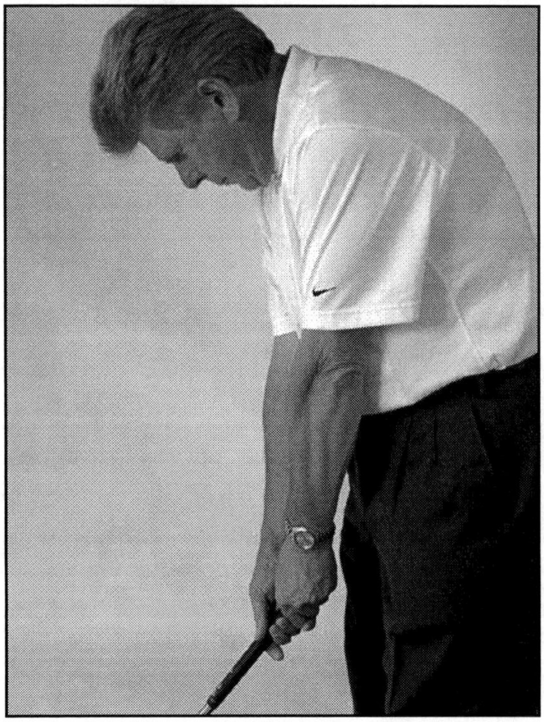

STEP 2: Then while keeping the shoulders and knees immobilized, the clubface grounded and the wrists and hands passive, drop the arms downward as far as possible – until the clubface stops rotating clockwise and begins to slide in toward the body.

STEP 3: The clubface must be held in such position and then the lifeline of the trail hand must be unlocked from the lead thumb without completely ungripping the club.

STEP 4: Continue to hold the clubface in the same position. Then the lifeline of the trail hand must be relocked squarely and securely on the lead thumb. *(The lifeline/thumb connection then must be unlocked and relocked once again.)*

Another critical discipline relating to the ARMS DROP-N-LOCK TECHNIQUE™ is the lifeline/thumb connection must be unlocked and relocked twice after the arms are pushed downward as far as possible. The lifeline/thumb connection may not be unlocked and relocked thereafter.

A most critical discipline associated with the assemblage and execution of the ARMS DROP-N-LOCK TECHNIQUE™ is to stand far enough away from the ball when the grip is assumed to cause the clubface to rotate fully clockwise when the arms are lowered as far as possible.

The ARMS DROP-N-LOCK TECHNIQUE™ requires a total of three "locks" of the lifeline/thumb connection. The first of the three "locks" of the lifeline/thumb connection necessary to assemble and execute the ARMS DROP-N-LOCK TECHNIQUE™ occurs when the grip is completed by locking the lifeline of the trail hand firmly on the lead thumb.

The second of the three "locks" of the lifeline/thumb connection occurs after the arms are pushed downward as far as possible when then the lifeline of the trail hand is unlocked from the lead thumb by at least an inch without completely ungripping the club and then relocked on the lead thumb. The third of the three "locks" occurs when the lifeline/thumb connection then once again is unlocked and relocked in the same manner.

If the lifeline/thumb connection is unlocked and relocked once more thereafter the forearms will rotate the wrists, clubface and elbows to some alignment other than a straight ball flight alignment.

The elbows must be disconnected from the rib cage during the proceedings. If either or both of the elbows are connected to the rib cage during the proceedings, the forearms will rotate the wrists, clubface and elbows to a different ball flight alignment at the completion of the proceedings.

Once the proceedings are completed, the SHOULDERS ONLY TEST™, ARMS-LIFT TEST™ and STRAIGHT-UP TEST™ must be conducted. If there is any counterclockwise or clockwise rotation of the clubface during any of the tests, the grip should be disassembled and the steps repeated until there is no such rotation.

Once the proceedings are completed and the three tests confirm the technique was assembled and executed correctly and a straight ball flight alignment has been established and locked-in, the remainder of the pre-shot routine must be addressed.

The sweet spot of the clubface then must be centered as near the back of the ball as possible (if not already so centered) and the shoulders simultaneously must be aligned squarely parallel with the intended target line at final address, followed by a non-manipulative golf swing.

Recommended Practice Sessions When Using the Arms Drop-N-Lock Technique™ in Combination with the Arrow Alignment Technique™

You should engage in some meaningful practice sessions before using the ARMS DROP-N-LOCK TECHNIQUE™ in actual play.

You should also use the ARROW ALIGNMENT TECHNIQUE™ to align your shoulders parallel with your intended target line in your practice sessions.

The steps below should be helpful during your practice routines:

STEP 1: Place a ball on the surface of your practice area. Identify a very narrow and specific target as well as your intended target line.

STEP 2: Ground the sole of your clubface in the middle of your stance and keep it grounded throughout the proceedings.

STEP 3: Assemble and execute the ARMS DROP-N-LOCK TECHNIQUE™, as instructed throughout this chapter. Remember to immobilize your shoulders and knees and keep your wrists inactive and passive during the procedure.

STEP 4: Once you have pushed your arms downward as far as possible while immobilizing your shoulders and knees and keeping your clubface grounded, you must then unlock the lifeline of your trail hand from your lead thumb by at least an inch without completely ungripping your club and then relock your trail lifeline on your lead thumb. Then, once again, you must unlock and relock your lifeline/thumb connection in the same manner.

STEP 5: Conduct the SHOULDERS ONLY TEST™, ARMS-LIFT TEST™ and STRAIGHT-UP TEST™ at the completion of the proceedings and repeat the steps, if necessary, until a properly assembled and executed ARMS DROP-N-LOCK TECHNIQUE™ is confirmed by the three tests.

STEP 6: Center the sweet spot of your clubface as near the back of your ball as possible (if not already so centered) and assume a comfortable posture and stance to your ball. Align your shoulders parallel with your intended target line to the best of your ability.

STEP 7: Conduct the ARROW ALIGNMENT TECHNIQUE™ and adjust your stance, if necessary, until your alignment

arrow points directly at your target when you turn your head and trail eye in the direction of your target as far as possible while immobilizing all other parts of your body.

STEP 8: Ensure the sweet spot of your clubface has remained centered as near the back of the ball as possible and then execute a non-manipulative golf shot.

Remember to select a safe and relatively flat practice area.

You should begin each practice session with your most lofted club and continue through your set, using each next most lofted club thereafter, in succession. With each club you should begin with a wrist swing, then with a ½ swing, on to a ¾ swing and conclude with a full swing.

SUMMARY POINTS

1. **The ARMS DROP-N-LOCK TECHNIQUE™ requires the sole of the clubface to be grounded in the middle of the stance throughout the proceedings.**

2. **The ARMS DROP-N-LOCK TECHNIQUE™ requires the arms to be pushed downward as far as possible and until the clubface stops rotating clockwise after a conventional style of grip is formed on a club and while immobilizing the shoulders and knees.**

3. **It also requires the wrists to remain passive and inactive during the proceedings and only move in response to the arms being lowered.**

4. **The ARMS DROP-N-LOCK TECHNIQUE™ requires the lead hand to be gripped on the club in a conventional (diagonal) manner.**

5. **When the arms are pushed downward after a conventional style of grip is formed on a club, the forearms will rotate the elbows to a parallel alignment with the shoulders to create an on-line swing path of the clubface.**

6. **The lowering of the arms in such manner also rotates the wrists and clubface to a square alignment.**

7. **The trail hand must be gripped on the club in a conventional manner, either in the form of an original Vardon overlap, modified Vardon overlap, traditional interlock or regular**

baseball (ten-fingers) style of grip. The grip is completed by locking the lifeline of the trail hand squarely and firmly on the lead thumb.

8. **Once the grip is completed and the arms are pushed downward as far as possible and until the clubface stops rotating clockwise, the lifeline of the trail hand must be unlocked from the lead hand by at least an inch and then relocked on the lead thumb. Then, once again, you must unlock and relock your lifeline/thumb connection in the same manner.**

9. **Once the proceedings are completed, the SHOULDERS ONLY TEST™, ARMS-LIFT TEST™ and STRAIGHT-UP TEST™ must be conducted to determine if the technique was assembled and executed correctly. If not confirmed, the proceedings should be repeated until confirmed.**

10. **The ARROW ALIGNMENT TECHNIQUE™ should be conducted to align the shoulders parallel with the intended target line when using the ARMS DROP-N-LOCK TECHNIQUE™.**

CHAPTER 9

INTRODUCTION OF THE TRIPLE-LOCK TECHNIQUE™

The TRIPLE-LOCK TECHNIQUE™ requires three "locks" of the lifeline/thumb connection – from which it derives its name. The TRIPLE-LOCK TECHNIQUE™ is compatible with all the conventional styles of grip. Therefore either an original Vardon overlap, modified Vardon overlap, traditional interlock or regular baseball (ten-fingers) style of grip may be used when assembling and executing it.

The first of the three "locks" of the lifeline/thumb connection is to lock the lifeline of the trail hand squarely and securely on the lead thumb to complete the grip.

The second of the three "locks" of the lifeline/thumb connection constitutes the body movement – believe it or not – that causes the forearms to rotate the wrists, clubface and elbows from a slice alignment to establish a straight ball flight alignment.

The third of the three "locks" secures and locks-in the straight ball flight alignment that is established by the second "lock" and prevents the forearms, wrists, clubface and elbows from rotating to a different ball flight alignment during the remainder of the pre-swing proceedings and the golf swing.

How to Assemble and Execute the Triple-Lock Technique™

The TRIPLE-LOCK TECHNIQUE™ is almost too simple to assemble and execute.

First, a conventional style of golf grip is formed on a golf club while the sole of the clubface is grounded in the middle of the stance. The lifeline of the trail hand is locked on the lead thumb to complete the grip. As noted above, this constitutes the first of the three "locks" of the lifeline/thumb connection that is necessary to assemble and execute the TRIPLE-LOCK TECHNIQUE™.

Second, without allowing the clubface to move or rotate in any manner, the lifeline of the trail hand must be unlocked from the lead thumb by at least an inch without completely ungripping the club and then relocked on the lead thumb. This constitutes the second of the three "locks" of the lifeline/thumb connection that is necessary to assemble the TRIPLE-LOCK TECHNIQUE™.

Third, then once again, without allowing the clubface to move or rotate in any manner, the lifeline of the trail hand must be unlocked from the lead thumb by at least an inch without completely ungripping the club and then, once again, relocked on the lead thumb to secure and lock-in the straight ball flight alignment and prevent the forearms, wrists, clubface and elbows from rotating to a different alignment during the remainder of the pre-shot routine and the backswing. This constitutes the third and last of the three "locks" of the lifeline/thumb connection that are necessary to assemble and execute the TRIPLE-LOCK TECHNIQUE™. (Figure 9-1).

Why the Triple-Lock Technique™ Works

The reason why the TRIPLE-LOCK TECHNIQUE™ works is when the lifeline/thumb connection is unlocked and relocked after the initial lock to complete the grip, the forearms will rotate the elbows to a parallel alignment with the shoulders to create an on-line swing path.

Figure 9-1

STEP 1: The first essential step to assemble the TRIPLE-LOCK TECHNIQUE™ is to grip both hands on the club in a conventional manner with the clubface grounded in the middle of the stance.

STEP 2: Then, while keeping the clubface grounded, shoulders and knees stabilized and the wrists, hands and arms passive, unlock the lifeline of the trail hand from the lead hand by at least an inch without completely ungripping the club.

STEP 3: Then, relock the lifeline of the trail hand squarely and securely on the lead thumb.

STEP 4: Once again, unlock the lifeline of the trail hand from your lead thumb by at least an inch without completely ungripping the club.

STEP 5: Then, once again relock the lifeline of the trail hand squarely and securely on your lead thumb to complete the proceedings.

When the elbows are rotated to a parallel alignment with the shoulders, the wrists correspondingly will rotate the clubface to a square alignment, all of which will establish a straight ball flight alignment.

Then when the lifeline/thumb connection is unlocked and relocked again (the "third" lock), the straight ball flight alignment will be locked-in.

You may find it difficult to unlock and relock your lifeline/thumb connection twice after completing your grip without rotating the clubface clockwise or counterclockwise when assembling and executing the TRIPLE-LOCK TECHNIQUE™. If so, simply lock both elbows against your rib cage before assuming your grip and keep them connected to your rib cage until your grip is completed and you have unlocked and relocked your lifeline/thumb connection twice thereafter.

Keeping your elbows locked against your rib cage in such manner and throughout the proceedings should help prevent the clubface from rotating clockwise during the procedure.

Disciplines Associated with the Triple-Lock Technique™

The TRIPLE-LOCK TECHNIQUE™ is amazingly simple, yet requires precision. Therefore, various disciplines apply when assembling and executing it.

The first discipline is the lead hand must be assembled on the club in a conventional (diagonal) manner. The clubface may not be allowed to move during the time the lead hand is being assembled on a club.

Neither can the lead hand be loosened and tightened or partially ungripped and re-gripped as long as it remains on the club handle. Any such loosening or tightening or partial ungripping and regripping of the lead hand after being assembled on the club will cause the forearms to rotate the wrists, clubface and elbows to a different ball flight alignment.

Also, once the lifeline of the trail hand is locked on the lead thumb to complete the grip, the clubface may not be allowed to rotate or move during the time the lifeline/thumb connection is unlocked and relocked (the second "lock") except for the rotation of the clubface caused by the procedure. In addition, the clubface cannot be allowed to move or rotate prior to or during the subsequent unlocking and relocking of the lifeline/thumb connection (the third "lock") except for any rotation caused by the procedure.

One way to help prevent the clubface from rotating during the gripping proceedings is to press the sole of the clubface into the surface before assembling the grip on the club.

Another way to keep the forearms and clubface from rotating during the procedure except for the rotation caused by unlocking and relocking the lifeline/thumb connection is to press the elbows against the rib cage before the grip is assumed and keep them connected to the rib cage until the proceedings are completed, as mentioned earlier.

If the lifeline/thumb connection is locked only once after a conventional style of grip is formed on a club rather than twice the forearms will not rotate the wrists, clubface and elbows to establish a straight ball flight alignment at the completion of the procedure.

Another discipline associated with the TRIPLE-LOCK TECHNIQUE™ is the lifeline/thumb connection may be locked only a total of three times and no more thereafter. If unlocked and relocked once more thereafter, the forearms will rotate the wrists, clubface and elbows to some alignment other than that of a straight ball flight alignment.

Remember also there can be no clubface rotation allowed when the trail hand is gripped on a club or between the time the lead hand and trail hand are gripped on a club.

If you can count to three, you should have no difficulty assembling and executing the TRIPLE-LOCK TECHNIQUE™.

The thirty-two LOCKED-IN TECHNIQUES™ addressed in this book are based in part on how many times the lifeline of the trail hand must be locked on the lead thumb to secure and lock-in a straight ball flight alignment and prevent the forearms from rotating the wrists, clubface and elbows to a different ball flight alignment during the remainder of the pre-shot routine and the backswing.

In some instances, only a double locking of the lifeline/thumb connection is required. In other instances, a triple locking of the lifeline/thumb connection is required. Please do not jump to any foregone conclusion as to how many times the lifeline of the trail hand must be locked on the lead thumb with respect to the remaining techniques to be discussed in this book.

When using the TRIPLE-LOCK TECHNIQUE™ in practice or play, at the completion of the procedure –

You Should Always Conduct the Shoulders Only Test™, the Arms-Lift Test™ and the Straight-Up Test™ to Determine Whether You Assembled and Executed the Triple-Lock Technique™ Correctly

First, you should conduct the SHOULDERS ONLY TEST™ at the completion of the TRIPLE-LOCK TECHNIQUE™. If you lock your knee joints, relax your arms and raise your shoulders very slowly at the completion of the proceedings and the clubface does not rotate counterclockwise or clockwise but instead slides freely in your direction it will indicate a straight ball flight alignment has been established and locked-in. However, if there is any resistance of the clubface sliding freely in your direction, it will indicate a straight ball flight alignment has not been established and locked-in.

Even when the SHOULDERS ONLY TEST™ confirms that the TRIPLE-LOCK TECHNIQUE™ has been assembled and executed correctly, you should nonetheless conduct the STRAIGHT-UP TEST™ as an additional precaution. Although it sometimes may be difficult to determine whether the clubface rotates counterclockwise or clockwise when conducting the SHOULDERS ONLY TEST™, if the clubface rotates counterclockwise or clockwise when conducting the STRAIGHT-UP TEST™, it is quite noticeable.

You should also conduct the ARMS-LIFT TEST™ just to make "triple-sure" you have established and locked-in a straight ball flight alignment. Conduct all three tests just to be on the safe side because if the TRIPLE-LOCK TECHNIQUE™ is compromised in any manner the result can be very ugly.

The TRIPLE-LOCK TECHNIQUE™ only aligns two of the four essential bone alignments that are required in the pre-shot proceedings: an on-line swing path and a square alignment of the clubface.

Two other alignments also must exist at the completion of the pre-swing proceedings to establish a straight ball flight alignment to a specific target. The shoulders must be aligned squarely parallel with the intended target line while, simultaneously, the sweet spot of the clubface must be centered as near the back of the ball as possible.

Therefore, once you have confirmed the TRIPLE-LOCK TECHNIQUE™, you must then ensure the sweet spot of your clubface is centered as near the back of your ball as possible (if not already so centered) and, simultaneously, your shoulders are aligned squarely parallel with your intended target line at the completion of your pre-shot routine. If these requirements are met and you then execute a non-manipulative golf swing so there is no inadvertent or intentional rotation of your wrists, clubface and elbows during your golf swing, your clubface will duplicate its address position when it contacts the ball and fly your ball on a straight path in the direction of your target.

Centering the sweet spot of your clubface as near the back of your ball as possible without allowing your clubface to touch or move your ball is the easy part. Ensuring your shoulders are aligned squarely parallel with your intended target line at the same time and at the completion of your pre-shot routine is more complex. As a result, once you have assembled and executed the TRIPLE-LOCK TECHNIQUE™ properly and centered the sweet spot of your clubface as near the back of the ball as possible, you should then conduct the ARROW ALIGNMENT TECHNIQUE™ to align your shoulders squarely parallel with your intended target line.

Recommended Practice Routines When Using the Triple-Lock Technique™ in Combination with the Arrow Alignment Technique™

When practicing while using the TRIPLE-LOCK TECHNIQUE™ in combination with the ARROW ALIGNMENT TECHNIQUE™, you should begin with a wedge and then progress through your set with each next most lofted club until each is used. With each respective club, you should begin with a simple wrist swing, followed by a ½ swing, then a ¾ swing and conclude with a full swing.

You also should follow the steps below during your practice sessions:

STEP 1: Select a safe hitting area and a relatively flat surface to practice, such as at a practice facility. Place a ball on the surface. Then identify a specific and narrow target as well as your intended target line.

STEP 2: Ground the sole of your club in the middle of your stance and keep it grounded throughout the proceedings. Assemble and execute the TRIPLE-LOCK TECHNIQUE™. Ensure the lifeline of your trail hand is locked three times on your lead thumb, and no more thereafter, counting the initial grip as the first of the three "locks."

STEP 3: Conduct the SHOULDERS ONLY TEST™, ARMS-LIFT TEST™ and STRAIGHT-UP TEST™ to determine whether the TRIPLE-LOCK TECHNIQUE™ properly has been assembled and executed. If not, repeat the procedure until all three tests confirm that it has been assembled correctly and a straight ball flight alignment has been established and locked-in.

STEP 4: Center the sweet spot of your clubface as near the back of your ball as possible (unless already so centered) without allowing your clubface to touch or move your ball. Assume a comfortable posture and stance to your ball and then align your shoulders squarely parallel with your intended target line to the best of your ability.

STEP 5: Conduct the ARROW ALIGNMENT TECHNIQUE™ and adjust your stance, if necessary, until your alignment arrow points directly at your intended target when you turn your trail eye and head in the direction of your target as far as possible. Only your trail eye and head may turn in the direction of your target. All other body parts must remain stable so there is no change in your spine angle during the procedure.

STEP 6: Once the ARROW ALIGNMENT TECHNIQUE™ confirms your shoulders are aligned squarely parallel with your intended target, ensure the sweet spot of your clubface has remained centered as near the back of the ball as possible, then execute a non-manipulative golf swing.

Some professional and low handicap amateurs unlock and relock their lifeline/thumb connections repeatedly. They instinctively have learned how many times to do so until their forearms, wrists, clubface and elbows have rotated to establish a straight ball flight alignment. They do so by what is known as "feel" or "muscle-memory". You may remember Sergio Garcia's gripping habits when he first entered the professional tour. He sometimes would unlock and relock his lifeline/thumb connection more than twenty times before beginning his golf swing.

You do not need to resort to "feel" or "muscle-memory" to rotate your forearms, wrists, clubface and elbows to establish a straight ball flight alignment when unlocking and relocking your lifeline/thumb connection.

You only need to lock your lifeline/thumb connection three times and no more in order to complete the TRIPLE-LOCK TECHNIQUE™.

Although simplistic in concept, the TRIPLE-LOCK TECHNIQUE™ may not become your most preferred of the thirty-two LOCKED-IN TECHNIQUES™ discussed in this book. It is most difficult to lock, then unlock and relock and then, once again, unlock and relock the lifeline/thumb connection without there being some clubface rotation in the process.

When there is any such clubface rotation, the technique will be compromised.

On the other hand, if you press your elbows against your rib cage during the procedure and faithfully conduct the confirmation tests until a properly assembled and executed TRIPLE LOCK TECHNIQUE™ is confirmed, this technique should become a "keeper."

SUMMARY POINTS

1. To assemble and execute the TRIPLE-LOCK TECHNIQUE™, either an original or modified Vardon, traditional interlock or baseball (ten-fingers) style of grip must be assembled on a golf club and completed by locking the lifeline of the trail hand on the lead thumb. This constitutes the first of the three "locks" of the lifeline/thumb connection that is necessary to assemble the TRIPLE-LOCK TECHNIQUE™.

2. The lifeline/thumb connection then must be unlocked and relocked to rotate the forearms, wrists, clubface and elbows to establish a straight ball flight alignment. This is the body movement required to cause the forearms to rotate the wrists, clubface and elbows to establish a straight ball flight alignment. This constitutes the second of the three "locks" of the lifeline/thumb connection that is necessary to assemble the TRIPLE-LOCK TECHNIQUE™.

3. Then the lifeline/thumb connection once again must be unlocked and relocked to secure and lock-in the straight ball flight alignment and prevent the forearms, wrists, clubface and elbows from rotating to a different ball flight during the remainder of the pre-shot routine and the backswing. This constitutes the third "lock" of the lifeline/thumb connection that is required to assemble the TRIPLE-LOCK TECHNIQUE™.

4. From the beginning to the end of the TRIPLE-LOCK™ proceedings there cannot be any rotation or movement of the clubface except by the indiscernible rotation caused by the unlocking and relocking of the lifeline/thumb connection.

5. If the lifeline/thumb connection is unlocked and relocked once after the third "lock," the forearms, wrists, clubface and elbows will rotate to establish a different ball flight alignment.

6. The lead hand must be assembled on the club in a conventional (diagonal) manner.

7. The sole of the clubface must be grounded throughout the proceedings to assemble and execute the TRIPLE-LOCK TECHNIQUE™.

8. You should conduct the three confirmation tests addressed in chapter one to determine whether the TRIPLE-LOCK TECHNIQUE™ is assembled correctly: the SHOULDERS ONLY TEST™, ARMS-LIFT TEST™ and the STRAIGHT-UP TEST™.

9. Once you have confirmed the TRIPLE-LOCK TECHNIQUE™ has been assembled and executed correctly and a straight ball flight alignment has been established and locked-in, you should then center the sweet spot of your clubface as near the back of your ball as possible (if not already so centered) and conduct the ARROW ALIGNMENT TECHNIQUE™ to align your shoulders squarely parallel with your intended target line.

10. Once you have aligned your shoulders squarely parallel with your intended target line, ensure your clubface has remained centered as near the back of the ball as possible and then execute a non-manipulative golf swing.

CHAPTER 10

INTRODUCTION OF THE LEAD ELBOW CONNECT-N-LOCK TECHNIQUE™

The LEAD ELBOW CONNECT-N-LOCK TECHNIQUE™ also rotates the forearms wrists, clubface and elbows to establish a straight ball flight alignment.

Both elbows must be disconnected from the rib cage prior to gripping the club when assembling and executing the LEAD ELBOW CONNECT-N-LOCK TECHNIQUE™.

Once both hands are gripped on a club and the lifeline of the trail hand is locked on the lead thumb to complete the grip, the lead elbow then must be connected to the rib cage. The lead elbow must remain connected to the rib cage until the proceedings are completed.

Connecting the lead elbow to the rib cage is what rotates the forearms, wrists, clubface and elbows to establish a straight ball flight alignment. However, it does not secure and lock-in a straight ball flight alignment.

To secure and lock-in a straight ball flight alignment, the lifeline/thumb connection then must be unlocked and relocked once but no more thereafter.

The LEAD ELBOW CONNECT-N-LOCK TECHNIQUE™ requires the lifeline/thumb connection to be locked a total of two times. The first "lock" of the lifeline/thumb connection occurs when the lifeline of the trail hand is locked on the lead thumb to complete the grip. The second "lock" of the lifeline/thumb connection occurs after the lead elbow is connected to the rib cage when then the lifeline/thumb connection is unlocked and relocked.

How to Assemble and Execute the Lead Elbow Connect-N-Lock Technique™

First, the sole of the clubface should be grounded in the middle of the stance with the elbows disconnected from the rib cage.

Second, the lead hand must be assembled on the club in a conventional (diagonal) manner.

Third, the trail hand must be assembled on the club with either an original or modified Vardon overlap, traditional interlock or regular baseball (ten-fingers) style of grip while both elbows remain disconnected from the body.

Fourth, the lead elbow then must be connected to the rib cage without allowing the clubface to rotate during the connecting maneuver. The connecting maneuver may be done quickly or slowly. However, once again, when the lead elbow is connected to the rib cage – whether quickly or slowly – the clubface may not be allowed to move or rotate in any manner.

Fifth, once the lead elbow is connected to the rib cage, the lifeline of the trail hand must be unlocked from the lead thumb by at least an inch without ungripping the club and then relocked on the lead thumb.

Sixth, after the lifeline/thumb connection is unlocked and relocked once to secure and lock-in the straight ball flight alignment, the lead elbow should be relaxed and allowed to disconnect from the rib cage. (Figure 10-1).

Disciplines That Apply to the Lead Elbow Connect-N-Lock Technique™

The first discipline in the procedure is to ground the clubface and ensure the elbows are disconnected from the rib cage.

Figure 10-1

STEP 1: The first essential step to assemble and execute the LEAD ELBOW CONNECT-N-LOCK TECHNIQUE™ is to grip both hands on the club in a conventional manner with the clubface grounded in the middle of the stance and the elbows disconnected from the rib cage.

STEP 2: Then, the lead elbow must be connected against the rib cage without allowing any clubface rotation.

STEP 3: While continuing to hold the lead elbow against the rib cage, unlock the lifeline of the trail hand from the lead thumb by at least an inch without completely ungripping the club.

STEP 4: Then, while continuing to hold the lead elbow against the rib cage, the lifeline of the trail hand must be relocked squarely and securely on the lead thumb. *(The lead elbow then may be disconnected from the rib cage.)*

The next discipline is to form a conventional (diagonal) grip with the lead hand.

After gripping the lead hand on the club, the grip may not be loosened and tightened or partially ungripped and regripped. If there is any such movement, the forearms will rotate the wrists, clubface and elbows to establish a different ball flight alignment at the completion of the proceedings.

There may be no rotation or movement of the clubface between the time the lead hand and the trail hand are assembled on the club. Likewise, the clubface may not be allowed to move or rotate when the lead elbow is connected securely against the lead rib cage or when the lifeline/thumb connection is then unlocked and relocked.

The LEAD ELBOW CONNECT-N-LOCK TECHNIQUE™ is compatible with all four conventional styles of grip. Irrespective of which conventional style of grip you prefer, your grip must be assembled correctly on your club. If you have difficulty gripping your club with your preferred style of grip or if the clubface tends to rotate and move when gripping your club you may want to change to a different style of grip.

If you prefer an original Vardon overlap style of grip, you must overlap the end of the little finger (just beneath the finger nail) of the trail hand on top of the middle knuckle of the index finger of the lead hand.

One way to help prevent the clubface from rotating during the proceedings is to press the sole of the clubface into the surface before assembling the grip on the club.

Once the lead elbow is connected to the rib cage it must remain connected to the lead rib cage until the lifeline/thumb connection is unlocked and relocked to secure and lock-in the straight ball flight alignment.

Another discipline that applies to the LEAD ELBOW CONNECT-N-LOCK TECHNIQUE™ is the lifeline/thumb connection cannot be unlocked and relocked before the lead elbow is connected to the lead rib cage. If unlocked and relocked before the lead elbow is connected to the rib cage, the forearms will not rotate the wrists, clubface and elbows to establish a straight ball flight alignment at the completion of the proceedings.

The lifeline/thumb connection may be unlocked and relocked only once after the lead elbow is connected to the rib cage. If unlocked and relocked once more thereafter, the forearms will rotate the wrists, clubface and elbows to establish a different ball flight alignment at the completion of the proceedings.

The trail elbow must remain disconnected from the rib cage throughout the proceedings. The trail elbow should remain inactive and passive from the beginning to the end of the procedure.

Finally, the lead elbow should be relaxed at the completion of the proceedings to allow it to disconnect from the rib cage.

Once the proceedings to assemble and execute the LEAD ELBOW CONNECT-N-LOCK TECHNIQUE™ are completed, the SHOULDERS ONLY TEST™, ARMS-LIFT TEST™ and STRAIGHT-UP TEST™ must be conducted to determine whether a straight ball flight alignment has been established and locked-in.

If there is any clockwise or counterclockwise rotation of the clubface during any of the three tests, the grip should be disassembled and the procedure repeated until there is no such clubface rotation when the three tests are conducted.

Why the Lead Elbow Connect-N-Lock Technique™ Works

This technique works because when the lead elbow is connected to the rib cage after a conventional grip is formed on a club, the forearms will rotate the elbows to a parallel alignment with the shoulders to create an on-line swing path of the clubface.

When the elbows are rotated to a parallel alignment with the shoulders the wrists correspondingly will rotate the clubface to a square alignment, all of which will establish a straight ball flight alignment.

Then when the lifeline/thumb connection is unlocked and relocked once while the lead elbow remains connected to the rib cage, the straight ball flight alignment will be locked-in.

A straight ball flight alignment only means the forearms have rotated the wrists and clubface to a square alignment and the elbows to an on-line swing path. It does not align the shoulders squarely parallel with the intended target line or center the sweet spot of the clubface as near the back of the ball as possible. It is necessary to do both once a straight ball flight alignment is established and locked-in if your objective is to produce a straight ball flight in the direction of your target.

Therefore, in your practice sessions as well as in actual play, when using the LEAD ELBOW CONNECT-N-LOCK TECHNIQUE™ you should conduct the ARROW ALIGNMENT TECHNIQUE™ to ensure your shoulders are aligned squarely parallel with your intended target line at the completion of your pre-shot routine.

Recommended Practice Routines When Using the Lead Elbow Connect-N-Lock Technique™ in Combination with the Arrow Alignment Technique™

You should follow the steps below in each of your practice sessions:

STEP 1: Select a safe hitting area and a relatively flat surface.

STEP 2: Place a ball on the surface, whether a practice mat or grass. Identify your specific target as well as your intended target line.

STEP 3: Ground the sole of your clubface in the middle of your stance and keep it grounded until the proceedings are completed. Ensure your elbows are disconnected from your rib cage and then assemble either an original or modified Vardon overlap, traditional interlock or regular baseball (ten-fingers) style of grip on your club and complete your grip by locking the lifeline of your trail hand squarely and securely on your lead thumb.

STEP 4: Next, connect your lead elbow to your rib cage without allowing your clubface to rotate or otherwise move.

STEP 5: While your lead elbow remains pressed against your rib cage, unlock and relock your lifeline/thumb connection once to secure and lock-in the straight ball flight alignment.

STEP 6: Then relax your lead elbow and allow it to disconnect from your rib cage.

STEP 7: Conduct the SHOULDERS ONLY TEST™, ARMS-LIFT TEST™, and the STRAIGHT-UP TEST™ to determine whether you assembled and executed the procedure correctly. If confirmed, proceed to the next step. If not confirmed, repeat the process until all three tests confirm the procedure has been assembled and executed correctly. Then proceed to the next step.

STEP 8: Center the sweet spot of your clubface as near the back of your ball as possible without allowing it to move or touch your ball. Assume a comfortable posture and stance to your ball and then align your shoulders squarely parallel with your intended target line to the best of your ability.

STEP 9: Next, conduct the ARROW ALIGNMENT TECHNIQUE™ and adjust your stance, if necessary, until your alignment arrow points directly at your intended target when you turn your trail eye and head

in the direction of your target as far as possible while immobilizing all other parts of your body.

STEP 10: Once the ARROW ALIGNMENT TECHNIQUE™ confirms your shoulders are aligned squarely parallel with your intended target line, ensure the sweet spot of your clubface has remained centered as near the back of your ball as possible and then execute a non-manipulative golf swing.

When practicing with the LEAD ELBOW CONNECT-N-LOCK TECHNIQUE™ you should not only begin with a wedge or some other short club but vary the extent of each swing. With each club, you should begin with a wrist swing, followed by a ½ swing, then a ¾ swing and finish with a full swing.

SUMMARY POINTS

1. The LEAD ELBOW CONNECT-N-LOCK TECHNIQUE™ locks the lead elbow against the rib cage.

2. Either an original or modified Vardon overlap, traditional interlock or regular baseball (ten-fingers) style of grip must be assembled on the club before the lead elbow is connected to the rib cage. Such grip is completed by locking the lifeline of the trail hand on the lead thumb. This constitutes the first of the two "locks" of the lifeline/thumb connection that is necessary to establish and lock-in a straight ball flight alignment.

3. One discipline that applies to the LEAD ELBOW CONNECT-N-LOCK TECHNIQUE™ is there may not be any clubface rotation allowed during the gripping process.

4. Once a conventional grip is assembled and completed, the lead elbow must be connected to the rib cage without allowing the clubface to move or rotate during the connecting maneuver. The lead elbow must remain connected to the rib cage until the entire proceedings are completed.

5. Once the lead elbow is connected to the rib cage, the lifeline of the trail hand then must be unlocked from the lead thumb by at least an inch without completely ungripping the club and then relocked on the lead thumb. This constitutes the second of the two "locks" of the lifeline/thumb connection that is necessary to establish and lock-in a straight ball flight alignment.

6. **The lifeline/thumb connection must not be unlocked and re-locked thereafter. To do so would cause the forearms to rotate the wrists, clubface and elbows to establish a different ball flight alignment.**

7. **Neither may the lifeline/thumb connection be unlocked and relocked before the lead elbow is connected to the lead rib cage. To do so would cause the forearms to rotate the wrists, clubface and elbows to establish a different ball flight alignment.**

8. **Once the LEAD ELBOW CONNECT-N-LOCK TECHNIQUE™ is completed, the SHOULDERS ONLY TEST™, ARMS-LIFT TEST™ and STRAIGHT-UP TEST™ should be conducted to determine whether it has been assembled and executed correctly.**

9. **The ARROW ALIGNMENT TECHNIQUE™ should be used to align the shoulders parallel with the intended target line.**

CHAPTER 11

INTRODUCTION OF THE TRAIL ELBOW CONNECT-N-LOCK TECHNIQUE™

The TRAIL ELBOW CONNECT-N-LOCK TECHNIQUE™ requires the trail elbow to be connected to the rib cage after a conventional grip is assumed.

However, once the trail elbow is connected to the rib cage, it must remain connected until the proceedings are complete.

Remember once the hands are gripped on a golf club in a conventional manner – either in the form of an original or modified Vardon overlap, traditional interlock or regular baseball style of grip – some body movement must take place in a specific way to cause the forearms to rotate the wrists, clubface and elbows from a slice alignment to a straight ball flight alignment.

In the case of the TRAIL ELBOW CONNECT-N-LOCK TECHNIQUE™, it is the connection between the trail elbow and the rib cage after the hands are gripped on the club that causes the forearms to rotate the wrists, clubface and elbows from a slice alignment to establish a straight ball flight alignment. However, this alone will not prevent the forearms from rotating to another ball flight during the golf swing. In order to lock-in the straight ball flight alignment, the lifeline/thumb connection must then be unlocked and relocked twice.

How to Assemble and Execute the Trail Elbow Connect-N-Lock Technique™

First, the sole of the clubface should be grounded in the middle of the stance and remain grounded until the proceedings are completed.

Second, the elbows must be disconnected from the rib cage and then the lead hand must be formed on a club in a conventional (diagonal) manner without allowing the clubface to rotate during the gripping process.

Third, the trail hand must be assembled on the club either in the form of an original or modified Vardon overlap, traditional interlock or baseball (ten-fingers) style of grip, followed by locking the lifeline of the trail hand squarely and firmly on the lead thumb to complete the grip. This is the first of the three "locks" of the lifeline/thumb connection that is necessary to assemble and execute the TRAIL ELBOW CONNECT-N-LOCK TECHNIQUE™.

Fourth, the trail elbow then must be connected to the rib cage without allowing any clubface rotation in the process and remain connected to the rib cage until the entire proceedings are completed.

Fifth, once the trail elbow is connected to the trail rib cage, the lifeline of the trail hand then must be unlocked from the lead thumb by at least an inch without completely ungripping the club and then relocked on the lead thumb. This is the second of the three "locks" of the lifeline/thumb connection that is necessary to assemble and execute the TRAIL ELBOW CONNECT-N-LOCK TECHNIQUE™.

Sixth, then once again the lifeline of the trail hand must be unlocked from the lead thumb by at least an inch without completely ungripping the club and then, once again, the lifeline of the trail hand must be relocked on the lead thumb. This is the third of the three "locks" that is necessary to assemble and execute the TRAIL ELBOW CONNECT-N-LOCK TECHNIQUE™.

Seventh, the trail elbow then should be relaxed and allowed to disconnect from the rib cage. (Figure 11-1).

Figure 11-1

STEP 1: The first essential step in assembling and executing the TRAIL ELBOW CONNECT-N-LOCK TECHNIQUE™ is to assume a conventional grip with both hands while the clubface is grounded in the middle of the stance and the elbows are disconnected from the rib cage.

STEP 2: Then the trail elbow must be pressed (connected) against the rib cage without allowing any clubface rotation and remain pressed against the rib cage until the proceedings are completed.

STEP 3: While continuing to hold the trail elbow against the rib cage, unlock the lifeline of the trail hand by at least an inch without completely ungripping the club.

STEP 4: Then relock the lifeline of the trail hand squarely and securely on the lead thumb. *(Then, once again, unlock and relock the lifeline/thumb connection while continuing to hold the trail elbow against the rib cage. The trail elbow then may be disconnected from the rib cage.)*

Disciplines That Apply to the Trail Elbow Connect-N-Lock Technique™

The first discipline that applies to the assemblage and execution of the TRAIL ELBOW CONNECT-N-LOCK TECHNIQUE™ is the lead hand cannot be loosened or tightened or partially ungripped and regripped after being assembled on the club. To do so will cause the forearms to rotate the wrists, clubface and elbows to establish a different ball flight alignment at the completion of the procedure.

There also may be no rotation or movement of the clubface between the time the lead hand and the trail hand are assembled on the club or during the time the trail hand is formed on the club. In addition, there may be no clubface rotation or movement after the hands are gripped on the club until the entire procedure is completed.

One way to help prevent the clubface from rotating during the proceedings is to press the sole of the clubface into the surface before assembling the grip on the club.

Remember the LOCKED-IN TECHNIQUES™ not only require a conventional style of grip but a properly assembled conventional style of grip.

The modified Vardon overlap and traditional interlock styles of grip probably are the two most difficult conventional styles of grip to assume, especially in attempting to keep the clubface from rotating during the gripping process.

If either of these is your preferred style of grip and you have difficulty gripping your club without allowing any rotation of your clubface, you may need to change to a different conventional style of grip.

However, if you use the original Vardon overlap style of grip, you must overlap the end of the little finger of the trail hand (just beneath the fingernail) on top of the middle finger of the index finger of the trail hand.

A most critical discipline is the hands must be assembled on the club in a conventional manner <u>before</u> the trail elbow is connected to the rib cage. In addition, there can be no movement or rotation of the clubface allowed when the trail elbow is connected to the rib cage. If any such movement or rotation of the clubface occurs during this maneuver, you should abandon the procedure and begin anew.

The lifeline of the trail hand must be locked on the lead thumb to complete the grip but the lifeline/thumb connection may not be unlocked and relocked before the trail elbow is connected to the rib cage.

Once the trail elbow is connected to the rib cage, it must remain connected until the entire proceedings are completed. If disconnected and reconnected, the forearms will rotate the wrists, clubface and elbows to establish a different ball flight alignment at the completion of the proceedings.

After the trail elbow is connected to the rib cage, the lifeline/thumb connection must be unlocked and relocked twice to secure and lock-in the straight ball flight alignment. It may not be unlocked and relocked thereafter. If unlocked and relocked once more thereafter the forearms will rotate the wrists, clubface and elbows to establish a different ball flight alignment.

The lead elbow must remain disconnected from the rib cage during the entire proceedings.

Why the Trail Elbow Connect-N-Lock Technique™ Works

The TRAIL ELBOW CONNECT-N-LOCK TECHNIQUE™ works because when the trail elbow is connected to the rib cage after the grip is assembled, the forearms will rotate the elbows to a parallel alignment with the shoulders to create an on-line swing path of the clubface. When the elbows are rotated to a parallel alignment with the shoulders the wrists correspondingly will rotate the clubface to a square alignment, all of which will establish a straight ball flight alignment.

Then when the lifeline/thumb connection is unlocked and relocked twice, a straight ball flight alignment will be locked-in.

Keep in mind the TRAIL ELBOW CONNECT-N-LOCK TECHNIQUE™ only establishes a straight ball flight in relation to the shoulders. In order to hit a golf ball on a straight path in the direction of an intended target and also on a straight path that parallels the shoulders, the shoulders must be aligned squarely parallel with the intended target line and the sweet spot of the clubface simultaneously must be centered as near the back of the ball as possible at final address.

When using the TRAIL ELBOW CONNECT-N-LOCK TECHNIQUE™, whether during practice or in play, you should conduct the ARROW ALIGNMENT TECHNIQUE™ to ensure your shoulders are aligned squarely parallel with your intended target line at the completion of your pre-shot routine.

When you have established a straight ball flight alignment, centered the sweet spot of your clubface as near the back of the ball as possible without allowing your clubface to touch or move the ball and simultaneously aligned your shoulders squarely parallel with your intended target line, you will have established an ideal "ball position." If you then execute a non-manipulative golf swing in that you do not intentionally or inadvertently rotate and re-route your forearms, wrists, clubface and elbows from their established alignments so the impact position of your clubface will duplicate its address position, the sweet spot of your clubface will contact the ball at the lowest point of its arc and the ball will fly on a straight path in the direction of your target and also on a straight path that parallels your shoulder line.

The most effective way to execute a non-manipulative golf swing is to keep your head steady and your feet planted during your golf swing.

Recommended Practice Routines When Using the Trail Elbow Connect-N-Lock Technique™ in Combination with the Arrow Alignment Technique™

You should begin your practice sessions with a short iron, such as a wedge and then proceed with each next most lofted club thereafter in succession until you have practiced with each club in your set. When practicing with each respective club you should begin with a wrist swing, then with a ½ swing, on to a ¾ swing and finally to a full swing.

When using the TRAIL ELBOW CONNECT-N-LOCK TECHNIQUE™, you should follow the steps below.

STEP 1: Select a safe and reasonably level hitting area such as at a practice facility. Place a ball on the hitting surface. Identify your specific target and your intended target line. Ground the sole of your clubface in the middle of your stance and keep it grounded until the TRAIL ELBOW CONNECT-N-LOCK TECHNIQUE™ is completed. Ensure your elbows are disconnected from your rib cage before you assume your grip.

STEP 2: Form either an original or modified Vardon overlap, traditional interlock or regular baseball (ten-fingers) style of grip on your club and complete the grip by locking the lifeline of your trail hand squarely and securely on your lead thumb.

STEP 3: Then connect your trail elbow to your rib cage and keep it connected until the proceedings are completed. Do not allow your clubface to rotate during this connecting maneuver.

STEP 4: After connecting your trail elbow to your rib cage, unlock the lifeline of your trail hand from your lead thumb by at least an inch without completely ungripping your club and then relock your trail lifeline on your lead thumb.

STEP 5: Then once again unlock the lifeline of your trail hand from your lead thumb by at least an inch without completely ungripping your club and then, once again, relock the lifeline of your trail

hand on your lead thumb to secure and lock-in the straight ball flight alignment. The lifeline/thumb connection may not be unlocked and relocked thereafter.

STEP 6: Disconnect your trail elbow from your rib cage and conduct the SHOULDERS ONLY TEST™, ARMS-LIFT TEST™ and STRAIGHT-UP TEST™ to determine whether you assembled and executed it correctly. If the three tests confirm you did, proceed to the next step. If not, repeat the procedure until they do so confirm and then move to the next step.

STEP 7: Next, center the sweet spot of your clubface as near the back of the ball as possible. Assume a comfortable posture and stance to the ball and then align your shoulders parallel with your intended target line to the best of your ability.

STEP 8: Conduct the ARROW ALIGNMENT TECHNIQUE™ and adjust your stance, if necessary, until your alignment arrow points directly at your target when you turn your trail eye and head in the direction of your target as far as possible while immobilizing all other parts of your body.

STEP 9: Ensure the sweet spot of your clubface has remained centered as near the back of the ball as possible and then execute a non-manipulative golf swing.

You should take extra precaution that you do not allow your clubface to touch or move your ball when conducting the ARROW ALIGNMENT TECHNIQUE™. Nonetheless, you should center the sweet spot of your clubface as near the back of the ball as possible at final address to the ball.

SUMMARY POINTS

1. When assembling and executing the TRAIL ELBOW CONNECT-N-LOCK TECHNIQUE™, both hands must be formed on the club in a conventional manner before the trail elbow is connected to the rib cage.

2. Once the trail elbow is connected to the rib cage, it cannot be disconnected until the entire proceedings are completed.

3. After the trail elbow is connected to the rib cage, the lifeline/thumb connection must be unlocked and relocked twice. The lifeline/thumb connection may not be unlocked and relocked thereafter.

4. If unlocked and relocked once more, the forearms will rotate the wrists, clubface and elbows to establish a different ball flight alignment.

5. The trail elbow should be disconnected from the rib cage when the proceedings are completed.

6. The SHOULDERS ONLY™, ARMS-LIFT TEST™ and STRAIGHT-UP TEST™ should always be conducted at the completion of the TRAIL ELBOW CONNECT-N-LOCK TECHNIQUE™.

7. Whether practicing or playing, the ARROW ALIGNMENT TECHNIQUE™ should be conducted to align the shoulders squarely parallel with the intended target line.

8. A non-manipulative golf swing is best executed when the head remains steady and both feet remain planted.

CHAPTER 12

INTRODUCTION OF THE LEAD ARM EXTEND-N-LOCK TECHNIQUE™

The LEAD ARM EXTEND-N-LOCK TECHNIQUE™ also rotates the wrists, clubface and elbows from a slice alignment – that is established when a conventional style of grip is formed on a club when there is no clubface rotation – to a straight ball flight alignment.

It, like the other thirty-one LOCKED-IN TECHNIQUES™ addressed in this book, requires the lifeline/thumb connection to be locked a precise number of times.

The body movement that causes the forearms to rotate the wrists, clubface and elbows to establish a straight ball flight alignment when the LEAD ARM EXTEND-N-LOCK TECHNIQUE™ is assembled and executed is the straightening of the lead arm from a very relaxed position after a conventional style of grip is assumed on the club.

The LEAD ARM EXTEND-N-LOCK TECHNIQUE™ is compatible with all four conventional styles of grip whether that of an original Vardon overlap, modified Vardon overlap, traditional interlock or regular baseball (ten-fingers) style of grip.

How to Assemble and Execute the Lead Arm Extend-N-Lock Technique™

First, ground the sole of your clubface and keep it grounded until the entire procedure is completed.

Second, relax your lead arm appreciably and then grip your lead hand on the club in a conventional (diagonal) manner without allowing your clubface to rotate during the process.

Third, then assume a conventional grip on your club with your trail hand. The conventional grip may be in the form of either an original or modified Vardon overlap, traditional interlock or regular baseball (ten-fingers) style of grip.

Fourth, lock the lifeline of your trail hand squarely and securely on your lead thumb to complete the grip. This is the first of a total of two "locks" of the lifeline/thumb connection that is necessary to assemble and execute the LEAD ARM EXTEND-N-LOCK TECHNIQUE™.

Fifth, after gripping the club with both hands in a conventional manner and locking the lifeline of the trail hand on the lead thumb to complete the grip, do not allow the clubface to rotate or move. Then straighten your lead arm to the fullest extent possible while keeping your trail arm very relaxed. Keep your lead arm straightened in this manner until the entire proceedings are completed.

Sixth, while continuing to keep your lead arm straightened to the fullest extent possible and keeping your trail arm relaxed, unlock the lifeline of your trail hand from your lead thumb by at least an inch without completely ungripping the club and then re-lock your trail lifeline on your lead thumb.

Seventh, relax your lead arm and allow it to return to a comfortable position. (Figure 12-1).

Figure 12-1

STEP 1: The first essential step in assembling and executing the LEAD ARM EXTEND-N-LOCK TECHNIQUE™ is to relax both arms appreciably and then grip the club with both hands in a conventional manner with the clubface grounded in the middle of the stance.

STEP 2: Then the trail arm must remain relaxed as the lead arm is straightened to the maximum extent possible. The lead arm must remain straightened to the maximum extent possible until the completion of the proceedings.

STEP 3: While the lead arm remains straightened to the fullest extent possible, the lifeline of the trail hand must be unlocked from the lead thumb by at least an inch without completely ungripping the club.

STEP 4: While continuing to keep the lead arm straightened to the maximum extent possible, the lifeline of the trail hand must be relocked squarely and securely on the lead thumb. *(Then the lead arm should be relaxed to a comfortable position.)*

Disciplines That Apply When Assembling and Executing the Lead Arm Extend-N-Lock Technique™

The first discipline is to ground the sole of your clubface in the middle of your stance and keep it grounded until the proceedings are completed.

Once your lead hand is gripped on the club in a conventional manner, it thereafter may not be loosened and tightened or partially ungripped and regripped. To do so would cause the forearms to rotate the wrists, clubface and elbows to establish a different ball flight alignment at the completion of the proceedings. Neither may the clubface be allowed to move or rotate while either hand is being gripped on a club or between the time the lead hand and the trail hand are gripped on the club.

One way to help prevent the clubface from rotating during the gripping proceedings is to press the sole of the clubface into the surface before assembling the grip on the club.

The most critical discipline associated with the LEAD ARM EXTEND-N-LOCK TECHNIQUE™ is to relax the lead arm appreciably when both hands are being gripped on a club in a conventional manner. The lead arm then must be straightened to the fullest extent possible while keeping the trail arm very relaxed. The lead arm must remain straightened to such an extent until the lifeline/thumb connection is unlocked and relocked once. The lifeline/thumb connection may not be unlocked and relocked thereafter.

If the lifeline/thumb connection is unlocked and relocked before the lead arm is straightened, the forearms will not rotate the wrists, clubface and elbows to establish a straight ball flight alignment at the completion of the proceedings.

An additional discipline associated with the assemblage and execution of the LEAD ARM EXTEND-N-LOCK TECHNIQUE™ is the elbows must be disconnected from the rib cage during the entire proceedings. If either or both elbows are connected to the rib cage at any stage of the proceedings, the forearms will rotate the wrists, clubface and elbows to a different ball flight alignment at the completion of the proceedings.

The LEAD ARM EXTEND-N-LOCK TECHNIQUE™ requires the hands to be assembled on a club in a conventional style of grip. Such a grip must be assembled correctly in order for the forearms to rotate the wrists, clubface and elbows to establish a straight ball flight alignment when the lead hand is straightened to the maximum extent possible.

If you are having difficulty in assembling your preferred conventional style of grip or keeping the clubface from rotating during the gripping process, you may want to consider a different conventional style of grip in the future.

Another discipline applicable to the LEAD ARM EXTEND-N-LOCK TECHNIQUE™ is once the lifeline/thumb connection is unlocked and relocked once after straightening the lead arm to the fullest extent possible, the lead arm then must be relaxed so it can return to a comfortable position.

Another discipline is you should always conduct the SHOULDERS ONLY TEST™, ARMS-LIFT TEST™ and the STRAIGHT-UP TEST™ at the completion of the proceedings.

If any of the confirmation tests indicate you did not assemble and execute the procedure correctly, you should disassemble your grip and repeat the procedure until the tests do confirm a properly assembled and executed LEAD ARM EXTEND-N-LOCK TECHNIQUE™.

Why the Lead Arm Extend-N-Lock Technique™ Works

When the lead arm is straightened to the fullest extent possible while keeping the trail arm relaxed after the hands have assembled a conventional style of grip on a club, the forearms will rotate the elbows to a parallel alignment with the shoulders to create an on-line swing path of the clubface.

When the elbows are rotated to a parallel alignment with the shoulders to create an on-line swing path of the clubface the wrists correspondingly will rotate the clubface to a square alignment, all of which will establish a straight ball flight alignment.

However, a straight ball flight alignment will not be locked-in at such point. To lock-in the straight ball flight alignment, the lifeline/thumb connection then must be unlocked and relocked once.

As with all the techniques addressed in this book, once the procedure is completed, only two of the four pre-shot requirements are satisfied to hit a golf ball to a specific target.

In order to hit a ball to a specific target, a correct "ball position" must exist, and simultaneously, a parallel shoulder alignment with the intended target line at the completion of the pre-shot routine also must exist, followed by a non-manipulative golf swing.

Therefore, once you have established and locked-in a straight ball flight alignment, you should center the sweet spot of your clubface as near the back of your ball as possible (if not already so centered) and simultaneously align your shoulders parallel with your intended target line. Then you must execute a non-manipulative golf swing if your objective is to flight your ball on a straight path in the direction of your target and on a straight path that parallels your shoulder line.

Before attempting to use the LEAD ARM EXTEND-N-LOCK TECHNIQUE™ in actual play, you first should gain confidence in doing so with some meaningful practice sessions.

Recommended Practice Routines When Using the Lead Arm Extend-N-Lock Technique™ in Combination with the Arrow Alignment Technique™

You should use the ARROW ALIGNMENT TECHNIQUE™ to align your shoulders squarely parallel with your intended target line, whether in practice of play.

You also should adhere to a specific routine when using the LEAD ARM EXTEND-N-LOCK TECHNIQUE™, such as outlined below:

STEP 1: **Select a safe practice area and one that has a relatively flat surface.**

STEP 2: **Place a ball on the surface, whether on a practice mat or grass. Identify your specific target as well as your intended target line. Then select your most lofted club, such as a wedge, to begin your practice.**

STEP 3: **Ground the sole of your clubface in the middle of your stance and keep it grounded until the proceedings are complete.**

STEP 4: **Relax your lead arm appreciably and then form a conventional grip on your club. Next, straighten your lead arm to the fullest extent possible while keeping your trail arm fully relaxed. Keep your lead arm straightened in such manner and then unlock and relock your lifeline/thumb connection <u>once</u> to secure and lock-in the straight ball flight alignment.**

STEP 5: **Relax your lead arm and allow it to return to a comfortable position.**

STEP 6: **Conduct the SHOULDERS ONLY TEST™, ARMS-LIFT TEST™ and STRAIGHT-UP TEST™ to determine whether the LEAD ARM EXTEND-N-LOCK TECHNIQUE™ has been assembled and executed correctly. If not, repeat the procedure until the three tests do confirm it has been properly assembled and executed.**

STEP 7: **Then center the sweet spot of your clubface as near the back of your ball as possible without allowing your clubface**

to move or touch the ball. Assume a comfortable posture and stance to the ball and then align your shoulders squarely parallel with your intended target line to the best of your ability.

STEP 8: Conduct the ARROW ALIGNMENT TECHNIQUE™ and adjust your stance, if necessary, until your alignment arrow points directly at your intended target when you turn your trail eye and head in the direction of the target as far as possible while immobilizing all other parts of your body.

STEP 9: Ensure the sweet spot of your clubface has remained centered as near the back of the ball as possible and then execute a non-manipulative golf swing.

In keeping with previous suggestions, you should begin your practice sessions with your most lofted club and then continue with each next most lofted club in succession thereafter until you have practiced with each club in your set. With each club, you should first begin with a wrist swing, then a ½ swing, on to a ¾ swing and finish with a full swing.

SUMMARY POINTS

1. The LEAD ARM EXTEND-N-LOCK TECHNIQUE™ requires the lifeline/thumb connection to be locked a total of two times in order to secure and lock-in a straight ball flight alignment.

2. The first of the two"locks" of the lifeline/thumb connection occurs when the lifeline of the trail hand is locked on the lead thumb to complete the grip.

3. The second of the two "locks" of the lifeline/thumb connection occurs after the lead arm is straightened to the fullest extent possible while keeping the trail arm relaxed when then the lifeline of the trail hand is unlocked from the lead thumb by at least an inch without completely ungripping the club and then relocked on the lead thumb.

4. The first step in the procedure is to ground the sole of the clubface and keep it grounded during the proceedings. Both arms should be fully relaxed when the lead hand is gripped on the club in a conventional (diagonal) manner.

5. The LEAD ARM EXTEND-N-LOCK TECHNIQUE™ is compatible with all the conventional styles of grip. Therefore, the trail hand may be gripped on the club either in the form of an original or modified Vardon overlap, traditional interlock or regular baseball (ten-fingers) style of grip.

6. Once a conventional style of grip is assembled on a club, the lead arm must be straightened to the fullest extent possible while keeping the trail arm relaxed.

7. **The lead arm must remain straightened in such a manner until the lifeline/thumb connection is unlocked and relocked <u>once</u>.**

8. **The lifeline/thumb connection must not be unlocked and relocked before the lead arm is straightened. If unlocked and relocked before the lead arm is straightened, it would not cause the forearms to rotate the wrists, clubface and elbows to establish a straight ball flight alignment at the completion of the proceedings.**

9. **The LEAD ARM EXTEND-N-LOCK TECHNIQUE™ only establishes a straight ball flight in relation to the shoulders. To establish a straight ball flight to a specific target, the sweet spot of the clubface must be centered as near the back of the ball as possible and, simultaneously, the shoulders must be aligned squarely parallel with the intended target line at final address, followed by a non-manipulative golf swing.**

10. **Whether practicing or playing, you should conduct the ARROW ALIGNMENT TECHNIQUE™ to align your shoulders squarely parallel with your intended target line.**

11. **You should always conduct the SHOULDERS ONLY TEST™, ARMS-LIFT TEST™ and STRAIGHT-UP TEST™ at the completion of the proceedings and repeat the procedure, if necessary, until such tests confirm a straight ball flight alignment has been established and locked-in.**

CHAPTER 13

INTRODUCTION OF THE LEAD ARM RELAX-N-LOCK TECHNIQUE™

The LEAD ARM RELAX-N-LOCK TECHNIQUE™ requires the lead arm to be straightened to the fullest extent possible prior to gripping the club. Then once the hands are gripped on the club, the lead arm then must be relaxed appreciably after which the lifeline/thumb connection must be unlocked and relocked twice but no more thereafter.

Before the lead arm is relaxed from a straightened position in such case, a conventional style of grip must be assembled on a club without allowing any clubface rotation during the time either the lead hand or trail hand is gripped or between the time the lead and trail hands are gripped.

The lead hand must be gripped on a club with a conventional (diagonal) style of grip. The trail hand must be assembled on the club either in the form of an original Vardon overlap, modified Vardon overlap, traditional interlock or regular baseball (ten-fingers) style of grip and the grip must be completed by locking the lifeline of the trail hand squarely and securely on the lead thumb.

How to Assemble the Lead Arm Relax-N-Lock Technique™

First, ground the sole of your clubface in the middle of your stance. It can be grounded either directly behind the ball or in the near vicinity of the ball. If grounded near the vicinity of the ball, once the proceedings are completed and a straight ball flight alignment is established and locked-in, the sweet spot of the clubface then can be centered as near the back of the ball as possible.

Second, keep your trail arm very relaxed but straighten your lead arm to the fullest extent possible and keep it straightened in such manner until after you have gripped your hands on your club and completed your grip by locking the lifeline of your trail hand squarely and firmly on your lead thumb.

Third, grip your lead hand on your club in a conventional (diagonal) manner while continuing to straighten your lead arm to the fullest extent possible and while keeping your trail arm relaxed.

Fourth, then while continuing to straighten your lead arm to the fullest extent possible with your trail arm relaxed, grip your trail hand on your club either in the form of an original Vardon overlap, modified Vardon overlap, traditional interlock or regular baseball (ten-fingers) style of grip. You should complete your grip by locking the lifeline of your trail hand squarely and firmly on your lead thumb.

Fifth, then relax your lead arm as much as possible from its straightened position while keeping your trail arm relaxed and passive.

Sixth, once you have relaxed your lead arm from its straightened position, unlock the lifeline of your trail hand from your lead thumb by at least an inch without completely ungripping your club and then relock the lifeline of your trail hand on your lead thumb.

Seventh, then once again unlock and relock your lifeline/thumb connection in the same manner. (Figure 13-1).

Eighth, once the proceedings are completed, the SHOULDERS ONLY TEST™, ARMS-LIFT TEST™ and STRAIGHT-UP TEST™ should be conducted to determine whether the grip has been assembled and executed correctly and whether a straight ball flight alignment has been established and locked-in.

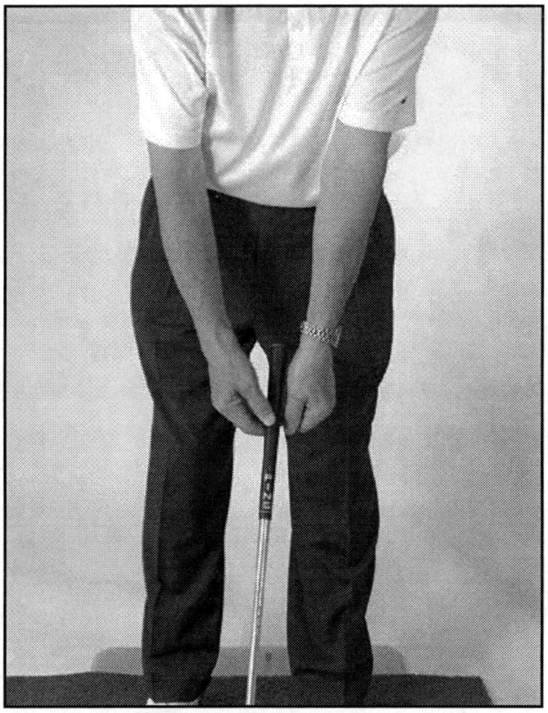

Figure 13-1

STEP 1: The first essential step to assemble and execute the LEAD ARM RELAX-N-LOCK TECHNIQUE™ is to straighten the lead arm to the maximum extent possible.

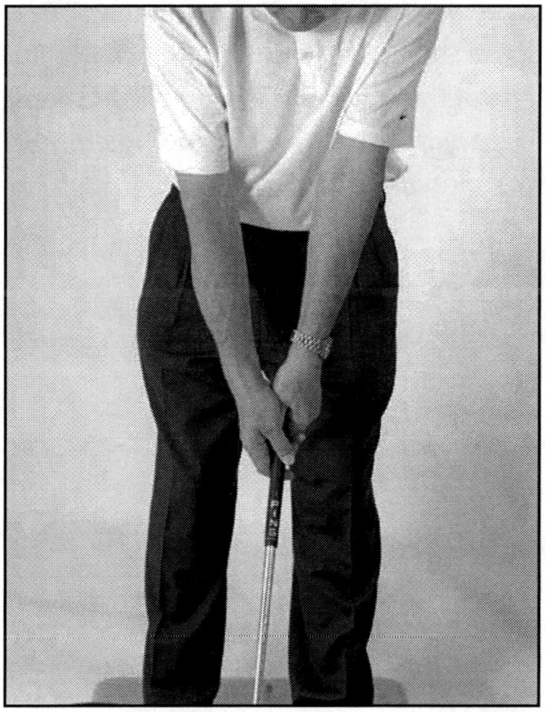

STEP 2: Continue to keep the lead arm straightened to the fullest extent possible and then grip both hands on the club in a conventional manner.

STEP 3: Then relax the lead arm appreciably from its straightened position.

STEP 4: Once the lead arm is relaxed from its straightened position, unlock the lifeline of the trail hand from the lead thumb by at least an inch without completely ungripping the club.

STEP 5: Then relock the lifeline of the trail hand squarely and securely on the lead thumb. *(Then once again, unlock and relock the lifeline/thumb connection in the same manner.)*

Why the Lead Arm Relax-N-Lock Technique™ Works

When the lead arm is straightened to the fullest extent possible while keeping the trail arm relaxed before a conventional grip is assembled on a club and then when the lead arm is relaxed after a conventional grip is formed on a club from its straightened position, the forearms will rotate the elbows to a parallel alignment with the shoulders to create an on-line swing path of the clubface.

When the elbows are aligned parallel with the shoulders to create an on-line swing path of the clubface the wrists correspondingly will rotate the clubface to a square alignment, all of which will establish a straight ball flight alignment.

However, the straight ball flight alignment will not be locked-in at such point.

In order to secure and lock-in the straight ball flight alignment the lifeline/thumb connection then must be unlocked and relocked twice but no more thereafter.

Disciplines Required to Assemble the Lead Arm Relax-N-Lock Technique™

The most critical discipline when assembling and executing the LEAD ARM RELAX-N-LOCK TECHNIQUE™ is to straighten your lead arm to the fullest extent possible while relaxing your trail hand before gripping the club with a conventional grip and then keeping the lead arm straightened in such a manner until the completion of the grip.

If the lead arm is relaxed – after being straightened – before a conventional style of grip is assembled on a club, the forearms will not rotate the elbows to a parallel alignment with the shoulders and will not cause the wrists correspondingly to rotate the clubface to a square alignment.

Another discipline is the lifeline/thumb connection must be locked a total of three times when assembling and executing the LEAD ARM RELAX-N-LOCK TECHNIQUE™.

The first of the three "locks" of the lifeline/thumb connection that is necessary to assemble and execute the LEAD ARM RELAX-N-LOCK TECHNIQUE™ occurs when the lifeline of the trail hand is locked squarely and securely on the lead thumb to complete the grip.

The second of the three "locks" of the lifeline/thumb connection occurs after the lead arm is relaxed from a straightened position when then the lifeline of the trail hand is unlocked from the lead thumb by at least an inch without completely ungripping the club and then relocked on the lead thumb. The third "lock" occurs when the lifeline/thumb connection once again must be unlocked and relocked in the same manner. If unlocked and relocked an additional time thereafter, the forearms will rotate the wrists, clubface and elbows to a different ball flight alignment at the completion of the proceedings.

The elbows must be disconnected from the rib cage during the proceedings. If either or both elbows are connected to the rib cage during the proceedings, the forearms will rotate the wrists, clubface and elbows to a different ball flight alignment at the completion of the proceedings.

There may not be any clubface rotation during the gripping process. If the clubface rotates counterclockwise or clockwise when either the lead or trail hand is gripped on the club, the grip should be disassembled and the procedure repeated.

The only clubface rotation allowed during the proceedings is the almost indiscernible rotation caused by the relaxation of the lead arm from a straightened position after a conventional style of grip is assumed on the club.

The trail arm should remain passive and inactive throughout the proceedings. There should be no relaxation of the trail arm when the lead arm is relaxed from a straightened position. It already should be relaxed.

The sole of the clubface should remain grounded in the middle of the stance throughout the proceedings.

At the completion of the proceedings, the SHOULDERS ONLY TEST™, ARMS-LIFT TEST™ and the STRAIGHT-UP TEST™ must be conducted to determine whether the grip has been assembled correctly. If not confirmed, the procedure should be repeated until a properly assembled and executed LEAD ARM RELAX-N-LOCK TECHNIQUE™ is confirmed by the three tests.

Recommended Practice Routines When Using the Lead Arm Relax-N-Lock Technique™ in Combination with the Arrow Alignment Technique™

Once the LEAD ARM RELAX-N-LOCK TECHNIQUE™ is confirmed and a straight ball flight alignment has been established and locked-in, you must then center the sweet spot of your clubface as near the back of your ball as possible (if not already so centered) and then align your shoulders squarely parallel with your intended target line, followed by a non-manipulative golf swing if your objective is to hit a ball in line with your target.

You should use the ARROW ALIGNMENT TECHNIQUE™ to align your shoulders squarely parallel with your intended target line when practicing or playing with the LEAD ARM RELAX-N-LOCK TECHNIQUE™.

You also should locate a safe and relatively flat practice area as well as follow the steps below in each of your practice sessions:

STEP 1: Place a ball on the surface of your practice area. Identify a very narrow and specific target. Also identify your intended target line.

STEP 2: Ground the sole of your clubface in the middle of your stance, either directly behind your ball or in its nearby vicinity.

STEP 3: Straighten your lead arm to the fullest extent possible while keeping your trail arm relaxed. While continuing to keep your lead arm straightened to the fullest extent possible, grip your club with a

conventional style of grip. Then relax your lead arm and unlock and relock your lifeline/thumb connection twice and no more thereafter.

STEP 4: Conduct the SHOULDERS ONLY TEST™, ARMS-LIFT TEST™ and STRAIGHT-UP TEST™ at the completion of the proceedings. If the clubface rotates counterclockwise or clockwise during any of the three tests, you should disassemble your grip and repeat the procedure until a properly assembled and executed LEAD ARM RELAX-N-LOCK TECHNIQUE™ is confirmed.

STEP 5: Center the sweet spot of your clubface as near the back of your ball as possible (if not already so centered) and assume a comfortable posture and stance to your ball. Align your shoulders parallel with your intended target line to the best of your ability.

STEP 6: Conduct the ARROW ALIGNMENT TECHNIQUE™ and adjust your stance, if necessary, until your alignment arrow points directly at your target when you turn your head and trail eye in the direction of your target <u>as far as possible</u> while immobilizing all other parts of your body.

STEP 7: Ensure the sweet spot of your clubface has remained centered as near the back of your ball as possible and execute a non-manipulative golf swing.

You should begin each practice session with your most lofted club and then with each next most lofted club thereafter in succession. With each club, you should begin with a wrist swing, on to a ½ swing, then with a ¾ swing and conclude with a full swing.

SUMMARY POINTS

1. The LEAD ARM RELAX-N-LOCK TECHNIQUE™ requires a straightening of the lead arm to the fullest extent possible while relaxing the trail arm prior to forming a conventional style of grip on a club.

2. Once a conventional style of grip then is assembled on a club, the straightened lead arm must be relaxed and remain relaxed until the lifeline/thumb connection is unlocked and relocked twice but no more thereafter.

3. The sole of the clubface should be grounded in the middle of the stance throughout the proceedings.

4. The LEAD ARM RELAX-N-LOCK TECHNIQUE™ is compatible with all four conventional styles of grip.

5. The lead hand must be gripped on the club in a conventional (diagonal) manner and must not be allowed to rotate during the gripping process.

6. The trail hand must be gripped on the club either in the form of an original Vardon overlap, modified Vardon overlap, traditional interlock or regular baseball (ten-fingers) style of grip.

7. The grip is completed by locking the lifeline of the trail hand firmly on the lead thumb.

8. Once a conventional style of grip is formed on the club, the straightened lead arm must be relaxed while the trail arm remains passive and inactive. Then the lifeline of the trail hand must be unlocked from the lead thumb by at least an inch without completely ungripping the club and then relocked on the lead thumb once to lock-in a straight ball flight alignment but no more thereafter. Then once again, the lifeline/thumb connection must be unlocked and relocked in the same manner.

9. The SHOULDERS ONLY TEST™, ARMS-LIFT TEST™ and STRAIGHT-UP TEST™ must be conducted at the completion of the proceedings. If the clubface rotates counterclockwise or clockwise during any of the three tests, the grip should be disassembled and the procedure repeated until there is no such clubface rotation during the tests.

10. The ARROW ALIGNMENT TECHNIQUE™ should be conducted to align the shoulders parallel with the intended target line when using the LEAD ARM RELAX-N-LOCK TECHNIQUE™.

CHAPTER 14

INTRODUCTION OF THE TRAIL ARM EXTEND-N-LOCK TECHNIQUE™

The TRAIL ARM EXTEND-N-LOCK TECHNIQUE™ requires the sole of the clubface to be grounded during the proceedings.

It also requires the trail arm to be straightened to the fullest extent possible from a relaxed position after a conventional style of grip has been assumed.

The TRAIL ARM EXTEND-N-LOCK TECHNIQUE™ is compatible with all four conventional styles of grip whether that of the original Vardon overlap, modified Vardon overlap, traditional interlock or regular baseball (ten-fingers) type of grip.

The TRAIL ARM EXTEND-N-LOCK TECHNIQUE™ requires a total of two "locks" of the lifeline/thumb connection, as will be addressed later in this chapter.

How to Assemble the Trail Arm Extend-N-Lock Technique™

First, ground the sole of your clubface in the middle of your stance and keep it grounded throughout the proceedings. It does not necessarily need to be grounded directly behind your ball during the proceedings. You can ground it near the vicinity of your ball and once the proceedings are completed, then transfer and center the sweet spot of your clubface as near the back of the ball as possible.

Second, relax both arms appreciably and then grip your lead hand on the club in a conventional (diagonal) manner. You must not allow any clubface rotation when gripping your lead hand on the club.

Third, then grip your trail hand on the club either in the form of an original Vardon overlap, modified Vardon overlap, traditional interlock or regular baseball (ten-fingers) style of grip. You must not allow the clubface to rotate during the time you trail hand is gripped on your club or between the time your lead and trail hands are being gripped on your club. You must lock the lifeline of your trail hand squarely and securely on your lead thumb to complete the grip.

Fourth, once you have gripped both hands on your club and completed your grip by locking the lifeline of your trail hand on your lead thumb, straighten your trail arm to the fullest extent possible while continuing to relax your lead arm.

Fifth, keep your trail arm straightened to the fullest extent possible and then unlock the lifeline of your trail hand by at least an inch from your lead thumb without completely ungripping your club and then relock your trail lifeline on your lead thumb. The lifeline/thumb connection may not be unlocked and relocked thereafter.

Sixth, once you have unlocked and relocked your lifeline/thumb connection, you then must relax your trail arm and allow it to return to a comfortable position. (Figure 14-1).

Seventh, conduct the SHOULDERS ONLY TEST™, ARMS-LIFT TEST™ and STRAIGHT-UP TEST™ at the completion of the proceedings. If the clubface rotates counterclockwise or clockwise during any of the three tests, you must disassemble your grip and repeat the procedure until there is no clubface rotation when the three tests are conducted.

Figure 14-1

STEP 1: The first essential step to assemble and execute the TRAIL ARM EXTEND-N-LOCK TECHNIQUE™ is to relax both arms appreciably and then grip both hands on the club in a conventional manner with the clubface grounded in the middle of the stance.

STEP 2: Then straighten the trail arm to the maximum extent possible and keep it straightened in such manner until the completion of the proceedings.

STEP 3: While continuing to keep the trail arm straightened to the fullest extent possible while relaxing the lead arm, unlock the lifeline of the trail hand from the lead thumb by at least an inch without completely ungripping the club.

STEP 4: Then, while continuing to keep the trail arm straightened to the fullest extent possible with the lead arm relaxed, relock the lifeline of the trail hand squarely and securely on the lead thumb. *(The trail arm then may be relaxed and allowed to return to a comfortable position.)*

Why the Trail Arm Extend-N-Lock Technique™ Works

When the trail arm is straightened to the fullest extent possible from a relaxed position – while the lead arm remains relaxed – after a conventional style of grip is formed on a club, the forearms will rotate the elbows to a parallel alignment with the shoulders to create an on-line swing path of the clubface.

When the forearms rotate the elbows to a parallel alignment with the shoulders the wrists correspondingly will rotate the clubface to a square alignment, all of which will establish a straight ball flight alignment.

However, the straight ball flight alignment will not be locked-in at such point. In order to lock-in the straight ball flight alignment, the trail arm then must remain in its straightened position while the lifeline of the trail hand is unlocked from the lead thumb by at least an inch without completely ungripping the club and then relocked on the lead thumb.

The TRAIL ARM EXTEND-N-LOCK TECHNIQUE™ requires a total of two "locks" of the lifeline/thumb connection.

The first of the two "locks" of the lifeline/thumb connection that is required to assemble and execute the TRAIL ARM EXTEND-N-LOCK TECHNIQUE™ occurs when the lifeline of the trail hand is locked squarely and securely on the lead thumb to complete the grip.

The second of the two "locks" of the lifeline/thumb connection to assemble and execute the technique correctly occurs after the trail arm is straightened to the fullest extent possible when then the lifeline of the trail hand is unlocked from the lead thumb by at least an inch without completely ungripping the club and then relocked on the lead thumb to lock-in the straight ball flight alignment.

Disciplines Required to Assemble and Execute the Trail Arm Extend-N-Lock Technique™

The most critical discipline required to assemble and execute this technique is the manner in which the trail arm is straightened after a conventional style of grip is formed on a club.

Both arms should be relaxed appreciably when a conventional grip is assumed. Only the trail arm is to be straightened during the procedure after the grip is completed. If both arms are straightened, the forearms will not rotate the elbows to a parallel alignment with the shoulders to create an on-line swing path of the clubface at the completion of the proceedings.

In order to straighten your trail arm to the fullest extent possible while keeping your lead arm relaxed, it will be necessary to raise your trail shoulder upward slightly.

It is most critical that the trail arm remain straightened to the fullest extent possible until the lifeline of the trail hand is unlocked and then relocked on the lead thumb. If the trail arm is relaxed after being straightened but before the lifeline/thumb connection is unlocked and relocked, the forearms will not rotate the elbows to a parallel alignment with the shoulders nor will the wrists rotate the clubface to a square alignment to establish a straight ball flight alignment.

The lead arm should remain relaxed during the proceedings and the lead hand and wrist should move only in response to the straightening of the trail arm.

If the trail arm is straightened only prior to a conventional grip being assembled on the club, it would not cause the forearms to rotate the elbows to a parallel alignment with the shoulders nor the wrists and clubface to a square alignment. If straightened only after the lifeline/thumb connection is unlocked and relocked, the forearms likewise would not rotate the wrists, clubface and elbows to establish a straight ball flight alignment at the completion of the proceedings.

Another discipline is the elbows must be disconnected from the rib cage during the proceedings. If either or both elbows are connected to the rib cage during the proceedings the forearms will rotate the wrists, clubface and elbows to a different ball flight alignment at the completion of the proceedings.

An additional discipline is the clubface may not be allowed to rotate counterclockwise or clockwise during the proceedings except for the rotation caused by the trail arm being straightened to the fullest extent possible after a conventional style of grip is formed on a club.

Once the lifeline of the trail hand is unlocked from the lead thumb and then relocked on the lead thumb after the trail arm is straightened to the maximum extent, the lifeline/thumb connection may not be unlocked or relocked an additional time. If unlocked and relocked once more thereafter the forearms will not rotate the wrists, clubface and elbows to lock-in a straight ball flight alignment.

The SHOULDERS ONLY TEST™, ARMS-LIFT TEST™ and the STRAIGHT-UP TEST™ must be conducted at the completion of the proceedings to determine whether the technique has been performed correctly. If not confirmed, the procedure should be repeated until all three tests do confirm such.

Once a straight ball flight alignment has been established and locked-in, the sweet spot of the clubface must be centered as near the back of the ball as possible (if not already so centered) and, simultaneously, the shoulders must be aligned squarely parallel with the intended target line at final address, followed by a non-manipulative golf swing if the objective is to hit the ball on a straight path in the direction of the target.

Recommended Practice Routines When Using the Trail Arm Extend-N-Lock Technique™ in Combination with the Arrow Alignment Technique™

You should engage in some meaningful practice sessions before using the TRAIL ARM EXTEND-N-LOCK TECHNIQUE™ in actual play.

In each of your practice sessions you should locate a safe and relatively flat practice area. You also should conduct the ARROW ALIGNMENT TECHNIQUE™ to align your shoulders parallel with your intended target line.

You also should follow the steps below when using the TRAIL ARM EXTEND-N-LOCK TECHNIQUE™ in your practice sessions:

STEP 1: Place a ball on the surface of your practice area. Identify a very narrow and specific target. Also identify your intended target line.

STEP 2: Ground the sole of your clubface in the middle of your stance either directly behind your ball or in its near vicinity. Keep it grounded throughout the proceedings.

STEP 3: Assemble the TRAIL ARM EXTEND-N-LOCK TECHNIQUE™, as instructed throughout this chapter. Remember to straighten your trail arm to the fullest extent possible after gripping your club and then keep it straightened to the fullest extent possible until you have unlocked and relocked your lifeline/thumb connection. Then relax your trail arm to a comfortable position.

STEP 4: Once the proceedings are completed, conduct the SHOULDERS ONLY TEST™, ARMS-LIFT TEST™ and STRAIGHT-UP TEST™. Repeat the procedure, if necessary, until the three tests confirm the technique was performed correctly and a straight ball flight alignment has been established and locked-in.

STEP 5: Center the sweet spot of your clubface as near the back of the ball as possible and assume a comfortable posture and stance to your ball. Align your shoulders parallel with your intended target line to the best of your ability.

STEP 6: Conduct the ARROW ALIGNMENT TECHNIQUE™ and adjust your stance, if necessary, until your alignment arrow points directly at your target when you turn your head and trail eye in the direction of your target as far as possible while immobilizing all other parts of your body.

STEP 7: Ensure the sweet spot of your clubface has remained centered as near the back of your ball as possible and then execute a non-manipulative golf swing.

You should begin each practice session with your most lofted club and then practice with each next most lofted club in succession thereafter. With each club you should begin with simply a wrist swing, then with a ½ swing, on to a ¾ swing and conclude with a full swing.

SUMMARY POINTS

1. **The TRAIL ARM EXTEND-N-LOCK TECHNIQUE™ requires the trail arm to be straightened to the fullest extent possible from a relaxed position after a conventional style of grip is formed on a club.**

2. **The sole of the clubface must be grounded in the middle of the stance during the proceedings.**

3. **Once a conventional style of grip is assembled on a club, the trail arm must be straightened to the fullest extent possible while relaxing the lead arm, and remain in such position until the lifeline/thumb connection is unlocked and relocked.**

4. **The TRAIL ARM EXTEND-N-LOCK TECHNIQUE™ is compatible with all four conventional styles of grip.**

5. **The lead hand therefore must be formed on a club in a conventional (diagonal) manner without allowing any clubface rotation during the gripping process.**

6. **The trail hand must be assembled on the club either in the form of an original Vardon overlap, modified Vardon overlap, traditional interlock or regular baseball (ten-fingers) style of grip.**

7. **The grip is completed by locking the lifeline of the trail hand firmly on the lead thumb.**

8. **Once the trail arm is extended and straightened to the fullest extent possible while keeping the lead arm relaxed, the lifeline of the trail hand then must be unlocked from the lead thumb by at least an inch without completely ungripping the club and then relocked on the lead thumb to complete the proceedings. The lifeline/thumb connection may not be unlocked and relocked thereafter.**

9. **The SHOULDERS ONLY TEST™, ARMS-LIFT TEST™ and STRAIGHT-UP TEST™ must be conducted at the completion of the proceedings to determine whether the technique was assembled and executed correctly. If not, the grip should be disassembled and the procedure repeated until the TRAIL ARM EXTEND-N-LOCK TECHNIQUE™ is confirmed as assembled and executed correctly.**

10. **The ARROW ALIGNMENT TECHNIQUE™ should be conducted to align the shoulders parallel with the intended target line when using the TRAIL ARM EXTEND-N-LOCK TECHNIQUE™.**

CHAPTER 15

INTRODUCTION OF THE TRAIL ARM RELAX-N-LOCK TECHNIQUE™

The TRAIL ARM RELAX-N-LOCK TECHNIQUE™ requires the trail arm to be relaxed from a straightened position after a conventional style of grip formed on a club. Once the trail hand is relaxed from a straightened position, the lifeline/thumb connection must be unlocked and relocked twice in order to lock-in a straight ball flight alignment. The lifeline/thumb connection may not be unlocked and relocked thereafter.

The TRAIL ARM EXTEND-N-LOCK TECHNIQUE™ is compatible with all four conventional styles of grip whether that of the original Vardon overlap, modified Vardon overlap, traditional interlock and regular baseball (ten-fingers) type of grip.

How to Assemble and Execute the Trail Arm Relax-N-Lock Technique™

First, ground the sole of your clubface in the middle of your stance and keep it grounded throughout the proceedings. It does not necessarily need to be grounded directly behind your ball during the proceedings. You may ground it near the vicinity of your ball and once the proceedings are completed, then transfer and center the sweet spot of the clubface as near the back of your ball as possible.

Second, straighten your trail arm to the fullest extent possible while relaxing your lead arm and then keep your trail arm straightened in such a manner until your grip is completed.

Third, then grip your lead hand on your club in a conventional (diagonal) manner without allowing any clubface rotation.

Fourth, grip your trail hand on your club either in the form of an original Vardon overlap, modified Vardon overlap, traditional interlock or regular baseball (ten-fingers) style of grip. Do not allow your clubface to rotate either clockwise or counterclockwise while gripping the club with your trail hand or between the time you grip your lead and trail hand on the club. Complete your grip by locking the lifeline of your trail hand squarely and securely on your lead thumb.

Fifth, then relax your trail arm from its straightened position.

Sixth, while your trail arm remains relaxed from its straightened position, unlock the lifeline of your trail hand from your lead thumb by at least an inch without completely ungripping the club and then relock the lifeline of your trail hand on your lead thumb.

Seventh, then once again unlock the lifeline of your trail hand from the lead thumb by at least an inch without completely ungripping your club and then, once again, relock the lifeline of your trail hand on your lead thumb to complete the proceedings. (Figure 15-1).

Eighth, conduct the SHOULDERS ONLY TEST™, ARMS-LIFT TEST™ and STRAIGHT-UP TEST™ at the completion of the proceedings. If the clubface rotates counterclockwise or clockwise during any of the three tests, you must disassemble your grip and repeat the procedure until there is no clubface rotation when the three tests are conducted.

Why the Trail Arm Relax-N-Lock Technique™ Works

When the trail arm is relaxed from a straightened position after a conventional style of grip is formed on a club, the forearms will rotate the elbows to a parallel alignment

Figure 15-1

STEP 1: The first essential step to assemble and execute the TRAIL ARM RELAX-N-LOCK TECHNIQUE™ is to relax the lead arm appreciably and straighten the trail arm to the fullest extent before the trail arm is gripped on the club.

STEP 2: Once the trail hand then is gripped on the club with the lead arm relaxed appreciably and the trail arm straightened to the maximum extent possible, relax the trail arm from its original position.

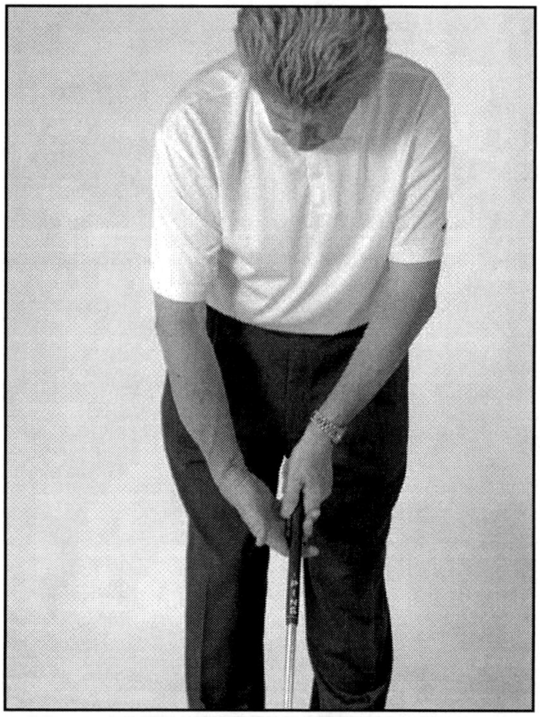

STEP 3: Then unlock the lifeline of the trail hand from the lead thumb by at least an inch without completely ungripping the club.

STEP 4: Then relock the lifeline of the trail hand squarely and securely on the lead thumb.

STEP 5: Then, once again, unlock the lifeline of the trail hand from the lead thumb by at least an inch without completely ungripping the club.

STEP 6: Then, once again, relock the lifeline of the trail hand squarely and securely on the lead thumb.

with the shoulders to create an on-line swing path of the clubface.

When the forearms rotate the elbows to a parallel alignment the wrists correspondingly will rotate the clubface to a square alignment, all of which will establish and lock-in a straight ball flight alignment.

However, a straight ball flight alignment will not be locked-in at this point. In order to lock-in a straight ball flight alignment, the trail arm must remain relaxed from its straightened position while the lifeline/thumb connection is unlocked and relocked twice.

The TRAIL ARM RELAX-N-LOCK TECHNIQUE™ requires a total of three "locks"of the lifeline/thumb connection.

The first of the three "locks" of the lifeline/thumb connection that is necessary to assemble and execute the TRAIL ARM RELAX-N-LOCK TECHNIQUE™ occurs when the lifeline of the trail hand is locked squarely and securely on the lead thumb to complete the grip.

The second of the three "locks" of the lifeline/thumb connection occurs after the trail arm is relaxed from its straightened position when then the lifeline of the trail hand is unlocked from the lead thumb by at least an inch without completely ungripping the club and then the trail lifeline is relocked on the lead thumb.

The third of the three "locks" occurs when then, once again, the lifeline of the trail hand is unlocked by at least an inch from the lead thumb without completely ungripping the club and then, once again, the lifeline of the trail hand is relocked on the lead thumb to complete the proceedings.

Disciplines Required to Assemble the Trail Arm Relax-N-Lock Technique™

The most critical discipline relating to the TRAIL ARM RELAX-N-LOCK TECHNIQUE™ is the manner in which the trail arm is relaxed from a straightened position after a conventional style of grip is formed on a club.

The lead arm should not be involved in the procedure whatsoever. It should remain passive and inactive during the proceedings.

In order to relax the trail arm sufficiently to cause the forearms to rotate the elbows to a parallel alignment with the shoulders and the wrists to rotate the clubface to a square alignment, it must be straightened to the fullest extent possible prior to assuming a conventional grip on the club. Then, once a conventional grip is formed on a club, the trail arm must be relaxed appreciably from its straightened position and remain relaxed until the lifeline/thumb connection is unlocked and relocked twice.

If both arms are relaxed evenly from a straightened position after a conventional grip is assembled on a club, the forearms will not rotate the wrists, clubface and elbows to establish a straight ball flight alignment at the completion of the proceedings.

The relaxation of the trail arm from a straightened position while the lead arm remains relaxed and passive must occur only after a conventional style of grip is assembled on a club but before the lifeline/thumb connection is unlocked and relocked twice to complete the proceedings.

Another discipline is the elbows must be disconnected from the rib cage during the proceedings. If either or both elbows are connected to the rib cage during the proceedings, the forearms will rotate the wrists, clubface and elbows to a different ball flight alignment at the completion of the proceedings.

An additional discipline is the clubface may not be allowed to rotate counterclockwise or clockwise during the proceedings except for the rotation caused by the trail arm being relaxed from a straightened position after a conventional grip is assembled on the club.

This means there may be no clubface rotation allowed when either the lead and trail hands are assembled on a club or between the time the lead and trail hands are gripped on the club. It also means the lead hand may not loosen or tighten the grip on the club or partially ungrip and then regrip the club during the proceedings.

The SHOULDERS ONLY TEST™, ARMS-LIFT TEST™ and STRAIGHT-UP TEST™ must be conducted at the completion of the proceedings to determine whether the procedure has been performed correctly. If not confirmed, the procedure should be repeated until all three tests confirm that it has.

Once the three tests confirm the procedure has been performed correctly and a straight ball flight alignment has been established and locked-in, the sweet spot of the clubface must be centered as near the back of the ball as possible (if not already so centered) and, simultaneously, the shoulders must be aligned squarely parallel with the intended target line at final address, followed by a non-manipulative golf swing if the objective is to hit a ball on a straight path in the direction of the target.

Recommended Practice Routines When Using the Trail Arm Relax-N-Lock Technique™ in Combination with the Arrow Alignment Technique™

You should engage in some meaningful practice sessions before using the TRAIL ARM RELAX-N-LOCK TECHNIQUE™ in actual play.

In each of your practice sessions you should locate a safe and relatively flat practice area. You also should conduct the ARROW ALIGNMENT TECHNIQUE™ to align your shoulders parallel with your intended target line.

In addition, you should follow the steps below when using the TRAIL ARM RELAX-N-LOCK TECHNIQUE™ in your practice sessions:

STEP 1: **Place a ball on the surface of your practice area. Identify a very narrow and specific target. Also identify your intended target line.**

STEP 2: **Ground the sole of your clubface either directly behind your ball or in its near vicinity. Keep it grounded throughout the proceedings.**

STEP 3: **Assemble the TRAIL ARM RELAX-N-LOCK TECHNIQUE™ as instructed throughout this chapter. Remember to straighten your trail arm to the fullest extent possible before gripping your club. Then, once you have gripped your club, relax your trail arm from its straightened position and keep it relaxed until you have unlocked and relocked your lifeline/thumb connection twice. Do not unlock and relock your lifeline/thumb connection thereafter.**

STEP 4: **Once you have completed the proceedings, conduct the SHOULDERS ONLY TEST™, ARMS-LIFT TEST™ and STRAIGHT-UP TEST™. Repeat the proceedings, if necessary, until the three tests confirm the technique was assembled and executed correctly and a straight ball flight alignment has been established and locked-in.**

STEP 5: **Center the sweet spot of your clubface as near the back of your ball as possible (if not already so centered) and assume a comfortable posture and stance to your ball. Align your shoulders parallel with your intended target line to the best of your ability.**

STEP 6: **Conduct the ARROW ALIGNMENT TECHNIQUE™ and adjust your stance, if necessary, until your alignment arrow points directly at your target when you turn your head and trail eye in the direction of your target <u>as far as pos-</u>**

sible while immobilizing all other parts of your body.

STEP 7: Ensure the sweet spot of your clubface has remained centered as near the back of your ball as possible and then execute a non-manipulative golf swing.

You should begin each practice session with your most lofted club and then practice with each next most lofted club in succession, thereafter. With each club you should begin with simply a wrist swing, then with a ½ swing, on to a ¾ swing and conclude with a full swing.

SUMMARY POINTS

1. The TRAIL ARM RELAX-N-LOCK TECHNIQUE™ requires a relaxation of the trail arm from a straightened position after a conventional grip is assembled on a club.

2. The sole of the clubface must be grounded during the proceedings when performing the TRAIL ARM RELAX-N-LOCK TECHNIQUE™.

3. The lead arm should remain relaxed during the proceedings.

4. The trail arm must be relaxed from its straightened position after the grip is completed and remain relaxed until the lifeline/thumb connection is unlocked and relocked twice.

5. The TRAIL ARM RELAX-N-LOCK TECHNIQUE™ is compatible with all four conventional styles of grip.

6. Therefore, the lead hand must be gripped on a club in a conventional (diagonal) manner.

7. The trail hand then must be assembled on the club either in the form of an original Vardon overlap, modified Vardon overlap, traditional interlock or regular baseball (ten-fingers) style of grip.

8. The grip is completed by locking the lifeline of the trail hand firmly on the lead thumb.

9. **The SHOULDERS ONLY TEST™, ARMS-LIFT TEST™ and STRAIGHT-UP TEST™ must be conducted at the completion of the proceedings to determine whether the procedure was assembled and executed correctly. If not, the grip should be disassembled and the proceedings repeated until a TRAIL ARM RELAX-N-LOCK TECHNIQUE™ is confirmed as assembled correctly.**

10. **The ARROW ALIGNMENT TECHNIQUE™ should be conducted to align the shoulders parallel with the intended target line when using the TRAIL ARM RELAX-N-LOCK TECHNIQUE™.**

CHAPTER 16

INTRODUCTION OF THE CLOCKWISE-N-LOCK TECHNIQUE™

This chapter will address the CLOCKWISE-N-LOCK TECHNIQUE™; the next chapter will address the COUNTERCLOCKWISE-N-LOCK TECHNIQUE™. Both are similar in concept but opposite in terms of application.

The CLOCKWISE-N-LOCK TECHNIQUE™ requires a twisting (rotation) of the forearms and wrists in a clockwise manner after a conventional style of grip has been assembled on a club. The COUNTERCLOCKWISE -N-LOCK TECHNIQUE™ requires a twisting (rotation) of the forearms and wrists in a counterclockwise direction after a conventional style of grip is formed on a club.

The shoulders and knees must be immobilized and the arms and hands must remain relaxed when the forearms and wrists are rotated clockwise to assemble and execute the CLOCKWISE-N-LOCK TECHNIQUE™.

How to Assemble and Execute the Clockwise-N-Lock Technique™

The ***first step*** is to ground the sole of the clubface and keep it grounded in the middle of the stance throughout the proceedings.

The sole of the clubface need not be grounded directly behind the ball when the hands are gripped on a club as long as the locked-in proceedings are completed before moving and centering the sweet spot of the clubface as near the back of the ball as possible.

Typically, I do not ground the sole of my clubface directly behind the ball when assembling and executing the LOCKED-IN TECHNIQUES™ addressed in this book. Instead, I assemble and execute the techniques with the sole of the clubface grounded in the near proximity of the ball and when the proceedings are completed, I then center the sweet spot of the clubface as near the back of the ball as possible.

The ***second step*** in the procedure is to form a conventional style of golf grip on the club. The grip may be in the form of an original or modified Vardon overlap, traditional interlock or regular baseball (ten-fingers) baseball style of grip. The grip must be completed in any such case by locking the lifeline of the trail hand firmly on the lead thumb.

The ***third step*** is to rotate or twist the forearms and wrists clockwise to the fullest extent possible – until the clubface stops rotating clockwise – without moving the shoulders or knees in the process.

The wrists can be rotated or twisted fully clockwise while immobilizing the shoulders and knees in two different ways. One is to rotate the arms, hands and wrists in a clockwise manner to the fullest extent possible while immobilizing the shoulders and knees. The second way is to immobilize the shoulders, knees and upper arms and then twist only the forearms and wrists fully clockwise to the maximum extent possible. In either case, once rotated or twisted clockwise to the fullest extent possible, the forearms and wrists must remain in such position until the proceedings are completed.

Once the upper arms, forearms and wrists or, merely the forearms and wrists, are rotated clockwise to the fullest extent possible while immobilizing the shoulders and knees, the ***fourth step*** then is to unlock the lifeline of the trail hand from the lead thumb by at least an inch without completely ungripping the club and then relock the trail lifeline on the lead thumb. The lifeline/thumb connection may not be unlocked and relocked thereafter.

The ***fifth step*** in the procedure is to relax the arms, hands and wrists and allow them to return to a comfortable position. (Figure 16-1).

Why the Clockwise-N-Lock Technique™ Works

The CLOCKWISE-N-LOCK TECHNIQUE™ works because when the forearms and wrists are rotated clockwise to the fullest extent possible while immobilizing the shoulders and knees after a conventional style of grip is assembled on a club, the forearms will rotate the elbows to a parallel alignment with the shoulders to create an on-line swing path of the clubface.

When the elbows are aligned squarely parallel with the shoulders to create an on-line swing path of the clubface the wrists correspondingly will rotate the clubface to a square alignment, all of which will establish a straight ball flight alignment.

However, the straight ball flight alignment will not be locked-in at this point. In order to lock-in the straight ball flight alignment, the forearms and wrists must remain rotated clockwise to the fullest extent possible while the lifeline/thumb connection is unlocked and relocked only once and no more thereafter.

Disciplines Required When Assembling and Executing the Clockwise-N-Lock Technique™

The first discipline is to ground the sole of your clubface and keep it grounded throughout the proceedings. The clubface should be grounded in the middle of the stance whether it is grounded directly behind the ball or in its near vicinity during the proceedings.

The second discipline is not to loosen and tighten or partially ungrip and regrip the lead hand after gripping it on the club. Any such movement will cause the clubface to rotate and, in turn, compromise the procedure. In addition, the clubface may not be allowed to move or rotate between the time the lead hand and the trail hand are gripped or during the time the trail hand is formed on the club. Neither may the clubface be allowed to move or rotate after both hands are gripped on the club except for the rotation caused when the forearms and wrists are rotated clockwise to the fullest extent while immobilizing the shoulders and knees.

On way to prevent the clubface from rotating during the gripping proceedings is to

Figure 16-1

STEP 1: The first essential step to assemble and execute the CLOCKWISE-N-LOCK TECHNIQUE™ is to grip the club with a conventional style of grip with the clubface grounded in the middle of the stance.

STEP 2: Then the shoulders and knees must be immobilized and the clubface grounded as the wrists and forearms or, the wrists, forearms and upper arms, are rotated clockwise as far as possible and held in such positions until the proceedings are completed.

STEP 3: While holding the wrists, forearms and clubface in such positions, the lifeline of the trail hand must be unlocked from the lead thumb by at least an inch without completely ungripping the club.

STEP 4: Then, while continuing to hold the wrists, forearms and clubface in such positions, the lifeline of the trail hand must be relocked squarely and securely on the lead thumb. *(The wrists, forearms and clubface must then be relaxed to allow them to return their original positions.)*

press the sole of the clubface into the surface before assembling the grip.

Whether the upper arms, forearms and wrists are rotated clockwise or, merely the forearms and wrists are rotated clockwise, they must remain rotated to the fullest extent possible until the lifeline/thumb connection is unlocked and relocked. You may find it helpful to rotate your upper arms, forearms and wrists to the maximum extent and then rotate them a little more while immobilizing your shoulders and knees in order to cause your forearms to rotate your wrists, clubface and elbows to establish a straight ball flight alignment. Then hold the position until the lifeline/thumb connection is unlocked and relocked.

An additional discipline relating to the CLOCKWISE-N-LOCK TECHNIQUE™ is the elbows must be disconnected from the rib cage during the entire proceedings. If either or both elbows are connected to the rib cage during any stage of the proceedings, the forearms will rotate the wrists, clubface and elbows to some alignment other than a straight ball flight alignment at the completion of the proceedings.

In order to assemble and execute the CLOCKWISE-N-LOCK TECHNIQUE™, the lifeline/thumb connection must be locked a total of two times.

The first of the two "locks" of the lifeline/thumb connection that is necessary to perform the CLOCKWISE-N-LOCK TECHNIQUE™ occurs when the lifeline of the trail hand is locked squarely and securely on the lead thumb to complete the grip. The second of the two "locks" of the lifeline/thumb connection occurs after the upper arms, forearms and wrists are rotated clockwise to the fullest extent possible while immobilizing the shoulders and knees when then the lifeline of the trail hand is unlocked by at least an inch from the lead thumb without completely ungripping the club and then relocked on the lead thumb.

Whether using the CLOCKWISE-N-LOCK TECHNIQUE™ in actual play or in your practice sessions you should –

Always Conduct the Shoulders Only Test™, Arms-Lift Test™ and Straight-Up Test™

There may be a tendency to relax your arms, hands and wrists slightly once they are rotated clockwise to the fullest extent before your lifeline/thumb connection is unlocked and relocked to complete the proceedings. There also may be a tendency to hurry the process and forget to unlock and relock your lifeline/thumb connection after rotating your forearms and wrists clockwise to the fullest extent.

Coupled with these and other possible compromises when assembling and executing the CLOCKWISE-N-LOCK TECHNIQUE™, it just makes good sense to conduct all three confirmation tests at the completion of the proceedings.

If your clubface rotates clockwise or counterclockwise from its original alignment when you conduct either the SHOULDERS ONLY TEST™, ARMS-LIFT TEST™ or STRAIGHT-UP TEST™ you will know you compromised the procedure in some way and will not have locked-in a straight ball flight alignment. In such an event, you should disassemble your grip and repeat the procedure until a properly assembled and executed CLOCKWISE-N-LOCK TECHNIQUE™ is indicated by the three confirmation tests.

The assemblage and execution of the CLOCKWISE-N-LOCK TECHNIQUE™ is only a part of a successful pre-shot routine. Whether using the CLOCKWISE-N-LOCK TECHNIQUE™ or one of the other thirty-one LOCKED-IN TECHNIQUES™ discussed in this book, the sweet spot of the clubface then must be centered as near the back of the ball as possible and, simultaneously, the shoulders must be aligned squarely parallel with the intended target line, followed by a non-manipulative golf swing if the objective is to hit a golf ball on a straight path in the direction of the intended target.

Recommended Practice Routines When Using the Clockwise-N-Lock Technique™ in Combination with the Arrow Alignment Technique™

Since aligning your shoulders squarely parallel with your intended target line at the completion of your pre-shot routine is so essential in producing a straight ball flight to an intended target, you should always conduct the ARROW ALIGNMENT TECHNIQUE™ as the final step in your pre-swing proceedings.

You also should follow a consistent routine such as the steps below when using the CLOCKWISE-N-LOCK TECHNIQUE™.

STEP 1: Select a safe and relatively flat hitting area. Place a ball on the surface of your hitting surface.

STEP 2: Identify a specific and narrow target as well as your intended target line. Ground the sole of your clubface in the middle of your stance, either near or directly behind your ball.

STEP 3: Assemble either an original or modified Vardon overlap, traditional inter-

lock or regular baseball (ten-fingers) style of grip on the handle of your club without allowing any clubface rotation during the gripping process. Then lock the lifeline of your trail hand firmly on your lead thumb to complete the grip.

STEP 4: **Immobilize your shoulders and feet, relax your arms and wrists and then rotate your upper arms, forearms and wrists in a clockwise manner to the fullest extent possible or, in the alternative, immobilize your shoulders, feet and upper arms and then twist your forearms and wrists clockwise to the fullest extent possible. Keep your forearms and wrists rotated fully clockwise and then unlock the lifeline of your trail hand from your lead thumb by at least an inch without completely ungripping your club and then relock your trail lifeline on your lead thumb.**

STEP 5: **Relax your arms, hands and wrists and allow them to return to a comfortable position.**

STEP 6: **Conduct the SHOULDERS ONLY TEST™, ARMS-LIFT TEST™ and STRAIGHT-UP TEST™ to determine if a straight ball flight alignment has been established and locked-in. If not, repeat the process until all three tests confirm the CLOCKWISE-N-LOCK TECHNIQUE™ was assembled and executed correctly and as a result, a straight ball flight alignment has been established and locked-in.**

STEP 7: **Center the sweet spot of your clubface as near the back of your ball as possible without allowing it to touch or move your ball. Assume a comfortable posture and stance to your ball and then align your shoulders parallel with your intended target line to the best of your ability.**

STEP 8: **Conduct the ARROW ALIGNMENT TECHNIQUE™ and adjust your stance, if necessary, until your alignment arrow points directly at your intended target when you turn your trail eye and head in the direction of your target <u>as far as possible</u> while immobilizing all other parts of your body.**

STEP 9: **Ensure the sweet spot of your clubface has remained centered as near the back of your ball as possible and then execute a non-manipulative golf swing.**

You should begin each practice session with your most lofted club and then with your next most lofted club in succession thereafter until you have practiced with each club in your set. With each club, you should begin with a simple wrist swing, followed by a ½ swing, on to a ¾ swing and finish with a full swing.

SUMMARY POINTS

1. The CLOCKWISE-N-LOCK TECHNIQUE™ rotates the forearms, wrists, clubface and elbows from a slice alignment – formed the instant a conventional style of grip is assumed when there is no clubface rotation during the gripping process – to establish a straight ball flight alignment.

2. The CLOCKWISE-N-LOCK TECHNIQUE™ requires the lead hand to be gripped on a club in a conventional (diagonal) manner.

3. The CLOCKWISE-N-LOCK TECHNIQUE™ then requires either an original or modified Vardon overlap, traditional interlock or regular baseball (ten-fingers) style of grip to be assembled on the club with the trail hand.

4. The lifeline of the trail hand then is locked on the lead thumb to complete the grip. This is the first of the two "locks" of the lifeline/thumb connection that is necessary to assemble and lock-in the CLOCKWISE-N-LOCK TECHNIQUE™.

5. The clubface may not be allowed to rotate clockwise or counterclockwise while either the lead or trail hand is gripped on the club or between the time the lead hand and trail hand are gripped on the club.

6. The shoulders and feet then must be immobilized as the upper arms, forearms, and wrists are rotated clockwise to the fullest extent possible or, as an alternative, the shoulders, feet and upper arms must be immobilized as the forearms and wrists are rotated clockwise to the fullest extent possible.

7. **Once the forearms and wrists are rotated fully clockwise they must be held in such position until the completion of the proceedings. The lifeline of the trail hand then must be unlocked from the lead thumb by at least an inch without completely ungripping the club and then relocked on the lead thumb to complete the proceedings. This is the second of the two "locks" of the lifeline/thumb connection that is required to assemble and execute the CLOCKWISE-N-LOCK TECHNIQUE™.**

8. **After the lifeline/thumb connection is unlocked and relocked once and no more thereafter, the arms, hands and wrists should be relaxed and allowed to return to a comfortable position.**

9. **The SHOULDERS ONLY TEST™, ARMS-LIFT TEST™ and STRAIGHT-UP TEST™ should always be conducted after completing the procedure to determine if it has been assembled and executed correctly. If not, the grip should be disassembled and the procedure should be repeated until all three tests confirm a straight ball flight alignment has been established and locked-in.**

10. **The ARROW ALIGNMENT TECHNIQUE™ should always be conducted to align the shoulders squarely parallel with the intended target line when using the CLOCKWISE TWIST-N-LOCK TECHNIQUE™.**

CHAPTER 17

INTRODUCTION OF THE COUNTER-CLOCKWISE-N-LOCK TECHNIQUE™

The COUNTERCLOCKWISE-N-LOCK TECHNIQUE™, in contrast to the CLOCKWISE-N-LOCK TECHNIQUE™, requires a rotation of the forearms and wrists in a counter-clockwise manner while immobilizing the shoulders and knees.

The COUNTERCLOCKWISE-N-LOCK TECHNIQUE™ requires a total of three "locks" of the lifeline/thumb connection rather than two "locks" as in the case of the CLOCKWISE-N-LOCK TECHNIQUE™.

When assembling and executing the COUNTERCLOCKWISE-N-LOCK TECHNIQUE™, the first "lock" of the lifeline/thumb connection occurs when a conventional style of grip is assembled on a club handle and completed by locking the lifeline of the trail hand on the lead thumb. The second "lock" of the lifeline/thumb connection occurs after the forearms and wrists are rotated counterclockwise to the fullest extent possible, while immobilizing the shoulders and knees, when then the lifeline/thumb connection is unlocked and relocked.

The third "lock" occurs when then, once again, the lifeline of the trail hand is unlocked from the lead thumb and then, once again, relocked on the lead thumb.

The COUNTERCLOCKWISE-N-LOCK TECHNIQUE™ is compatible with either an original Vardon overlap, modified Vardon overlap, traditional interlock or regular baseball (ten-fingers) style of grip.

How to Assemble and Execute the Counterclockwise-N-Lock Technique™

The ***first step*** is to ground the sole of the clubface in the middle of the stance.

The ***second step*** is to grip the lead hand on the club in a conventional (diagonal) manner without allowing the clubface to rotate during the process.

The ***third step*** is to grip the trail hand on the club in a conventional manner and then complete the grip by locking the lifeline of the trail hand squarely and securely on the lead thumb.

The ***fourth step*** of the process requires the shoulders and knees to be immobilized after which the upper arms, forearms and wrists must be rotated counterclockwise to the fullest extent possible – until the clubface stops rotating counterclockwise. As an alternative, the shoulders, feet and upper arms must be mobilized after which only the forearms and wrists must be rotated counterclockwise to the fullest extent possible – until the clubface stops rotating counterclockwise.

In either case, once the forearms and wrists are rotated counterclockwise to the fullest extent possible, they must be held in that position until the proceedings are completed.

The ***fifth step*** in the process is the lifeline of the trail hand then must be unlocked from the lead thumb by at least an inch without completely ungripping the club and then relocked on the lead thumb.

The ***sixth step*** in the procedure is to then, once again, unlock the lifeline of the trail hand from the lead thumb by at least an inch without completely ungripping the club and then, once again, relock the trail lifeline on the lead thumb. Once the lifeline/thumb connection is unlocked and relocked twice the shoulders, knees, arms and wrists should be relaxed and allowed to return to a comfortable position. (Figure 17-1).

Why the Counterclockwise-N-Lock Technique™ Works

The COUNTERCLOCKWISE-N-LOCK TECHNIQUE™ works because when the forearms and wrists are rotated counterclockwise to the fullest extent possible while the shoulders and knees are immobilized, the forearms will rotate the elbows to a parallel alignment with the shoulders to create an on-line swing path of the clubface.

When the elbows are rotated to a parallel alignment with the shoulders to create an on-line swing path the wrists correspondingly will rotate the clubface to a square alignment, all of which will establish a straight ball flight alignment.

However, the straight ball flight alignment will not be locked-in at this point.

In order to lock-in the straight ball flight alignment, the lifeline/thumb connection then must be unlocked and relocked <u>twice</u> while the forearms and wrists are rotated counterclockwise to the fullest extent possible.

Disciplines Required When Assembling and Executing the Counterclockwise-N-Lock Technique™

The lead hand should not be loosened and tightened or partially ungripped and regripped once assembled on the club. Neither should the clubface be allowed to rotate between the time the lead hand and the trail hand are gripped on the club or at any time after both hands are gripped on the club except for the rotation caused by the counterclockwise rotation or twisting of the forearms and wrists.

The lifeline/thumb connection may not be unlocked and relocked before the wrists are rotated counterclockwise as far as possible. Neither may the lifeline/thumb connection be unlocked and relocked an additional time after being unlocked and relocked <u>twice</u>. If the lifeline/thumb connection is unlocked and relocked an additional time, the forearms will rotate the wrists, clubface and elbows to a different alignment at the completion of the proceedings.

An additional discipline associated with the COUNTERCLOCKWISE-N-LOCK TECHNIQUE™ is the elbows must be disconnected from the rib cage during the entire proceedings. If either or both elbows are connected to the rib cage during the proceedings a straight ball flight alignment will not be locked-in at the completion of the procedure.

Figure 17-1

STEP 1: The first essential step in assembling and executing the COUNTERCLOCKWISE-N-LOCK TECHNIQUE™ is to grip both hands on the club in a conventional manner with the clubface grounded in the middle of the stance.

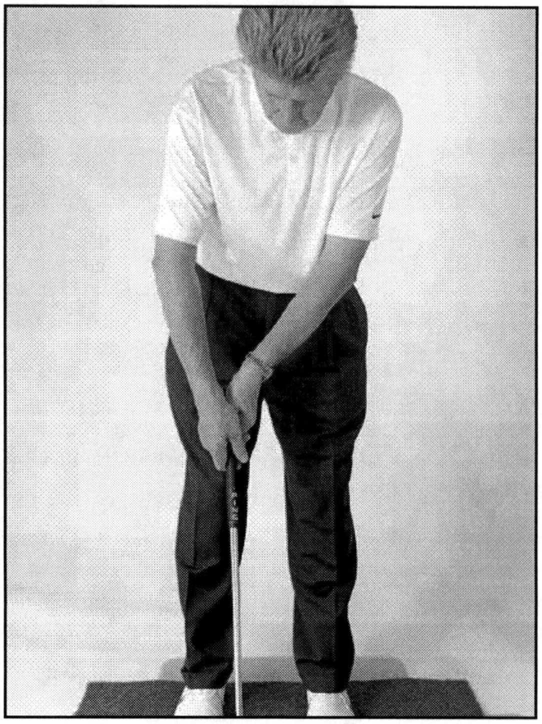

STEP 2: Then, while immobilizing the shoulders and knees and keeping the clubface grounded, the clubface must be rotated counterclockwise as far as possible with the wrists and forearms or, with the wrists, upper arms and forearms. They must be held in such a fully counterclockwise position until the completion of the proceedings.

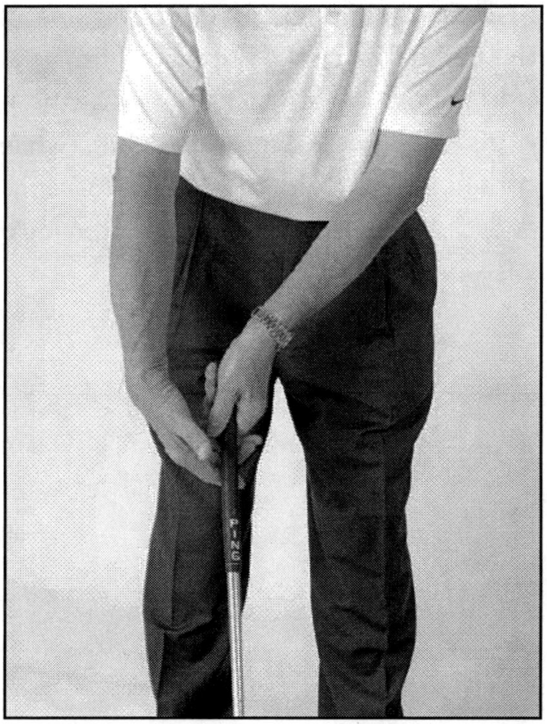

STEP 3: While the wrists, forearms and clubface are held in a fully counterclockwise position, the lifeline of the trail hand must be unlocked from the lead thumb by at least an inch without completely ungripping the club.

STEP 4: Then, while continuing to hold the wrists, forearms and clubface in a fully counterclockwise position, the lifeline of the trail hand must be relocked squarely and securely on the lead thumb.

STEP 5: Then, once again, the lifeline of the trail hand must be unlocked from the lead thumb by at least an inch without completely ungripping the club, while continuing to hold the wrists, forearms and clubface rotated fully counterclockwise.

STEP 6: While continuing to hold the wrists, forearms and clubface rotated fully counterclockwise, the lifeline of the trail hand once again must be relocked squarely and securely on the lead thumb. *(The wrists, forearms and clubface then must be relaxed and allowed to rotate back to their original positions.)*

When assembling and executing the COUNTERCLOCKWISE-N-LOCK TECHNIQUE™ you should always conduct the SHOULDERS ONLY TEST™, ARMS-LIFT TEST™ and STRAIGHT-UP TEST™ at the completion of the procedure to determine whether a straight ball flight alignment has been established and locked-in.

Once the forearms, wrists, clubface and elbows are rotated to establish and lock-in a straight ball flight alignment, there remains two additional steps that must be completed during the pre-shot routine if the objective is to hit a golf ball on a straight path in the direction of a specific target: the sweet spot of the clubface must be centered as near the back of the ball as possible and the shoulders simultaneously must be aligned squarely parallel with the intended target line at final address, followed by a non-manipulative golf swing.

Recommended Practice Routines When Using the Counterclockwise-N-Lock Technique™ in Combination with the Arrow Alignment Technique™

You should begin your practice sessions with your most lofted club, then progress through your set, practicing with each next most lofted club in succession thereafter. With each club you should begin with simply a wrist swing, then with a ½ swing, on to a ¾ swing and finally with a full swing.

Select a safe hitting area and a relatively flat surface and follow the steps below during your practice routine when using the COUNTERCLOCKWISE-N-LOCK TECHNIQUE™:

STEP 1: Place a ball on the surface, whether that of a practice mat or ground. Identify a specific and narrow target and your intended target line.

STEP 2: Ground the sole of your clubface in the middle of your stance and then assume either an original or modified Vardon overlap, traditional interlock or regular baseball (ten-fingers) style of grip – whichever you prefer. Complete your grip by locking the lifeline of your trail hand firmly on your lead thumb.

STEP 3: Immobilize your shoulders and knees and then rotate your upper arms, forearms and wrists counterclockwise to the fullest extent possible and hold them in such position until the proceedings are completed. As an alternative, immobilize your shoulders, feet and upper arms, then twist your forearms and wrists counterclockwise to the fullest extent possible and hold your forearms and wrists in such position until the proceedings are completed.

STEP 4: After your forearms and wrists are rotated or twisted counterclockwise to the fullest extent possible, unlock the lifeline of your trail hand from your lead thumb by at least an inch without completely ungripping your club and then relock your trail lifeline on your lead thumb. Then, once again, unlock the lifeline of your trail hand from your lead thumb by at least an inch without completely ungripping your club and then, once again, relock the lifeline of your trail hand on your lead thumb.

STEP 5: Next, relax your shoulders, knees and wrists to allow them to return to a comfortable position.

STEP 6: Conduct the SHOULDERS ONLY TEST™, ARMS-LIFT TEST™ and the STRAIGHT-UP TEST™ to determine whether the COUNTERCLOCKWISE-N-LOCK TECHNIQUE™ has been assembled and executed correctly. If not confirmed, repeat the procedure until confirmed.

STEP 7: Center the sweet spot of your clubface as near the back of your ball as possible without allowing it to touch or move the ball. Assume a comfortable posture and stance to the ball and then align your shoulders parallel with your intended target line to the best of your ability.

STEP 8: Conduct the ARROW ALIGNMENT TECHNIQUE™ and adjust your stance, if necessary, until your alignment arrow points directly at your target when you turn your trail eye and head in the direction of your target as far as possible while immobilizing all other parts of your body.

STEP 9: Ensure the sweet spot of your clubface has remained centered as near the back of the ball as possible and then execute a non-manipulative golf swing.

You should not center your clubface so near the back of your ball as to cause it to move when you begin your backswing. It is a very unpleasant experience to perfect your pre-shot routine only to mis-hit the ball because the sweet spot of your clubface was centered too near the back of the ball at final address. It nonetheless should be centered as near the back of the ball as possible as long as it does not cause the ball to move.

SUMMARY POINTS

1. **The COUNTERCLOCKWISE-N-LOCK TECHNIQUE™ requires the shoulders and knees to be immobilized as the forearms and wrists are rotated counterclockwise to the fullest extent possible after assuming a conventional grip on a club.**

2. **This maneuver supplies the body movement to cause the forearms to rotate the wrists, clubface and elbows from a slice alignment to establish a straight ball flight alignment at the completion of the proceedings.**

3. **As an alternative maneuver, the shoulders, knees and upper arms should be immobilized as only the forearms and wrists are twisted counterclockwise to the fullest extent possible after assuming a conventional style of grip on the club.**

4. **Irrespective of which maneuver is used, once the forearms and wrists are rotated or twisted counterclockwise to the fullest extent possible, they must remain in that position until the proceedings are completed.**

5. **Once the forearms and wrists are rotated counterclockwise to the fullest extent possible, the lifeline/thumb connection must be unlocked and relocked twice to secure and lock-in the straight ball flight alignment and to prevent the forearms, wrists, clubface and elbows from rotating to a different ball flight alignment during the remainder of the pre-shot routine and the backswing.**

6. **The shoulders, knees, arms and wrists should be relaxed after the lifeline/thumb connection is unlocked and relocked twice to allow them to return to a comfortable position.**

7. **After the shoulders, knees, arms and wrists are relaxed to allow them to return to a comfortable position at the completion of the proceedings, the SHOULDERS ONLY TEST™, ARMS-LIFT TEST™ and the STRAIGHT-UP TEST™ must be conducted to determine whether the procedure established and locked-in a straight ball flight alignment. If not, the procedure should be repeated until the three tests confirm such.**

8. **The COUNTERCLOCKWISE-N-LOCK TECHNIQUE™ is compatible with all four conventional styles of grip, whether that of an original Vardon overlap, modified Vardon overlap, traditional interlock or regular baseball (ten-fingers) type of grip.**

9. **The clubface must be grounded in the middle of the stance and remain grounded throughout the proceedings.**

10. **The clubface may not be allowed to rotate during the time either the lead hand or trail hand is gripped on the club or between the time the lead and trail hands are gripped on the club.**

11. **The ARROW ALIGNMENT TECHNIQUE™ should be conducted to align the shoulders squarely parallel with the intended target line when using the COUNTERCLOCKWISE-N-LOCK TECHNIQUE™.**

CHAPTER 18

INTRODUCTION OF THE HINGE UP-N-LOCK TECHNIQUE™

The HINGE UP-N-LOCK TECHNIQUE™ requires the club-face to be grounded throughout the entire proceedings.

It then requires the lead elbow to be connected to the rib cage before a conventional style of grip is assembled on a club. The lead elbow must remain connected to the rib cage until the completion of the proceedings.

Then once a conventional style of grip is completed, the wrists must be hinged upward to the fullest extent possible and held in such position until the lifeline of the trail hand is unlocked from the lead thumb by at least an inch without completely ungripping the club and then relocked on the lead thumb.

How to Assemble and Execute the Hinge Up-N-Lock Technique™

The ***first step*** in the process of assembling and executing the HINGE UP-N-LOCK TECHNIQUE™ is to ground the sole of the clubface in the middle of the stance. The sole of the clubface does not need to be grounded directly behind the ball necessarily at this point in the procedure. Once the HINGE UP-N-LOCK TECHNIQUE™ is assembled and executed, the clubface can be moved to a different location or position as long as the lifeline/thumb connection remains locked in place. This means that once the proceedings to assemble and execute the HINGE UP-N-LOCK TECHNIQUE™ are completed, the sweet spot of the clubface then can be centered as near the back of the ball as possible.

The ***second step*** in the procedure is to connect the lead elbow to the rib cage and keep it connected until the proceedings are completed.

The ***third step*** is to grip the lead hand on the club in a conventional (diagonal) manner without allowing the clubface to rotate during the process.

The ***fourth step*** is to assemble either an original or modified Vardon overlap, traditional interlock or regular baseball (ten-fingers) style of grip on the club with the trail hand and lock the lifeline of the trail hand squarely and securely on the lead thumb to complete the grip. This is the first of the two "locks" of the lifeline/thumb connection that is required to assemble and execute the HINGE UP-N-LOCK TECHNIQUE™.

The ***fifth step*** is to immobilize the shoulders and knees, keep the arms and hands relaxed and then hinge the wrists upward to the fullest extent possible and hold the wrists in such position until the proceedings are completed.

The ***sixth step*** is to unlock the lifeline of the trail thumb from the lead thumb by at least an inch without completely ungripping the club and then relock the trail lifeline on the lead thumb to lock-in the straight ball flight alignment.

Once the lifeline/thumb connection is unlocked and relocked, the lead elbow should be disconnected from the rib cage. The wrists should be relaxed and allowed to unhinge. The shoulders, knees, arms and hands also should be relaxed to allow them to return to their original positions. (Figure 18-1).

Why the Hinge Up-N-Lock Technique™ Works

This technique works because when the grip is completed after the lead elbow is connected to the rib cage and the wrists then are hinged upward to the fullest extent possible while immobilizing the shoulders and knees and while keeping the arms and hands

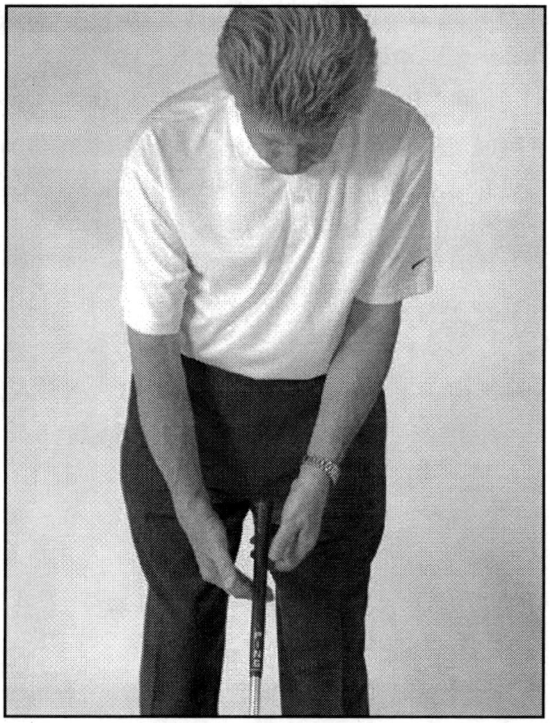

Figure 18-1

STEP 1: The first essential step to assemble and execute the HINGE UP-N-LOCK TECHNIQUE™ is to connect the lead elbow to the rib cage and keep it so connected until the completion of the grip. The clubface should be grounded in the middle of the stance during such time.

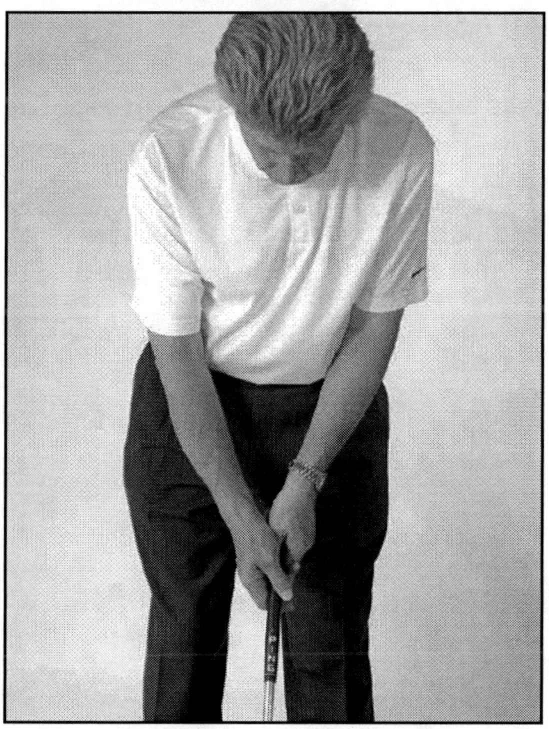

STEP 2: Then a conventional style of grip should be assembled on the club while continuing to keep the lead elbow connected to the rib cage.

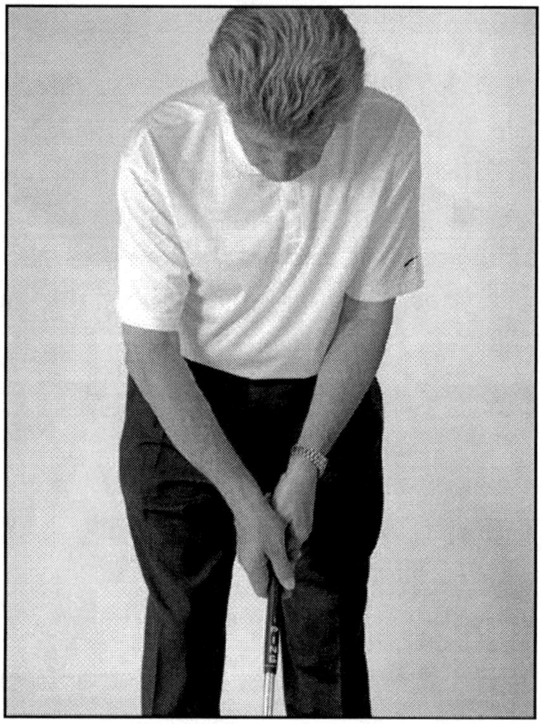

STEP 3: Immobilize the shoulders and knees, keep the arms and hands passive, and, the lead elbow connected to the rib cage and then hinge the wrists upward as far as possible – until the clubface stops rotating counterclockwise.

STEP 4: Continue to keep the wrists hinged upward as far as possible and the lead elbow connected to the rib cage and then unlock the lifeline of the trail hand from the lead hand by at least an inch without completely ungripping the club.

STEP 5: Then, while continuing to keep the lead elbow connected to the rib cage and the wrists hinged upward as far as possible, relock the lifeline of the trail hand squarely and securely on the lead thumb. *(Then disconnect the lead elbow from the rib cage. Also relax the wrists and allow them to return to a comfortable position.)*

relaxed and passive, the forearms will rotate the elbows to a parallel alignment with the shoulders to create an on-line swing path of the clubface.

When the elbows are rotated to a parallel alignment with the shoulders the wrists correspondingly will rotate the clubface to a square alignment, all of which will establish a straight ball flight alignment.

However, the straight ball flight alignment will not be locked-in at this point. In order to lock-in the straight ball flight alignment, the lifeline of the trail hand then must be unlocked from the lead thumb by at least an inch and then relocked on the lead thumb.

Disciplines Associated with the Hinge Up-N-Lock Technique™

The clubface may not be allowed to rotate during the proceedings except for that caused by the hinging upward maneuver of the wrists.

If the lead hand is loosened and tightened or partially ungripped and regripped after being assembled on the club, the clubface will rotate and move to some degree, even indiscernibly, and the forearms will rotate the wrists, clubface and elbows to establish a different alignment at the completion of the proceedings.

If the clubface is allowed to move or rotate between the time the lead hand and trail hand are assembled on a club or, after both hands are assembled on a golf club, except for the hinging upward maneuver of the wrists, the forearms likewise will rotate the wrists, clubface and elbows to establish a different ball flight at the completion of the proceedings. In addition, there can be no clubface rotation allowed during the time either the lead hand or trail hand is assembled on a club.

One way to help prevent the clubface from rotating is to press the sole of the clubface into the surface before assembling the grip on the club.

Another discipline relating to the HINGE UP-N-LOCK TECHNIQUE™ is the lifeline of the trail hand may not be unlocked and relocked on the lead thumb before the wrists are hinged upward. Neither may the lifeline/thumb connection be unlocked and relocked a second time after the wrists are hinged upward.

However, the lifeline/thumb connection must be unlocked and relocked once after the wrists are hinged upward – but only once.

Another discipline associated with the assemblage and execution of the HINGE UP-N-LOCK TECHNIQUE™ is the manner in which the lead elbow is connected to the rib cage.

Unless the lead elbow is connected to the rib cage during the proceedings the arms may become too active when the wrists are hinged upward and could cause the forearms to rotate the wrists, clubface and elbows to some alignment other than a straight ball flight alignment at the completion of the proceedings.

Only the wrists are to be active in causing the forearms to rotate the wrists, clubface and elbows to establish a straight ball flight alignment when this technique is used. The arms should move only in response to the upward hinging of the wrists.

Another discipline is the shoulders and knees must be immobilized during the entire proceedings. If the shoulders and knees are allowed to move when the wrists are hinged upward, the forearms will rotate the wrists, clubface and elbows to establish a different ball flight alignment at the completion of the proceedings.

Once the lifeline/thumb connection is unlocked and relocked to complete the proceedings, the forearms and wrists as well as the shoulders and knees should then be relaxed to allow them to return to a comfortable position.

Although the HINGE UP-N-LOCK TECHNIQUE™ establishes and locks-in a straight ball flight alignment, it does so only in relation to the shoulder line.

If your objective is to hit a ball on a straight path to a specific target, the sweet spot of your clubface then must be centered as near the back of your ball as possible without allowing it to touch or move your ball and, simultaneously, your shoulders must be aligned squarely parallel with your intended target line at the completion of your pre-shot proceedings, followed by a non-manipulative golf swing.

You should gain confidence in assembling and executing the HINGE UP-N-LOCK TECHNIQUE™ during some meaningful practice sessions before using it in actual play.

Recommended Practice Routines When Using the Hinge Up-N-Lockk Technique™ in Combination with the Arrow Alignment Technique™

One of the essential requirements in establishing a straight ball flight alignment at final address is to ensure your shoulder line is aligned squarely parallel with your intended target line. Therefore, you should use the ARROW ALIGNMENT TECHNIQUE™ in combination with the HINGE UP-N-LOCK TECHNIQUE™ in both practice and play.

Also, in each practice session you should begin by executing a wrist swing, then a ½ swing, on to a ¾ swing and finally to a complete swing with respect to each club in your set. You should begin with your most lofted club, typically a wedge, and then progress through your entire set, using each next most lofted club in succession thereafter.

Here are the steps you should use when practicing with the HINGE UP-N-LOCK TECHNIQUE™ :

STEP 1: **As always, select some safe and reasonably flat surface as your hitting area.**

STEP 2: **Place a ball on the surface. Identify your specific target as well as your intended target line.**

STEP 3: **Ground the sole of your clubface in the middle of your stance and then connect your lead elbow to your rib cage and keep it connected until the proceedings are completed.**

STEP 4: **Then form a conventional style of grip on your club. Complete your grip by locking the lifeline of your trail hand on your lead thumb.**

STEP 5: **Immobilize your shoulders and knees, keep your arms passive and inactive and then hinge your wrists upward to the fullest extent possible.**

STEP 6: **Continue to keep your wrists hinged upward to the fullest extent and then unlock and relock your lifeline/thumb connection to lock-in the straight ball flight alignment.**

STEP 7: **Disconnect your lead elbow from your rib cage and relax your shoulders, knees, forearms and wrists to allow them to return to a comfortable position.**

STEP 8: **Conduct the SHOULDERS ONLY TEST™, ARMS-LIFT TEST™ and STRAIGHT-UP TEST™ to determine if the HINGE UP-N-LOCK TECHNIQUE™ was assembled and executed correctly and whether a straight ball flight alignment has been established and locked-in. If not confirmed, repeat the procedure until confirmed.**

STEP 9: **Center the sweet spot of your clubface as near the back of your ball as possible (unless already so centered). Assume a comfortable posture and stance to the ball and then align your shoulders parallel with your intended target line to the best of your ability.**

STEP 10: **Conduct the ARROW ALIGNMENT TECHNIQUE™ and adjust your stance, if necessary, until your alignment arrow points directly at your intended target when you turn your trail eye and head in the direction of your target as far as possible while immobilizing all other parts of your body.**

STEP 11: **Ensure the sweet spot of your clubface has remained centered as near the back of your ball as possible and then execute a non-manipulative golf swing.**

Until your ball is in play, your clubface may touch or move the ball without you incurring a penalty. However, once in play, typically you will incur a penalty if your clubface moves the ball while your clubface is grounded, whether accidental or intentional.

There are some players who emulate such "greats" as Jack Nicklaus and Greg Norman in that they do not ground the sole of their clubface during their pre-shot routine in order to prevent a possible penalty.

If it is your preference not to ground the sole of your clubface behind your ball during your pre-shot routine, you nonetheless can use the thirty-two LOCKED-IN TECHNIQUES™ discussed in this book, including the HINGE UP-N-LOCK TECHNIQUE™.

Once you have locked-in a straight ball flight alignment, position the sole of your clubface above the surface but as near the back of your ball as possible when you align your shoulders parallel with your intended target line. Then begin your golf swing with the clubface so positioned.

Remember that although the sole of the clubface should be grounded when assuming and executing the HINGE UP-N-LOCK TECHNIQUE™, it does not need to be grounded behind the ball, it can be grounded elsewhere and then moved behind the ball – even in such a hovering manner as described above if you desire.

SUMMARY POINTS

1. **The HINGE UP-N-LOCK TECHNIQUE™ requires the lead elbow to be connected to the rib cage prior to forming a conventional style of grip on a club and then keeping the lead elbow connected in such manner until the completion of the proceedings.**

2. **The sole of the clubface must be grounded – preferably in the middle of the stance – during the entire proceedings.**

3. **Only the wrists are actively involved in the hinging up maneuver that causes the forearms to rotate the wrists, clubface and elbows to a straight ball flight alignment when performing the HINGE UP-N-LOCK TECHNIQUE™. The shoulders and knees must be immobilized and the arms must remain passive and inactive during the hinging-up maneuver.**

4. **The first step in the process of assembling and executing the HINGE UP-N-LOCK TECHNIQUE™ is to ground the sole of the clubface in the middle of the stance.**

5. **The second step is to connect the lead elbow to the rib cage.**

6. **The third step is to form either an original or modified Vardon overlap, traditional interlock or regular baseball (ten-fingers) style of grip on the club. Then the lifeline of the trail hand must be locked on the lead thumb to complete the grip.**

7. The next step is to hinge the wrists upward to the fullest extent possible while the shoulders and knees remain immobilized and the arms remain passive.

8. While the wrists are hinged upward to the fullest extent possible, the lifeline of the trail hand must be unlocked from the lead thumb and then relocked on the lead thumb to lock-in the straight ball flight alignment.

9. Once the lifeline/thumb connection is unlocked and relocked, the shoulders, knees, arms and wrists should be relaxed and allowed to return to a comfortable position and the lead elbow should be relaxed and allowed to disconnect from the rib cage.

10. The SHOULDERS ONLY TEST™, ARMS-LIFT TEST™ and STRAIGHT-UP TEST™ should be conducted at the completion of the proceedings.

11. Practice sessions are encouraged when learning how properly to assemble and execute the HINGE UP-N-LOCK TECHNIQUE™.

12. The ARROW ALIGNMENT TECHNIQUE™ should be used to align the shoulders squarely parallel with the intended target line when assembling and executing the HINGE UP-N-LOCK TECHNIQUE™.

CHAPTER 19

INTRODUCTION OF THE HINGE DOWN-N-LOCK TECHNIQUE™

The HINGE DOWN-N-LOCK TECHNIQUE™ is similar to the HINGE-UP-N-LOCK TECHNIQUE™, conceptionally. Instead of immobilizing the shoulders and knees and then hinging the wrists upward as far as possible when assembling and executing the HINGE UP-N-LOCK TECHNIQUE™, the wrists are hinged downward as far as possible when performing the HINGE DOWN-N-LOCK TECHNIQUE™.

The two techniques are similar, however, in that only the wrists are actively involved in the maneuver to cause the forearms to rotate the wrists, clubface and elbows to establish a straight ball flight alignment. They also are similar in that the shoulders and knees must be immobilized and the arms must remain inactive and passive and only respond to the downward hinging of the wrists.

They also are similar in that the lead elbow should be connected to the rib cage during the proceedings to keep the arms from becoming too active in the procedure.

How to Assemble and Execute the Hinge Down-N-Lock Technique™

First, the sole of the clubface must be grounded in the middle of the stance throughout the proceedings.

Second, as noted above, the lead elbow must be connected to the rib cage prior to the grip being assumed and remain so connected until the proceedings are completed.

Third, either an original or modified Vardon overlap, traditional interlock or regular baseball (ten-fingers) style of grip must be assembled on the club and the lifeline of the trail hand must be securely and squarely locked on the lead thumb to complete the grip. This is the first of a total of three "locks" of the lifeline/thumb connection that is necessary to assemble and execute the HINGE DOWN-N-LOCK TECHNIQUE™.

The ***fourth step*** in the process is to immobilize the shoulders and knees, keep the arms passive and then hinge the wrists downward to the fullest extent possible.

Fifth, once the wrists are hinged downward to the fullest extent possible, they must be held in such position until the lifeline of the trail hand is unlocked from the lead thumb by at least an inch without completely ungripping the club and then relocked on the lead thumb. This is the second of the three "locks" of the lifeline/thumb connection that is required to assemble and execute the HINGE DOWN-N-LOCK TECHNIQUE™.

Sixth, the wrists must remain hinged downward to the fullest extent until the lifeline of the trail hand once again is unlocked from the lead thumb by at least an inch without completely ungripping the club and then, once again, the lifeline of the trail hand is relocked on the lead thumb. This is the third of the three "locks" of the lifeline/thumb connection that is required to assemble and execute the HINGE DOWN-N-LOCK TECHNIQUE™.

The lifeline/thumb connection may not be unlocked and relocked thereafter.

Seventh, after the lifeline/thumb is unlocked and relocked twice, the lead elbow should be relaxed and allowed to disconnect from the rib cage. The shoulders, knees, arms and wrists also should be relaxed and allowed to return to a comfortable position. (Figure 19-1).

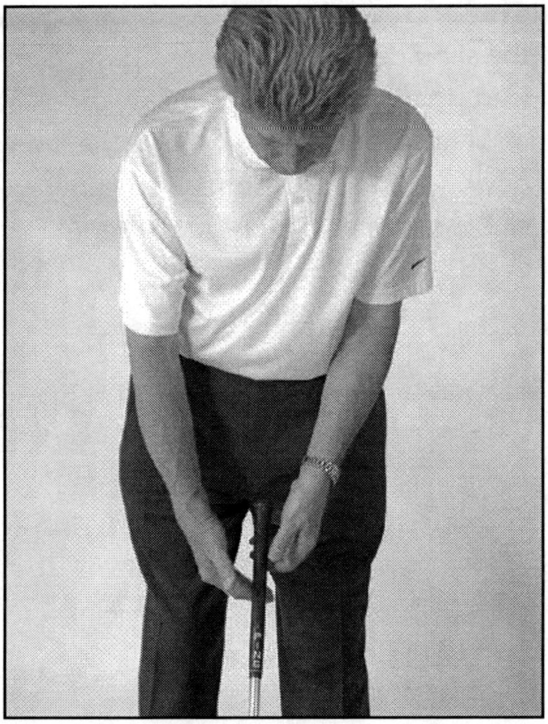

Figure 19-1

STEP 1: The first essential step in assembling and executing the HINGE DOWN-N-LOCK TECHNIQUE™ is to connect the lead elbow to the rib cage and keep it so connected until the completion of the proceedings.

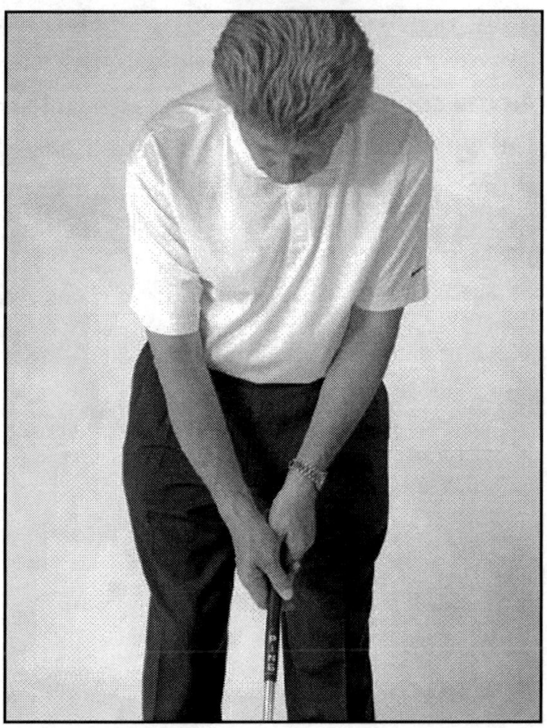

STEP 2: Then grip the club with both hands in a conventional manner with the lead elbow connected to the rib cage and the clubface grounded in the middle of the stance.

STEP 3: The next step is to immobilize the shoulders, keep the arms passive, the lead elbow connected to the rib cage, the clubface grounded and hinge the wrists downward as far as possible – until the clubface stops rotating clockwise.

STEP 4: Then, while the wrists are hinged downward as far as possible with the lead elbow connected to the rib cage, unlock the lifeline of the trail hand from the lead thumb by at least an inch without completely ungripping the club.

STEP 5: Then relock the lifeline of the trail hand squarely and securely on the lead thumb while the wrists remain hinged down as far as possible and the lead elbow remains connected to the rib cage. *(Then unlock and relock the lifeline/thumb connection in the same manner after which the lead elbow should be disconnected from the rib cage and the wrists, arms, hands, shoulders and knees should be relaxed and allowed to return to a comfortable position.)*

Disciplines That Apply When Assembling and Executing the Hinge Down-N-Lock Technique™

Once the lead hand is gripped on the club it may not be loosened and tightened or partially ungripped and regripped thereafter. Neither may the clubface be allowed to move or rotate after both hands are gripped on the club except for the rotation of the clubface caused by the wrists being hinged downward to the fullest extent possible.

This is one reason why the sole of the clubface should be grounded during the assemblage and execution of all the LOCKED-IN TECHNIQUES™. Otherwise, if the sole of the clubface is lifted above the surface before assuming the grip, it is very difficult to prevent the clubface from moving or rotating when the hands are gripped on the club.

As mentioned previously, one way to help prevent the clubface from rotating during the gripping process is to press the sole of the clubface into the surface before assembling the grip on the club.

Since the wrists must be hinged downward to the fullest extent possible, you must stand far enough from the ball when you assume your grip to allow the wrists sufficient room to hinge down to the maximum degree.

You may have a tendency to relax your wrists slightly, without realizing it, after you have completed the hinging downward maneuver. You should make an additional effort not to relax your wrists at such point. If you do not continue to hinge your wrists downward to the fullest extent possible until you unlock and relock your lifeline/thumb connection twice, your forearms will not rotate your wrists, clubface and elbows to establish a straight ball flight alignment at the completion of the proceedings.

The lifeline/thumb connection must be unlocked and relocked twice after the wrists are hinged downward in order to secure and lock-in the straight ball flight alignment. The lifeline/thumb connection may not be unlocked and relocked thereafter.

Considering the wrists must be hinged downward to the fullest extent possible while immobilizing the shoulders and knees and keeping the arms passive and inactive – and then held in such position until the lifeline/thumb connection is unlocked and relocked twice – you should always conduct the SHOULDERS ONLY TEST™, ARMS-LIFT TEST™ as well as the STRAIGHT-UP TEST™ at the completion of the proceedings to determine if a straight ball flight alignment has been established and locked-in.

If any of the tests indicate the HINGE DOWN-N-LOCK TECHNIQUE™ has not been assembled and executed properly, and, as a result, a straight ball flight alignment has not been established and locked-in, you should disassemble your grip and repeat the procedure until they do confirm such.

Why the Hinge Down-N-Lock Technique™ Works

This technique works because when the wrists are hinged downward as far as possible after a conventional style of grip is formed on a club and while the shoulders and knees are immobilized and the arms relaxed, the forearms will rotate the elbows to a parallel alignment with the shoulders to create an on-line swing path of the clubface.

When the elbows are rotated to a parallel alignment with the shoulders the wrists correspondingly will rotate the clubface to a square alignment, all of which will establish a straight ball flight alignment.

However, a straight ball flight alignment will not be locked-in at this point.

Only when the lifeline/thumb connection

then is unlocked and relocked twice will a straight ball flight alignment be locked-in.

The techniques discussed in this book, including the HINGE DOWN-N-LOCK TECHNIQUE™, only establish and lock-in a straight ball flight alignment in relation to the shoulders (the "effective" target line). If your desire is to hit a straight golf shot to a specific target, then you must also have the sweet spot of your clubface centered as near the back of the ball as possible and, simultaneously, your shoulders aligned parallel with your intended target line at the completion of your pre-shot routine, followed by a non-manipulative golf swing.

You should practice using the HINGE DOWN-N-LOCK TECHNIQUE™ before using it in play.

Recommended Practice Routines When Using the Hinge Down-N-Lock Technique™ in Combination with the Arrow Alignment Technique™

You should use the ARROW ALIGNMENT TECHNIQUE™ to align your shoulders squarely parallel with your intended target line when practicing with the HINGE DOWN-N-LOCK TECHNIQUE™ .

During your practice sessions, you should begin with a short iron, such as a wedge, then progress through your set, using each next most lofted club in succession thereafter. Also with each club, you should begin with a wrist swing, then with a ½ swing, on to a ¾ swing and finally with a full swing.

Here are the steps you should follow during your practice routine when using the HINGE DOWN-N-LOCK TECHNIQUE™.

STEP 1: Always select a safe and relative flat hitting area. Place a ball on the surface, whether that of a practice mat or grass. Identify a specific and narrow target and also your intended target line.

STEP 2: Ground the sole of your clubface in the middle of your stance. Connect your lead elbow against your rib cage and then assemble a conventional grip on your club, either in the form of an original or modified Vardon overlap, traditional interlock or regular baseball (ten-fingers) style of grip. Complete the grip by locking the lifeline of your trail hand firmly on your lead thumb.

STEP 3: Immobilize your shoulders and knees and keep your arms relaxed and passive while continuing to hold your lead elbow against your rib cage. Then hinge your wrists downward as far as possible. Hold your wrists in this position until the proceedings are completed.

STEP 4: Then unlock the lifeline of your trail hand from your lead thumb by at least an inch without completely ungripping your club and then relock the lifeline of your trail hand on your lead thumb.

STEP 5: Then, once again, unlock the lifeline of your trail hand from your lead thumb by at least an inch without completely ungripping your club and then, once again, relock the lifeline of your trail hand on your lead thumb.

STEP 6: Once you have unlocked and relocked your lifeline/thumb connection twice to secure and lock-in the straight ball flight alignment, disconnect your lead elbow from your rib cage and relax your shoulders, knees, arms and wrists to allow them to return to a comfortable position.

STEP 7: Conduct the SHOULDERS ONLY TEST™, ARMS-LIFT TEST™ and STRAIGHT-UP TEST™to determine whether the HINGE DOWN-N-LOCK TECHNIQUE™ has been assembled and executed correctly. If not, repeat the procedure until all three tests confirm a straight ball flight alignment has been established and locked-in.

STEP 8: Center the sweet spot of your clubface as near the back of your ball as possible without allowing your clubface to touch or move the ball. Assume a comfortable posture and stance to the ball and then align your shoulders parallel with your intended target line to the best of your ability.

STEP 9: Conduct the ARROW ALIGNMENT TECHNIQUE™ and adjust your stance, if necessary, until your alignment arrow points directly at your target when your trail eye and head are turned in the direction of the target <u>as far as possible</u> while immobilizing all other parts of your body.

STEP 10: Ensure the sweet spot of your clubface has remained as near the back of the ball as possible and then execute a non-manipulative golf swing.

Remember the best way to execute a non-manipulative golf swing is to keep your feet planted and your head steady during the backswing and allow the clubface to return to the ball reflexively without any "steering" of the club during the downswing.

SUMMARY POINTS

1. The HINGE DOWN-N-LOCK TECHNIQUE™ involves a downward hinging of the wrists to the fullest extent possible after assembling a conventional style of grip on the club.

2. Prior to gripping the club, the lead elbow should be connected to the rib cage and remain in such position during the proceedings. In addition, the clubface must be grounded during the proceedings.

3. Once the sole of the clubface is grounded and the lead elbow is connected to the rib cage, the next step in assembling and executing the HINGE DOWN-N-LOCK TECHNIQUE™ is to assume a conventional grip on a golf club, then complete the grip by locking the lifeline of the trail hand firmly on the lead thumb.

4. While immobilizing the shoulders and knees and while keeping the arms relaxed, the wrists then must be hinged downward to the fullest extent possible and held in such position until the lifeline/thumb connection is unlocked and relocked twice.

5. Once the lifeline/thumb connection is unlocked and relocked twice , the lead elbow should be disconnected from the rib cage and the shoulders, knees, arms and wrists should be relaxed to allow them to return to a more comfortable position.

6. **Considering the possibility the wrists may not be hinged downward properly, or not held in such position until the proceedings are completed, the SHOULDERS ONLY TEST™, ARMS-LIFT TEST™ and STRAIGHT-UP TEST™ should be conducted at the completion of the procedure. If a locked-in straight ball flight alignment is not confirmed, the procedure should be repeated until the three tests do confirm such.**

7. **There may not be any clubface rotation allowed at any stage of the gripping process.**

8. **Once the HINGE DOWN-N-LOCK TECHNIQUE™ is confirmed, the sweet spot of the clubface must be centered as near the back of the ball as possible and, simultaneously, the shoulders must be aligned parallel with the intended target line at final address, followed by a non-manipulative golf swing in order to hit a ball on a straight path in the direction of the intended target.**

9. **The ARROW ALIGNMENT TECHNIQUE™ should be conducted to align the shoulders squarely parallel with the intended target line when using the HINGE DOWN-N-LOCK TECHNIQUE™.**

CHAPTER 20

INTRODUCTION OF THE ARCH-N-LOCK TECHNIQUE™

The ARCH-N-LOCK TECHNIQUE™ also requires a "wrist action only" maneuver.

Once a conventional style of grip is formed on a club, the procedure requires the shoulders and knees to be immobilized while arching the wrists on a parallel line with the shoulders to the fullest extent possible. When the arching maneuver is executed correctly, it will cause the forearms to rotate the wrists, clubface and elbows to establish a straight ball flight alignment.

The arching of the wrists in this case means the wrists must be "bowed" on a parallel line with the shoulders and in the direction of the target without allowing them to rotate either clockwise or counterclockwise. Not only must the shoulders and knees be immobilized when the wrists are arched to the fullest extent possible but the arms should remain passive and inactive and only move in response to the wrist action during the arching maneuver.

How to Assemble and Execute the Arch-N-Lock Technique™

The ***first step*** in assembling and executing the ARCH-N-LOCK TECHNIQUE™ is to ground the sole of the clubface.

The ***second step*** in the procedure is to grip the lead hand on the club in a conventional (diagonal) manner.

The ***third step*** is to grip the club with the trail hand either in the form of an original or modified Vardon overlap, traditional interlock or regular baseball (ten-fingers) style of grip. The lifeline of the trail hand then must be firmly locked on the lead thumb to complete the grip. This constitutes the first of the three "locks" of the lifeline/thumb connection that is necessary to assemble and execute the ARCH-N-LOCK TECHNIQUE™.

The ***fourth step*** is to immobilize the shoulders and knees, keep the arms relaxed and then arch the wrists on a parallel line with the shoulders in the direction of the intended target to the fullest extent possible. The wrists must remain in this arched position until the procedure is completed.

The ***fifth step*** is the lifeline of the trail hand then must be unlocked from the lead thumb by at least an inch without completely ungripping the club and then relocked on the lead thumb. This constitutes the second of the three "locks" of the lifeline/thumb connection that is necessary to assemble and execute the ARCH-N-LOCK TECHNIQUE™.

The ***sixth step*** then is to once again unlock the lifeline of the trail hand from the lead thumb by at least an inch without completely ungripping the club and then, once again, relock the lifeline of the trail hand on the lead thumb. This constitutes the third of the three "locks" that is required to assemble and execute the ARCH-N-LOCK TECHNIQUE™.

The shoulders, knees, arms and wrists should then be relaxed and allowed to return to a comfortable position. (Figure 20-1).

Why the Arch-N-Lock Technique™ Works

This technique works because when the wrists are arched on a parallel line with the shoulders after a conventional style of grip is formed on a club, the forearms will rotate the elbows to a parallel alignment with the

Figure 20-1

STEP 1: The first essential step to assemble and execute the ARCH-N-LOCK TECHNIQUE™ is to grip the club with both hands in a conventional manner with the clubface grounded in the middle of the stance.

STEP 2: Immobilize the shoulders, knees and hips, keep the arms passive and the clubface grounded and then arch (bow) the wrists on a parallel line with the shoulders as far as possible – until the clubface no longer moves.

STEP 3: While continuing to arch the wrists in the direction of the target as far as possible, unlock the lifeline of the trail hand from the lead thumb by at least an inch without completely ungripping the club.

STEP 4: Then, while continuing to arch the wrists to the maximum extent, relock the lifeline of the trail hand squarely and securely on the lead thumb.

STEP 5: Then, once again, unlock the lifeline of the trail hand from the lead thumb by at least an inch without completely ungripping the club while continuing to keep the wrists fully arched.

STEP 6: Once again relock the lifeline of the trail hand squarely and securely on the lead thumb while continuing to keep the wrists fully arched. *(Then relax the wrists, shoulders and knees and allow them to return to their original position.)*

shoulders to create an on-line swing path of the clubface.

When the elbows are rotated to parallel alignment with the shoulders the wrists correspondingly will rotate the clubface to a square alignment, all of which will establish a straight ball flight alignment.

Then when the lifeline/thumb connection is unlocked and relocked <u>twice</u> the straight ball flight alignment will be locked-in.

The lifeline/thumb connection may not be unlocked and relocked thereafter. If unlocked and relocked once more thereafter, the forearms will rotate the wrists, clubface and elbows to establish a different ball flight alignment.

Disciplines Required When Assembling and Executing the Arch-N-Lock Technique™

One of the most important disciplines relative to the ARCH-N-LOCK TECHNIQUE™ is to ensure the wrists are arched on a parallel line with the shoulders. This may feel as though the wrists are being arched somewhat downward instead of on a line parallel with the shoulders but when executed correctly, the wrists will be arched in a manner to cause the forearms to rotate the wrists, clubface and elbows to establish a straight ball flight alignment.

The real test in determining whether the wrists are being arched on a parallel line with the shoulders is to observe whether the clubface rotates clockwise or counterclockwise during the arching maneuver. If the clubface rotates either clockwise or counterclockwise during the arching maneuver, the wrists will not be arched on a parallel alignment with the shoulders in which case, the grip should be disassembled and the procedure repeated.

Although the arms and hands will move somewhat in response to the arching of the wrists, they must not otherwise be actively engaged in the arching movement. The shoulders, knees and hips may not be moved at all during the procedure.

An additional discipline relating to the assemblage and execution of the ARCH-N-LOCK TECHNIQUE™ is the elbows must be disconnected from the rib cage during the entire proceedings. If either or both elbows are connected to the rib cage at any stage of the proceedings, the forearms will rotate the wrists, clubface and elbows to establish a different ball flight alignment.

Also, it is imperative that a conventional style of grip be properly formed on the club. The lead hand must grip the club in a conventional (diagonal) manner. If the club is gripped in the fingers of the lead hand rather than in a diagonal manner, the procedure will not cause the forearms to rotate the wrists, clubface and elbows to establish a straight ball flight alignment.

Also, the trail hand must be formed on the club in a properly assembled conventional manner.

Other fundamental disciplines apply when assembling and executing the ARCH-N-LOCK TECHNIQUE™.

For example, once the lead hand is gripped on the club handle, it may not thereafter be loosened and tightened or partially un-gripped and regripped. Also, after the lead hand is gripped on the club, the clubface must not be allowed to move or rotate while the trail hand is being assembled on the club. Indeed, when both hands are gripped on the club, the clubface must not be allowed to move or rotate other than that caused by the arching maneuver of the clubface.

One way to help prevent the clubface from rotating during the gripping procedure is to press the sole of the clubface into the surface before assembling the grip on the club.

Once arched, the wrists must be held in such position until the lifeline/thumb connection is unlocked and relocked twice and no more thereafter.

The lifeline/thumb connection may not be unlocked and relocked before the wrists are arched. Neither may the wrists be arched before assembling the grip on a club. In such an instance, there would be no room to allow the wrists to be arched properly after a conventional style of grip is formed on a club.

Whether practicing or playing you should conduct the SHOULDERS ONLY TEST™, ARMS-LIFT TEST™ and STRAIGHT-UP TEST™ at the completion of the ARCH-N-LOCK TECHNIQUE™.

Considering the sweet spot of your clubface must be centered as near the back of your ball as possible without allowing it to touch or move your ball and, simultaneously, your shoulders must be aligned squarely parallel with your intended target line at final address, followed by a non-manipulative golf swing, in order to hit a golf ball on a straight path in the direction of your intended target, you should always incorporate into your pre-shot routine the ARROW ALIGNMENT TECHNIQUE™.

Recommended Practice Routines When Using the Arch-N-Lock Technique™ in Combination with the Arrow Alignment Technique™

With respect to each of the LOCKED-IN TECHNIQUES™ discussed in this book, you should establish a consistent pre-shot routine. The following is recommended when using the ARCH-N-LOCK TECHNIQUE™.

STEP 1: As always, select a safe and relatively flat practice area. Choose a short iron such as a wedge to begin your practice and place a ball on the surface, whether the surface is that of a practice mat or grass.

STEP 2: Identify a specific and defined target as well as your intended target line. Ground the sole of your clubface in the middle of your stance and then assemble a grip on your club in a conventional manner. Complete your grip by locking the lifeline of your trail hand squarely and firmly on your lead thumb.

STEP 3: Immobilize your shoulders, knees and hips, keep your arms relaxed and then arch (bow) your wrists to the fullest extent possible in the direction of your target and on a line that parallels your shoulders. Do not allow your wrists to rotate clockwise or counterclockwise in any manner when executing this arching maneuver.

STEP 4: After you have arched your wrists on a parallel line with your shoulders to the fullest extent possible, you must hold your wrists in such position and then unlock and relock your lifeline/thumb connection twice to secure and lock-in the straight ball flight alignment.

STEP 5: Relax your shoulders, knees, arms and wrists to allow them to return to a comfortable position.

STEP 6: Conduct the SHOULDERS ONLY TEST™, ARMS-LIFT TEST™ and STRAIGHT-UP TEST™ to determine whether you assembled and executed the ARCH-N-LOCK TECHNIQUE™ correctly. If not, repeat the process until all three confirmation tests validate a straight ball flight alignment has been established and locked-in.

STEP 7: Center the sweet spot of your clubface as near the back of your ball as possible. Assume a comfortable posture and stance to your ball and then align your shoulders parallel with your intended target line to the best of your ability.

STEP 8: Conduct the ARROW ALIGNMENT TECHNIQUE™ and adjust your stance, if necessary, until your alignment arrow points directly at your intended target when you turn your trail eye and head in the direction of your target as far as possible while immobilizing all other parts of your body.

STEP 9: Ensure the sweet spot of your clubface has remained centered as near the back of the ball as possible and then execute a non- manipulative golf swing.

You should begin your practice sessions with a short club and progress through your set with each next most lofted club in succession thereafter. With each respective club, you should begin with a simple wrist swing, then with a ½ swing, on to a ¾ swing and conclude with a full swing.

SUMMARY POINTS

1. **The ARCH-N-LOCK TECHNIQUE™ involves only the wrists in converting a slice ball flight alignment to a straight ball flight alignment.**

2. **Once a conventional style of grip is assembled on a golf club and the lifeline/thumb connection is locked to complete the grip, the shoulders and knees must be immobilized and the arms relaxed.**

3. **The wrists then must be arched to the fullest extent possible on a line that parallels the shoulders. The wrists must remain in such position until the proceedings are completed.**

4. **Neither the wrists nor the clubface may be allowed to rotate either clockwise or counterclockwise during the arching maneuver.**

5. **Once the wrists are arched to the fullest extent possible, the lifeline of the trail hand must be unlocked from the lead thumb and then relocked on the lead thumb.**

6. **Then, once again, the lifeline/thumb connection must be unlocked and relocked in the same manner.**

7. **Once the lifeline/thumb connection has been unlocked and relocked twice, the shoulders, knees, arms and wrists should be relaxed and allowed to return to a comfortable position.**

8. The lifeline/thumb connection may not be unlocked and relocked before the arching maneuver nor may it be unlocked and relocked a third time after the arching maneuver.

9. The sole of the clubface must be grounded throughout the proceedings.

10. The ARROW ALIGNMENT TECHNIQUE™ should be incorporated into the pre-shot routine when using the ARCH-N-LOCK TECHNIQUE™.

CHAPTER 21

INTRODUCTION OF THE CUP-N-LOCK TECHNIQUE™

The CUP-N-LOCK TECHNIQUE™ is somewhat similar to the ARCH-N-LOCK TECHNIQUE™ in that the shoulders, knees and hips must be immobilized when the wrists are activated.

Instead of arching the wrists as in the ARCH-N-LOCK TECHNIQUE™, the wrists must be cupped on a parallel line with the shoulders and in an opposite direction from the target to cause the forearms to rotate the wrists, clubface and elbows to establish a straight ball flight alignment.

The CUP-N-LOCK TECHNIQUE™ only requires a total of two "locks" of the lifeline/thumb connection whereas the ARCH-N-LOCK TECHNIQUE™ requires three "locks."

The first of the two "locks" of the lifeline/thumb connection to assemble and execute the CUP-N-LOCK TECHNIQUE™ occurs when the lifeline of the trail hand is locked squarely and securely on the lead thumb to complete the grip.

The second of the two "locks" of the lifeline/thumb connection occurs after the wrists are cupped to the fullest extent possible on a parallel line with the shoulders when then the lifeline of the trail hand is unlocked from the lead hand by at least an inch without completely ungripping the club and then re-locked on the lead thumb.

How to Assemble and Execute the Cup-N-Lock Technique™

The ***first step*** in assembling and executing the CUP-N-LOCK TECHNIQUE™ is to ground the sole of the clubface in the middle of the stance.

The ***second step*** is to grip the lead hand on the club in a conventional (diagonal) manner without allowing the clubface to rotate.

The ***third step*** is to grip the trail hand on the club in a conventional manner, either in the form of an original or modified Vardon overlap, traditional interlock or regular base-ball (ten-fingers) style of grip. The lifeline of the trail hand must be firmly locked on the lead thumb to complete the grip.

The ***fourth step*** in the procedure then is to immobilize the shoulders, knees and hips, relax the arms and then cup the wrists on a parallel line with the shoulders to the fullest extent possible.

The hands and arms should not be actively engaged during the cupping maneuver. They should move only in response to the cupping of the wrists. Although the arms and hands may move in response to the cupping effect of the wrists, the shoulders, knees and hips must remain immobilized. Neither the shoulders, knees or hips may be allowed to move from the time the grip is assumed until the proceedings are completed.

Once the wrists are cupped to the fullest extent possible, the ***fifth step*** then is to unlock the lifeline of the trail hand from the lead thumb by at least an inch without completely ungripping the club and then relock the trail lifeline on the lead thumb. The lifeline/thumb connection may not be unlocked and relocked thereafter.

Once the lifeline of the trail hand is unlocked from the lead thumb and then relocked on the lead thumb, the shoulders, knees, arms and wrists should be relaxed and allowed to return to a comfortable position. (Figure 21-1).

Figure 21-1

STEP 1: The first essential step to assemble and execute the CUP-N-LOCK TECHNIQUE™ is to grip the club with both hands in a conventional manner with the clubface grounded in the middle of the stance.

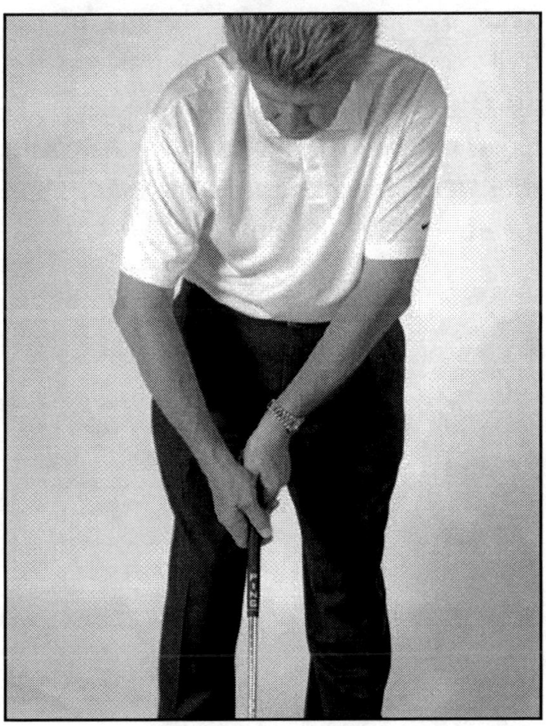

STEP 2: The next step is to immobilize the shoulders, knees and hips, keep the arms passive and the clubface grounded and then cup the wrists on a parallel line with the shoulders in the opposite direction from the target to the fullest extent possible – until the clubface stops moving.

STEP 3: While keeping the shoulders, knees and hips immobilized, the clubface grounded and the wrists cupped to the maximum extent possible, unlock the life-line of the trail hand from the lead thumb by at least an inch without completely un-gripping the club.

STEP 4: Then relock the lifeline of the trail hand squarely and securely on the lead thumb while continuing to keep the wrists cupped fully. *(Then relax the wrists, shoulders, knees and arms and allow them to return to a comfortable position.)*

Why the Cup-N-Lock Technique™ Works

This procedure works because when the wrists are cupped on a parallel line with the shoulders to the fullest extent possible after a conventional style of grip is formed on a club, the forearms will rotate the elbows to a parallel alignment with the shoulders to create an on-line swing path of the clubface.

When the elbows are rotated to a parallel alignment with the shoulders to create an on-line swing path of the clubface the wrists correspondingly will rotate the clubface to a square alignment, all of which will establish a straight ball flight alignment.

However, the straight ball flight alignment will not be locked-in at this point.

In order to lock-in the straight ball flight alignment, the lifeline of the trail hand then must be unlocked from the lead thumb by at least an inch without completely ungripping the club and then the lifeline of the trail hand must be relocked on the lead thumb.

Disciplines Associated with the Cup-N-Lock Technique™

The first discipline is once the lead hand is gripped on the club it cannot be loosened and tightened or partially ungripped and regripped thereafter. The clubface may not be allowed to move or rotate between the time the lead hand and trail hand are gripped nor when the hands are assembled on the club. Neither is any movement or rotation of the clubface allowed after both hands are gripped on the club except for that caused by the cupping maneuver.

The second discipline is the wrists must be cupped on a line parallel with the shoulders in the opposite direction from the target. This may feel as though the wrists are being cupped in an awkward manner. However, when cupped correctly, they instead will be cupped on a parallel line with the shoulders.

The best way to ensure the wrists are cupped on a parallel line with the shoulders is to observe whether the clubface rotates either clockwise or counterclockwise during the cupping maneuver. If the clubface rotates either clockwise or counterclockwise when the wrists are cupped, the wrists will not be cupped on a parallel line with the shoulders. If not, the grip should be disassembled and the procedure repeated.

An additional discipline is the wrists must be held in their cupped position until the lifeline/thumb connection is unlocked and relocked to secure and lock-in the straight ball flight alignment.

The lifeline/thumb connection may not be unlocked and relocked before the cupping maneuver nor unlocked and relocked a second time after the cupping maneuver.

The wrists may not be cupped before the grip is assembled. If so, there would be insufficient room to allow the wrists to be cupped properly after a conventional style of grip is assembled on the club.

An additional discipline is the elbows must be disconnected from the rib cage during the entire proceedings.

The SHOULDERS ONLY TEST™, ARMS-LIFT TEST™and STRAIGHT-UP TEST™ must be conducted at the completion of the proceedings to determine if a straight ball flight alignment has been established and locked-in. If they do not confirm such, you should disassemble your grip and repeat the procedure until a properly assembled and executed CUP-N-LOCK TECHNIQUE™ is confirmed and, as a result, a straight ball flight alignment has been established and locked-in.

Once a locked-in straight ball flight alignment has been confirmed, the sweet spot of the clubface must be centered as near the back of the ball as possible (if not already so centered) and, simultaneously, the shoulders must be aligned parallel with the intended target line. All that will remain will be to execute a non-manipulative golf swing if the objective is to flight the ball on a straight path in the direction of the target.

Recommended Practice Routines When Using the Cup-N-Lock Technique™ in Combination with the Arrow Alignment Technique™

You should practice using the CUP-N-LOCK TECHNIQUE™ before attempting to use it in actual play. During your practice sessions, you should follow the steps below.

STEP 1: Select a safe and relatively flat practice area. Place a ball on the surface and then identify your target as well as your intended target line.

STEP 2: Choose a short iron to begin your practice session such as a wedge.

STEP 3: Ground the sole of your clubface in the middle of your stance. Then assume a conventional grip either in the form of an original or modified Vardon overlap, traditional interlock or regular baseball (ten-fingers) style of grip. Lock the lifeline of your trail hand firmly and squarely on your lead thumb to complete the grip.

STEP 4: Immobilize your shoulders, knees and hips, relax your arms and hands, then cup your wrists to the fullest extent possible on a line that parallels your shoulders without allowing any clockwise or counterclockwise rotation of the clubface.

STEP 5: **Continue to cup your wrists to the fullest extent possible until you unlock the lifeline of your trail hand from your lead thumb and then relock your trail lifeline on your lead thumb. Your lifeline/thumb connection may not be unlocked and relocked thereafter.**

STEP 6: **Relax your wrists, shoulders and arms and allow them to return to a comfortable position. Then conduct the SHOULDERS ONLY TEST™, ARMS-LIFT TEST™ and STRAIGHT-UP TEST™ to determine whether the procedure was performed correctly. If not, repeat the procedure until a locked-in straight ball flight alignment is confirmed by all three tests.**

STEP 7: **Center the sweet spot of your clubface as near the back of your ball as possible without allowing your clubface to touch or move the ball. Assume a comfortable posture and stance to the ball and then align your shoulders parallel with your intended target line to the best of your ability.**

STEP 8: **Conduct the ARROW ALIGNMENT TECHNIQUE™ and adjust your stance, if necessary, until your alignment arrow points directly at your intended target when your trail eye and head are turned in the direction of the target <u>as far as possible</u> while immobilizing all other parts of your body.**

STEP 9: **Ensure the sweet spot of your clubface has remained centered as near the back of your ball as possible and then execute a non-manipulative golf swing.**

During your practice routines, you should begin with your most lofted club and progress through your set, using each next most lofted club thereafter in succession. With each club, you should begin with a wrist swing, then with a ½ swing, on to a ¾ swing and finish with a full swing.

SUMMARY POINTS

1. The CUP-N-LOCK TECHNIQUE™ rotates the forearms, wrists, clubface and elbows to establish a straight ball flight alignment.

2. The sole of the clubface should be grounded in the middle of the stance when the hands are gripped on the club in a conventional manner. The club may be gripped with either an original or modified Vardon overlap, traditional interlock or regular baseball (ten-fingers) style of grip.

3. The lifeline of the trail hand must then be locked on the trail thumb to complete the grip. This constitutes the first of a total of two "locks" of the lifeline/thumb connection that is necessary to assemble and execute the CUP-N-LOCK TECHNIQUE™.

4. Once the hands are gripped on the club, the shoulders, knees and hips must be immobilized, the arms relaxed and the wrists cupped to the fullest extent possible on a parallel line with the shoulders.

5. The shoulders, knees and hips should not be allowed to move at any point during the cupping maneuver.

6. Once the wrists are cupped to the fullest extent possible, they must be held in such position until the lifeline/thumb connection is unlocked and relocked. This constitutes the second of the two "locks"of the lifeline/thumb connection that is required to assemble and execute the CUP-N-LOCK TECHNIQUE™ correctly.

7. **Once the lifeline/thumb connection is unlocked and relocked to secure and lock-in the straight ball flight alignment, the shoulders, knees, arms and wrists should be relaxed and allowed to return to a comfortable position.**

8. **Once the proceedings are completed, the SHOULDERS ONLY TEST™, ARMS-LIFT TEST™ and STRAIGHT-UP TEST™ should be conducted to determine whether a straight ball flight alignment has been established and locked-in. If not, the procedure should be repeated until all three tests confirm the CUP-N-LOCK TECHNIQUE™ was assembled and executed correctly and, as a result, a straight ball flight alignment has been established and locked-in.**

9. **Whether practicing or playing, the ARROW ALIGNMENT TECHNIQUE™ should be conducted to align the shoulders squarely parallel with the intended target line when using the CUP-N-LOCK TECHNIQUE™.**

CHAPTER 22

INTRODUCTION OF THE SHOULDERS UP-N-LOCK TECHNIQUE™

When performing the SHOULDERS UP-N-LOCK TECHNIQUE™, the sole of the clubface must be grounded in the middle of the stance throughout the proceedings.

The SHOULDERS UP-N-LOCK TECHNIQUE™ is compatible with all four conventional styles of grip. The lead hand must be gripped on the club in a conventional (diagonal) manner. Then the trail hand must be assembled on the club either in the form of an original Vardon overlap, modified Vardon overlap, traditional interlock or regular baseball (ten-fingers) type of grip.

Once a conventional style of grip is formed on a club without allowing any clubface rotation in the process, you then must raise only your shoulders until your clubface stops rotating counterclockwise and begins to slide in toward the body. This will rotate your wrists, clubface and elbows to establish a straight ball flight alignment.

Then you must unlock and relock your lifeline/thumb connection once to secure and lock-in the straight ball flight alignment. Your lifeline/thumb connection may not be unlocked and relocked thereafter.

How to Assemble and Execute the Shoulders Up-N-Lock Technique™

First, ground the sole of your clubface and keep it grounded throughout the proceedings. It doesn't necessarily need to be grounded directly behind the ball. The sole of the clubface may be grounded near the ball and once the proceedings are completed, the sweet spot of the clubface then can be centered as near the back of the ball as possible.

Second, grip your lead hand on your club in a conventional (diagonal) manner without allowing any clubface rotation during the process.

Third, then assume a conventional grip on your club with your trail hand either in the form of an original Vardon overlap, modified Vardon overlap, traditional interlock or regular baseball (ten-fingers) style of grip without allowing any clubface rotation during the time the trail hand is gripped on the club or between the time the lead hand and trail hand are gripped on the club. Complete your grip by locking the lifeline of your trail hand squarely and securely on your lead thumb.

Fourth, stabilize your knees, relax your arms, wrists and hands and raise your shoulders upward until your clubface stops rotating fully counterclockwise and begins to slide toward your body. Your arms, hands and wrists should only move in response to the upward lifting of your shoulders. Your knees should not be allowed to move at all. Your clubface must remain grounded even though the sole of your clubface should begin to slide in toward your body.

Fifth, once you have raised your shoulders upward until your clubface stops rotating counterclockwise and then begins to slide in your direction, you must then unlock the lifeline of your trail hand from your lead thumb by at least an inch without completely ungripping your club and then relock the lifeline of your trail hand on your lead thumb. Your lifeline/thumb connection may not be unlocked and relocked thereafter. (Figure 22-1).

Sixth, once the proceedings are completed, the SHOULDERS ONLY TEST™, ARMS-LIFT

Figure 22-1

STEP 1: The first essential step to assemble and execute the SHOULDERS UP-N-LOCK TECHNIQUE™ is to grip the club in a conventional manner with the clubface grounded in the middle of the stance.

STEP 2: The knees should be stabilized, the wrists and arms relaxed with the clubface grounded and then the shoulders should be raised upward until the clubface stops rotating counterclockwise and begins to slide in the direction of the body.

STEP 3: The shoulders and clubface must remain in such position and then the lifeline of the trail hand must be unlocked from the lead thumb by at least an inch without completely ungripping the club.

STEP 4: Then the lifeline of the trail hand must be relocked squarely and securely on the lead thumb while the shoulders and clubface remain in such positions. *(Then the shoulders, arms and knees may be relaxed and allowed to return to their original positions.)*

TEST™ and STRAIGHT-UP TEST™ must be conducted to determine whether a straight ball flight alignment has been established and locked-in. If not, the grip should be disassembled and the procedure repeated until the three tests confirm a straight ball flight alignment has been established and locked-in.

Disciplines Required to Assemble and Execute the Shoulders Up-N-Lock Technique™

The first discipline is to ground the sole of your clubface in the middle of your stance.

The second discipline is to form a conventional grip on your club with your lead hand. This is a diagonal grip across the lead hand as opposed to a "fingers only" type of grip. When forming the lead hand on the club, the clubface should not be allowed to rotate or move during the gripping process.

The third discipline is to grip the trail hand on the club without allowing the clubface to rotate during the gripping process.

The fourth and most essential discipline is to raise only your shoulders upward until your clubface stops rotating counterclockwise and begins to slide in toward the body.

When the knees become too active during the proceedings, the forearms will not rotate the wrists, clubface and elbows to establish and lock-in a straight ball flight alignment. They should be stabilized throughout the proceedings.

Another critical discipline is once the shoulders are raised upward until the clubface stops rotating counterclockwise, the clubface must be held in such position until the lifeline of the trail hand is unlocked from the lead thumb by at least an inch without completely ungripping the club and then relocked on the lead thumb.

An additional discipline associated with the SHOULDERS UP-N-LOCK TECHNIQUE™ is the elbows must be disconnected from the rib cage during the entire proceedings. If either or both elbows are connected to the rib cage during any part of the proceedings, the forearms will rotate the wrists, clubface and elbows to a different ball flight alignment.

Although you may observe other golfers, including professional tour players, unlock and relock their lifeline/thumb connection repeatedly during their pre-shot routines, the SHOULDERS UP-N-LOCK TECHNIQUE™ will not permit such a practice. As noted above, the lifeline/thumb connection must be unlocked and relocked once and no more after the shoulders are raised upward.

Another discipline is once the SHOULDERS UP-N-LOCK TECHNIQUE™ is completed, it must be tested to determine whether a straight ball flight alignment has been established and locked-in. The SHOULDERS ONLY TEST™, ARMS-LIFT TEST™ and the STRAIGHT-UP TEST™ therefore must be conducted at the completion of the proceedings.

Why the Shoulders Up-N-Lock Technique™ Works

When the shoulders are raised upward until the clubface stops rotating counter-clockwise after a conventional grip is formed on a club – while the sole of the clubface remains grounded – the forearms will rotate the elbows to a parallel alignment with the shoulders to create an on-line swing path of the clubface.

When the elbows are rotated to a parallel alignment with the shoulders the wrists correspondingly will rotate the clubface to a square alignment, all of which will establish a straight ball flight alignment.

However, the straight ball flight alignment will not be locked-in at such point.

In order to lock-in the straight ball flight alignment, the lifeline/thumb connection then must be unlocked and relocked once and no more thereafter.

Assembling and executing the SHOULDERS UP-N-LOCK TECHNIQUE™ correctly is just a part of the pre-shot requirements. Neither the SHOULDERS UP-N-LOCK TECHNIQUE™ nor any of the other LOCKED-IN TECHNIQUES™ addressed in this book are of much value unless you first learn how to align your shoulders squarely parallel with your intended target line and center the sweet spot of your clubface as near the back of the ball as possible without touching or moving the ball.

Unless you have assembled and executed the SHOULDERS UP-N-LOCK TECHNIQUE™ correctly, centered the sweet spot of your clubface as near the back of the ball as possible and aligned your shoulders squarely parallel with your intended target line at final address, you cannot expect to hit a golf ball on a straight path in the direction of your intended target.

Recommended Practice Routines When Using the Shoulders Up-N-Lock Technique™ in Combination with the Arrow Alignment Technique™

In your practice sessions when using a combination of the SHOULDERS UP-N-LOCK TECHNIQUE™ and the ARROW ALIGNMENT TECHNIQUE™, you should begin with a wedge.

After you have wrist swung several golf shots with your wedge to a specific target, you should then execute about a ½ swing, then on to a ¾ swing and finally, to a full swing. You should then choose your next most lofted club and swing in the same sequence. You should continue using each next most lofted club in succession until you have practiced with each club in your set.

In each case, you should follow the steps below:

STEP 1: Place a ball on the surface of your practice area. Identify a specific target such as a flag on a practice green in a safe hitting area. Also identify your intended target line.

STEP 2: Ground the sole of your clubface in the middle of your stance and keep it grounded until the proceedings are completed.

STEP 3: Then assemble and execute the SHOULDERS UP-N-LOCK TECHNIQUE™ as instructed throughout this chapter. Once your grip is completed you must stabilize your knees, relax your arms, wrists and hands and then raise only your shoulders upward until your clubface stops rotating counterclockwise and begins to slide in toward your body. Then you must unlock and relock your lifeline/thumb connection once but no more thereafter.

STEP 4: Once you have assembled and executed the SHOULDERS UP-N-LOCK TECHNIQUE™, you must conduct the ARMS-LIFT TEST™, SHOULDERS ONLY TEST™ and STRAIGHT-UP TEST™ to determine whether it was assembled and executed correctly. If the clubface rotates counterclockwise or clockwise when conducting the ARMS-LIFT TEST™, SHOULDERS ONLY TEST™ or STRAIGHT-UP TEST™, you can trust the technique was not assembled and executed correctly. On the other hand, if the clubface does not rotate counterclockwise or clockwise when the three tests are conducted, a properly assembled and executed SHOULDERS UP-N-LOCK TECHNIQUE™ will be indicated as well as a locked-in straight ball flight alignment. If confirmed, go to the next step. If not, repeat the procedure until the ARMS-LIFT TEST™, SHOULDER ONLY TEST™ and STRAIGHT-UP TEST™ confirm the technique has been assembled and executed correctly.

STEP 5: Next, center the sweet spot of your clubface as near the back of your ball as possible without touching or moving the ball. Then assume a comfortable stance and posture to the ball. Align your shoulders parallel with your intended target line to the best of your ability.

STEP 6: Conduct the ARROW ALIGNMENT TECHNIQUE™ and adjust your stance, if necessary, until your alignment arrow

points directly at your intended target when you turn your trail eye and head in the direction of your target as far as possible while immobilizing all other body parts.

STEP 7: Ensure the sweet spot of your clubface has continued to remain as near the back of your ball as possible and execute a non-manipulative golf swing.

Once you become confident in your practice sessions when using the SHOULDERS UP-N-LOCK TECHNIQUE™ in combination with the ARROW ALIGNMENT TECHNIQUE™ with each club in your set, you will then be prepared to take both to the golf course.

SUMMARY POINTS

1. The SHOULDERS UP-N-LOCK TECHNIQUE™ is compatible with the four conventional styles of grip.

2. The sole of the clubface must be grounded throughout the proceedings, preferably in the middle of the stance.

3. The lead hand then must be assembled on the club in a conventional (diagonal) manner without allowing the clubface to rotate during the process.

4. Next, the trail hand must be gripped on the club with a modified or original Vardon overlap, traditional interlock or a regular baseball (ten-fingers) style of grip.

5. The lifeline of the trail hand must be locked squarely and securely on the lead thumb to complete the grip.

6. Once the lifeline of the trail hand is locked on the lead thumb to complete the grip, all body parts other than the shoulders must remain passive. The shoulders then must be raised upward until the clubface stops rotating counterclockwise and begins to slide in toward the body.

7. Once the clubface stops rotating fully counterclockwise the lifeline/thumb connection must be unlocked and relocked once.

8. **The ARMS-LIFT TEST™, SHOULDERS ONLY TEST™ and STRAIGHT-UP TEST™ should be conducted at the completion of the proceedings to ensure the procedure was assembled and executed correctly.**

9. **The SHOULDERS UP-N-LOCK TECHNIQUE™ should be used in combination with the ARROW ALIGNMENT TECHNIQUE™ to ensure the shoulders are aligned parallel with the intended target line at the completion of the proceedings.**

CHAPTER 23

INTRODUCTION OF THE SHOULDERS DOWN-N-LOCK TECHNIQUE™

The SHOULDERS DOWN-N-LOCK TECHNIQUE™ is similar to the SHOULDERS UP-N-LOCK TECHNIQUE™, as addressed in the previous chapter, but instead of raising your shoulders until your clubface stops rotating fully counterclockwise after forming a conventional grip on a club, you must lower your shoulders until the clubface stops rotating fully clockwise. As with the SHOULDERS UP-N-LOCK TECHNIQUE™, you must ground the sole of the clubface prior to assuming your grip and keep it grounded throughout the proceedings.

The SHOULDERS DOWN-N-LOCK TECHNIQUE™ is compatible with all four conventional styles of grip whether that of an original Vardon overlap, modified Vardon overlap, traditional interlock or regular baseball (ten-fingers) style of grip.

How to Assemble and Execute the Shoulders Down-N-Lock Technique™

First, the sole of the clubface must be grounded in the middle of the stance throughout the proceedings. It does not necessarily need to be grounded directly behind the ball during the proceedings. It can be grounded in the near vicinity of the ball and once the proceedings are completed the sweet spot of the clubface then can be transferred and centered as near the back of the ball as possible.

Second, your lead hand must be assembled on the club in a conventional (diagonal) manner without allowing your clubface to rotate during the gripping process.

Third, your trail hand then must be assembled on the club in a conventional manner without allowing your clubface to rotate clockwise or counterclockwise during the process or between the time your lead and trail hands are being gripped on the club.

Fourth, keep your arms, wrists and hands relaxed, stabilize your knees and then lower your shoulders until your clubface stops rotating clockwise.

Fifth, once your shoulders are lowered until your clubface stops rotating fully clockwise, the lifeline of your trail hand then must be unlocked from your lead thumb by at least an inch without completely ungripping the club and then relocked on your lead thumb. Then, once again, your lifeline/thumb connection must be unlocked and relocked in the same manner.

Sixth, once the proceedings are completed, your knees, shoulders, arms and wrists should be relaxed and allowed to return to a comfortable position. (Figure 23-1).

Seventh, once the proceedings to assemble and execute the SHOULDERS DOWN-N-LOCK TECHNIQUE™are completed, the SHOULDERS ONLY TEST™, ARMS-LIFT TEST™ and STRAIGHT-UP TEST™ must be conducted to determine whether it was assembled and executed correctly.

Why the Shoulders Down-N-Lock Technique™ Works

The SHOULDERS DOWN-N-LOCK TECHNIQUE™ works because when the shoulders

Figure 23-1

STEP 1: The first essential step to assemble and execute the SHOULDERS DOWN-N-LOCK TECHNIQUE™ is to ground the clubface in the middle of the stance and then grip the club in a conventional manner.

STEP 2: Stabilize the knees, relax the wrists and arms and with the clubface remaining grounded, lower the shoulders downward until the clubface stops rotating clockwise.

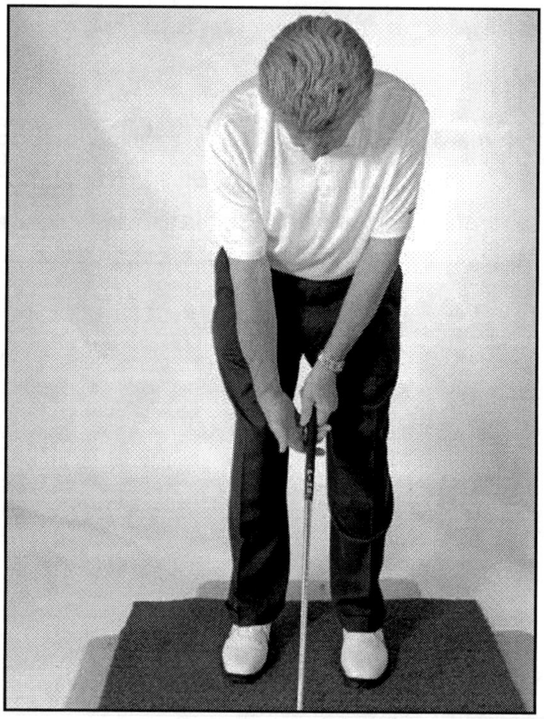

STEP 3: While holding the shoulders in their lowered position with the clubface rotated fully clockwise, unlock the lifeline of the trail hand from the lead thumb by at least an inch without completely ungripping the club.

STEP 4: Then relock the lifeline of the trail hand squarely and securely on the lead thumb while the shoulders remain lowered and the clubface rotated fully clockwise.

STEP 5: Then, once again, unlock the lifeline of the trail hand from the lead hand by at least an inch without completely ungripping the club while the shoulders remain lowered and the clubface rotated fully clockwise.

STEP 6: Then, once again, relock the lifeline of the trail hand squarely and securely on the lead thumb while the shoulders remain lowered and the clubface rotated fully clockwise. *(Then relax the shoulders, knees, wrists and arms and allow them to return to a comfortable position.)*

are lowered until the clubface stops rotating fully clockwise after a conventional grip is formed on the club, the forearms will rotate the elbows to a parallel alignment with the shoulders to create an on-line swing path of the clubface.

When the forearms rotate the elbows to a parallel alignment with the shoulders to create an on-line swing path of the clubface the wrists correspondingly will rotate the clubface to a square alignment, all of which will establish a straight ball flight alignment.

However, the straight ball flight alignment will not be locked in at such point.

In order to lock-in the straight ball flight alignment the lifeline/thumb connection must then be unlocked and relocked twice – but no more thereafter.

The SHOULDERS DOWN-N-LOCK TECHNIQUE™ requires the lifeline/thumb connection to be locked a total of three times. The first of the three "locks" occurs when the lifeline of the trail hand is locked squarely and securely on the lead thumb to complete the grip. The second of the three "locks" occurs after the shoulders are lowered until the clubface stops rotating clockwise when then the lifeline of the trail hand is unlocked from the lead thumb by at least an inch without completely ungripping the club and then relocked on the lead thumb. The third of the three "locks" occurs when then, once again, the lifeline/thumb connection is unlocked and relocked in the same manner.

Disciplines Required to Assemble the Shoulders Down-N-Lock Technique™

The most critical discipline relating to the assemblage and execution of the SHOULDERS DOWN-N-LOCK TECHNIQUE™ is the lowering of the shoulders after a conventional style of grip is formed on a club and while the sole of the clubface remains grounded.

The knees must be stabilized during the lowering of the shoulders. If the knees are flexed upward or downward while the shoulders are being lowered, it will prevent the forearms from rotating the wrists, clubface and elbows to establish a straight ball flight alignment.

In addition to the knees being stabilized during the proceedings, the arms, hands and wrists should remain passive and inactive and only move in response to the lowering of the shoulders during the proceedings.

The shoulders must be lowered only after a conventional style of grip is formed on a club but before the lifeline/thumb connection is unlocked and relocked twice. If the shoulders are lowered only before a conventional grip is formed on a club, it will not cause the forearms to rotate the wrists, clubface and elbows to establish a straight ball flight at the completion of the proceedings.

If the shoulders are lowered only after the lifeline/thumb connection is unlocked and relocked twice, the forearms will not rotate the wrists, clubface and elbows to establish a straight ball flight alignment.

Grounding the sole of the clubface during the proceedings also is an important discipline when assembling the SHOULDERS DOWN-N-LOCK TECHNIQUE™. It provides an anchor against which the clubface can rotate clockwise when the shoulders are lowered during the proceedings. It also enables you to observe the clockwise rotation of the clubface when the shoulders are lowered.

Another discipline relating to the assemblage and execution of the SHOULDERS DOWN-N-LOCK TECHNIQUE™ is there should be no clubface rotation when the lead and trail hands are gripped on the club or between the time the hands are gripped on the club.

The only clubface rotation allowed during the proceedings is the clockwise rotation of the clubface caused by lowering the shoulders after a conventional style of grip is assembled on the club.

The elbows must be disconnected from the rib cage during the proceedings. If either or both elbows are connected to the rib cage during the proceedings, the forearms will rotate the wrists, clubface and elbows to a different ball flight alignment at the completion of the proceedings.

An additional discipline associated with the assemblage and execution of the SHOULDERS DOWN-N-LOCK TECHNIQUE™ is the lifeline/thumb connection must be unlocked and relocked twice after the shoulders are lowered. If the lifeline/thumb connection is unlocked and relocked once more thereafter, the forearms will rotate the wrists, clubface and elbows to some alignment other than a straight ball flight alignment.

The SHOULDERS ONLY TEST™ , ARMS-LIFT TEST™ and STRAIGHT-UP TEST™ must be conducted at the completion of the proceedings. If the clubface rotates counterclockwise or clockwise during any of the three tests, the grip should be disassembled and the proceedings repeated until there is no such clubface rotation during the three tests.

Establishing and locking-in a straight ball flight alignment is just a part of the pre-shot routine. In addition, the sweet spot of the clubface must be centered as near the back of the ball as possible (if not already so centered) and, simultaneously, the shoulders must be aligned squarely parallel with the intended target line at final address, followed by a non-manipulative golf swing if the objective is to hit a golf ball on a straight path in the direction of a specific target.

You should engage in some meaningful practice sessions when using the SHOULDERS DOWN-N-LOCK TECHNIQUE™ before using it in actual play.

Recommended Practice Routines When Using the Shoulders Down-N-Lock™ in Combination with the Arrow Alignment Technique™

In your practice sessions you should conduct the ARROW ALIGNMENT TECHNIQUE™ to align your shoulders squarely parallel with your intended target line when using the SHOULDERS DOWN-N-LOCK TECHNIQUE™.

You always should locate a safe and reasonably flat surface on which to practice as well as to follow the steps below in your practice routine:

STEP 1: Place a ball on the surface of your practice area. Identify a very narrow and specific target. Also identify your intended target line.

STEP 2: Ground the sole of your clubface either directly behind your ball or in its nearby vicinity and keep it grounded throughout the proceedings.

STEP 3: Assemble and execute the SHOULDERS DOWN-N-LOCK TECHNIQUE™ in accordance with the instructions in this chapter. Remember to keep your knees stabilized and your arms, hands and wrists passive and inactive as you lower your shoulders until your clubface stops rotating clockwise after forming a conventional style of grip on your club.

STEP 4: Once you have lowered your shoulders until your clubface stops rotating clockwise, unlock the lifeline of your trail hand from your lead thumb by at least an inch without completely ungripping your club and then relock your trail lifeline on your lead thumb. Then, once again, unlock and relock your lifeline/thumb connection in the same manner. Do not unlock and relock your lifeline/thumb connection thereafter.

STEP 5: Then conduct the SHOULDERS ONLY TEST™, ARMS-LIFT TEST™ and STRAIGHT-UP TEST™ and repeat the proceedings, if necessary, until a straight ball flight alignment is confirmed as established and locked-in.

STEP 6: Center the sweet spot of your clubface as near the back of your ball as possible (unless already so centered) and then assume a comfortable posture and stance to your ball. Align your shoulders parallel with your intended target line to the best of your ability.

STEP 7: Conduct the ARROW ALIGNMENT TECHNIQUE™ and adjust your stance, if necessary, until your alignment arrow points directly at your target when you turn your head and trail eye in the direction of your target as far as possible while immobilizing all other parts of your body.

STEP 8: Ensure the sweet spot of your clubface has remained centered as near the back of your ball as possible and then execute a non-manipulative golf swing.

In each practice session you should begin with your most lofted club and then with your next most lofted club in succession thereafter until you have practiced with each club in your set. With each club, you should begin with a simple wrist swing, then with a ½ swing, on to a ¾ swing and conclude with a full swing.

SUMMARY POINTS

1. The SHOULDERS DOWN-N-LOCK TECHNIQUE™ requires a lowering of the shoulders after a conventional style of grip is formed on a club.

2. The sole of the clubface must be grounded, the knees must be stabilized and the arms, hands and wrists must remain passive and inactive as the shoulders are lowered until the clubface stops rotating clockwise after the formation of a conventional grip on the club.

3. When the shoulders are lowered until the clubface stops rotating clockwise, the forearms will rotate the elbows to a parallel alignment with the shoulders to create an on-line swing path of the clubface.

4. When the elbows are rotated to a parallel alignment with the shoulders, the wrists correspondingly will rotate the clubface to a square alignment.

5. The lead hand must be gripped on the club in a conventional (diagonal) manner without allowing any clubface rotation during the gripping process.

6. The trail hand must be assembled on the club either in the form of an original Vardon overlap, modified Vardon overlap, traditional interlock or regular baseball (ten-fingers) style of golf grip.

7. **The grip must be completed by locking the lifeline of the trail hand firmly on the lead thumb.**

8. **Once the shoulders are lowered until the clubface stops rotating clockwise, the lifeline of the trail hand must be unlocked from the lead thumb by at least an inch without completely ungripping the club and then relocked on the lead thumb. Then, once again, the lifeline/thumb connection must be unlocked and relocked in the same manner.**

9. **The SHOULDERS ONLY TEST™, ARMS-LIFT TEST™ and STRAIGHT-UP TEST™ must be conducted once the proceedings are completed and the procedure repeated, if necessary, until the three tests confirm the technique was assembled and executed correctly and a straight ball flight alignment has been established and locked-in.**

10. **The ARROW ALIGNMENT TECHNIQUE™ should be conducted to align the shoulders squarely parallel with the intended target line when using the SHOULDERS DOWN-N-LOCK TECHNIQUE™.**

CHAPTER 24

INTRODUCTION OF THE LEAD FOOT OUT-N-LOCK TECHNIQUE™

The LEAD FOOT OUT-N-LOCK TECHNIQUE™ requires the club to be gripped with a conventional style of grip, followed by moving the lead foot outward toward the target by at least the width of one shoe and then unlocking and relocking the lifeline/thumb connection once but no more thereafter.

The LEAD FOOT OUT-N-LOCK TECHNIQUE™ is compatible with all four conventional styles of grip whether that of an original Vardon overlap, modified Vardon overlap, traditional interlock or regular (ten-fingers) style of grip.

How to Assemble and Execute the Lead Foot Out-N-Lock Technique™

First, the sole of the clubface must be grounded and then the lead hand must be gripped on a club in a conventional (diagonal) manner. The clubface may not be allowed to rotate either clockwise or counterclockwise during the gripping of the lead hand on the club.

Second, the trail hand then must be gripped on the club either in the form of an original Vardon overlap, modified Vardon overlap, traditional interlock, or regular baseball (ten-fingers) style of grip. The grip must be completed by locking the lifeline of the trail hand squarely and firmly on the lead thumb.

Third, the lead foot then must be moved outward – in the direction of the target – by at least the width of one shoe.

Fourth, once the lead foot is moved outward in the direction of the target by at least the width of one shoe, the lifeline of the trail hand must be unlocked by at least an inch from the lead thumb without ungripping the club and then relocked on the lead thumb.

Fifth, the lead foot then should be moved back to its original position. (Figure 24-1).

Sixth, the SHOULDERS ONLY TEST™, ARMS-LIFT TEST™ and STRAIGHT-UP TEST™ then must be conducted to determine if all of the above steps were performed correctly and whether a straight ball flight alignment has been established and locked-in. If there is any clockwise or counterclockwise rotation during any of the three tests, simply disassemble the grip and repeat the steps correctly until the three tests confirm the technique was assembled and executed correctly and a straight ball flight alignment has been established and locked-in as a result.

Why the Lead Foot Out-N-Lock Technique™ Works

This technique works because when the lead foot is moved outward in the direction of the target by at least the width of one shoe after the grip is completed and the clubface rotates fully clockwise, the forearms will rotate the elbows to a parallel alignment with the shoulders to establish an on-line swing path of the clubface.

When the elbows are rotated to a parallel alignment with the shoulders to establish an on-line swing path of the clubface the wrists correspondingly will rotate the clubface to a square alignment, all of which will establish a straight ball flight alignment.

However, the straight ball flight alignment will not be locked-in at this point. In order to lock-in the straight ball flight alignment,

Figure 24-1

STEP 1: The first essential step in assembling and executing the LEAD FOOT OUT-N-LOCK TECHNIQUE™ is to grip the club with a conventional grip with the clubface grounded in the middle of the stance.

STEP 2: Then move the lead foot outward in the direction of the target in a lateral manner by at least one shoe and until the clubface is rotated fully clockwise.

STEP 3: Continue to maintain the lead foot in such position with the clubface rotated fully clockwise and then unlock the lifeline of the trail hand from the lead thumb by at least an inch without ungripping the club.

STEP 4: Then relock the lifeline of the trail hand squarely and securely on the lead thumb with the lead foot held in such position with the clubface rotated fully clockwise. *(Then move the lead foot back to its original position.)*

the lifeline/thumb connection then must be unlocked and relocked once but no more thereafter.

The LEAD FOOT OUT-N-LOCK TECHNIQUE™ requires a total of two "locks" of the lifeline/thumb connection.

The first of the two "locks" of the lifeline/thumb connection occurs when the lifeline of the trail hand is locked squarely and securely on the lead thumb to complete the grip. The second of the two "locks" of the lifeline/thumb connection occurs after the grip is completed and the lead foot is moved outward when then the lifeline of the trail hand must be unlocked from the lead thumb and then relocked on the lead thumb.

The lifeline/thumb connection may not be unlocked and relocked thereafter. If the lifeline/thumb connection is unlocked and relocked an additional time, the forearms will rotate the wrists, clubface and elbows to a different ball flight alignment and the straight ball flight alignment will no longer exist.

Disciplines Necessary to Perform the Lead Foot Out-N-Lock Technique™

One of the necessary disciplines to assemble and execute the LEAD FOOT OUT-N-LOCK TECHNIQUE™ correctly is there must not be any clubface rotation during the gripping process. The clubface may not be allowed to rotate clockwise or counterclockwise during the time the lead hand is gripped on the club or during the time the trail hand is gripped on the club.

If there is any such rotation, you should disassemble the grip and repeat the procedure in accordance with the aforementioned instructions.

The clubface should be grounded in the middle of the stance when the FOOT OUT-N-LOCK TECHNIQUE™ is performed. It is not necessary to center the sweet spot of the clubface directly behind the ball during the proceedings. The proceedings may be performed with the clubface placed in the near vicinity of the ball and, once completed, the sweet spot of the clubface then can be centered as near the back of the ball as possible.

Another discipline is the lead foot must be moved outward in the direction of the target by the width of one shoe only after a conventional style of grip is assembled on a club. If the lead foot is moved outward in such manner only prior to the time the hands are gripped on the club, it will not cause the forearms to rotate the wrists, clubface and elbows to establish a straight ball flight alignment.

The lead foot must be moved outward in the direction of the target by at least the width of one shoe between the time the grip is completed and the lifeline/thumb connection is unlocked and relocked.

Another discipline necessary to perform the LEAD FOOT OUT-N-LOCK TECHNIQUE™ correctly is to ensure both elbows are disconnected from the rib cage during the entire proceedings. If either or both elbows are connected to the rib cage during any step in the proceedings, the forearms will rotate the elbows and clubface to establish a different straight ball flight alignment at the completion of the proceedings.

Another discipline that cannot be neglected is to conduct the SHOULDERS ONLY TEST™, ARMS-LIFT TEST™ and STRAIGHT-UP TEST™ at the completion of the proceedings. Considering each step to complete the procedure must be performed precisely, it is easy to compromise one or more steps inadvertently in the process.

The three confirmation steps are critical to ensure the proceedings have been performed correctly. If there is any rotation of the clubface during any of the three tests, the grip should be disassembled and the procedure repeated until a locked-in straight ball flight alignment is confirmed by the three tests.

Once the three tests confirm the LEAD FOOT OUT-N-LOCK TECHNIQUE™ has been assembled and executed correctly, the sweet spot of the clubface must be centered as near the back of the ball as possible (if not already so centered) and the shoulders simultaneously must be aligned squarely parallel with the shoulders, followed by the execution of a non-manipulative golf swing in order to fly the ball on a straight path in the direction of the target and on a straight path that parallels the shoulder line.

Recommended Practice Routines When Using the Lead Foot Out-N-Lock Technique™ in Combination with the Arrow Alignment Technique™

Prior to using the LEAD FOOT OUT-N-LOCK TECHNIQUE™ in actual play, you first should engage in some meaningful practice sessions.

You should always select a safe and reasonably level surface for your practice sessions.

Since the sweet spot of your clubface must be centered as near the back of your ball as possible without allowing your clubface to move the ball in the process and, simultaneously, your shoulders must be aligned squarely parallel with your intended target line at final address in order to hit a ball straight to a chosen target, you should conduct the ARROW ALIGNMENT TECHNIQUE™ when practicing or playing while using the LEAD FOOT OUT-N-LOCK TECHNIQUE™.

Also, you should follow the steps below in your practice routine when using the LEAD FOOT OUT-N-LOCK TECHNIQUE™.

STEP 1: Place a ball on the surface of your practice area. Select a specific target as well as identify your intended target line.

STEP 2: Ground the sole of your clubface either directly behind your ball or in the near vicinity of your ball.

STEP 3: Perform the steps to complete the LEAD FOOT OUT-N-LOCK TECHNIQUE™ as instructed throughout this chapter. Do not allow your clubface to rotate from the time your lead hand is gripped on the club until your grip is completed. Remember to move your lead foot outward in the direction of your target by at least the width of one shoe and until the clubface rotates fully clockwise before your lifeline/thumb connection is unlocked and relocked.

STEP 4: Once the proceedings are completed, conduct the SHOULDERS ONLY TEST™, ARMS-LIFT TEST™ and STRAIGHT-UP TEST™ to determine whether the procedure has been performed correctly. If there is any clubface rotation during the three tests, disassemble the grip and repeat the steps precisely until the three tests confirm the technique has been performed correctly and a straight ball flight alignment has been established and locked-in.

STEP 5: Center the sweet spot of your clubface as near the back of your ball as possible (if not already so centered) and assume a comfortable stance and posture to your ball. Align your shoulders parallel with your intended target to the best of your ability.

STEP 6: Conduct the ARROW ALIGNMENT TECHNIQUE™ and adjust your stance, if necessary, until your alignment arrow points directly at your target when you turn your head and trail eye in the direction of your target <u>as far as possible</u> while immobilizing all other parts of your body.

STEP 7: Ensure the sweet spot of your clubface has remained as near the back of your ball as possible and then execute a non-manipulative golf swing.

If the above steps are performed correctly, your ball should fly on a straight path in the direction of your target.

During your practice sessions, you should begin with your most lofted club and practice with each next most lofted club in succession thereafter until you have practiced with each club in your set. You should begin with a simple wrist swing with each club, followed by a ½ swing, on to a ¾ swing and conclude with a full swing.

SUMMARY POINTS

1. The LEAD FOOT OUT-N-LOCK TECHNIQUE™ is compatible with all four conventional styles of grip.
2. The first order of business is to ground the sole of the clubface in the middle of the stance.
3. The lead hand must be gripped on the club in a conventional (diagonal) manner. The clubface may not be allowed to rotate during the time the lead hand is being gripped on the club.
4. The trail hand then must be gripped on the club either in the form of an original Vardon overlap, modified Vardon overlap, traditional interlock or regular baseball (ten-fingers) style of grip.
5. The clubface may not be allowed to move during the time the trail hand is gripped on the club or between the time the lead and trail hands are gripped on the club.
6. The grip is completed by locking the lifeline of the trail hand squarely and securely on the lead thumb. This is the first of the two "locks" of the lifeline/thumb connection that is necessary to complete the LEAD FOOT OUT-N-LOCK TECHNIQUE™.
7. Once the grip is completed, the lead foot must be moved outward in the direction of the target by at least the width of one shoe.

8. **Once the lead foot is moved outward by at least the width of one shoe, the lifeline of the trail hand then must be unlocked from the lead thumb by at least an inch without completely ungripping the club and then relocked on the lead thumb. This is the second of the two "locks" of the lifeline/thumb connection that is necessary to perform the LEAD FOOT OUT-N-LOCK TECHNIQUE™.**

9. **Once the proceedings are completed, the SHOULDERS ONLY TEST™, ARMS-LIFT TEST™ and STRAIGHT-UP TEST™ must be conducted to determine if the technique was performed correctly and whether a straight ball flight alignment has been established and locked-in. If not, the grip should be disassembled and the procedure repeated until the three tests confirm such.**

10. **The ARROW ALIGNMENT TECHNIQUE™ should be conducted to align the shoulders squarely parallel with the intended target line when using the LEAD FOOT OUT-N-LOCK TECHNIQUE™.**

CHAPTER 25

INTRODUCTION OF THE TRAIL FOOT OUT-N-LOCK TECHNIQUE™

The TRAIL FOOT OUT-N-LOCK TECHNIQUE™ requires the club to be gripped with a conventional style of grip, followed by moving the trail foot outward and away from the target by at least the width of one shoe and then unlocking and relocking the lifeline/thumb connection twice but no more thereafter.

The TRAIL FOOT OUT-N-LOCK TECHNIQUE™ is compatible with all four conventional styles of grip whether that of an original Vardon overlap, modified Vardon overlap, traditional interlock or regular (ten-fingers) style of grip.

How to Assemble and Execute the Trail Foot Out-N-Lock Technique™

First, the sole of the clubface must be grounded and then the lead hand must be gripped on a club in a conventional (diagonal) manner. The clubface may not be allowed to rotate either clockwise or counterclockwise during the gripping of the lead hand on the club.

Second, the trail hand then must be gripped on the club either in the form of an original Vardon overlap, modified Vardon overlap, traditional interlock, or regular baseball (ten-fingers) style of grip. The grip must be completed by locking the lifeline of the trail hand squarely and firmly on the lead thumb.

Third, the trail foot then must be moved outward and away from the target by at least the width of one shoe and until the clubface rotates fully counterclockwise.

Fourth, once the trail foot is moved outward and away from the target by at least the width of one shoe and until the clubface is rotated fully counterclockwise, the lifeline of the trail hand must be unlocked by at least an inch from the lead thumb without ungripping the club and then relocked on the lead thumb. Then, once again, the lifeline/thumb connection must be unlocked and relocked (Figure 25-1).

Fifth, the SHOULDERS ONLY TEST™, ARMS-LIFT TEST™ and STRAIGHT-UP TEST™ then must be conducted to determine if all of the above steps were performed correctly and whether a straight ball flight alignment has been established and locked-in. If there is any clockwise or counterclockwise rotation during the three tests, the grip should be disassembled and the steps repeated correctly until the three tests confirm the technique has been assembled and executed correctly and a straight ball flight alignment has been established and locked-in as a result.

Why the Trail Foot Out-N-Lock Technique™ Works

The TRAIL FOOT OUT-N-LOCK TECHNIQUE™ works because when the trail foot is moved laterally outward and away from the target by at least the width of one shoe and until the clubface is rotated fully counterclcokwise after the grip is completed, the forearms will rotate the elbows to a parallel alignment with the shoulders to establish an on-line swing path of the clubface.

When the elbows are rotated to a parallel alignment with the shoulders to establish an on-line swing path of the clubface the wrists correspondingly will rotate the clubface to a square alignment, all of which will establish and lock-in a straight ball flight alignment.

Figure 25-1

STEP 1: The first essential step in assembling and executing the TRAIL FOOT OUT-N-LOCK TECHNIQUE™ is to grip the club in a conventional manner with the clubface grounded in the middle of the stance.

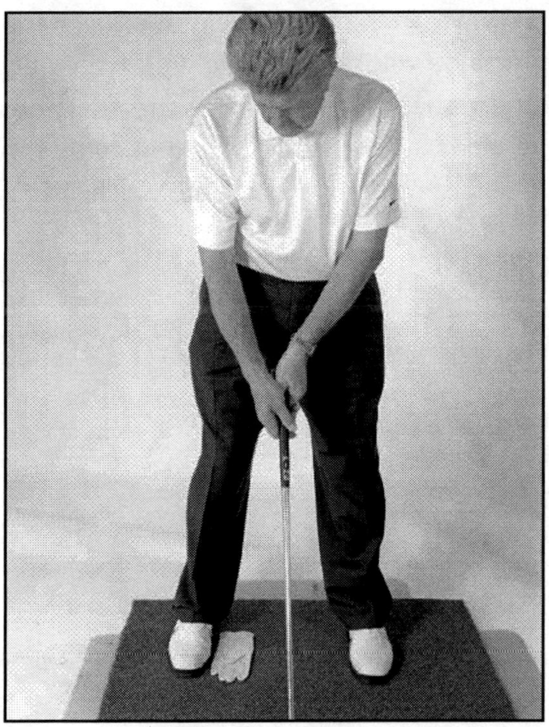

STEP 2: Then the trail foot must be moved outward and away from the target in a lateral manner by at least the width of one shoe and until the clubface is rotated fully counterclockwise.

STEP 3: The trail foot must remain in such position with the clubface rotated fully counterclockwise and then the lifeline of the trail hand must be unlocked from the lead thumb by at least an inch without completely ungripping the club.

STEP 4: Then the lifeline of the trail hand must be relocked squarely and securely on the lead thumb while the trail foot remains in the same position with the clubface rotated fully counterclockwise.

STEP 5: Then, once again, the lifeline of the trail hand must be unlocked from the lead thumb while the trail foot remains in the same position with the clubface rotated fully counterclockwise.

STEP 6: Then, once again, the lifeline of the trail hand must be relocked squarely and securely on the lead thumb with the clubface remaining rotated fully counterclockwise. *(The trail foot then may be moved back to its original position.)*

However, the straight ball flight alignment will not be locked-in at this point. In order to lock-in the straight ball flight alignment, the lifeline/thumb connection then must be unlocked and relocked twice but no more thereafter.

The TRAIL FOOT OUT-N-LOCK TECHNIQUE™requires a total of three "locks" of the lifeline/thumb connection.

The first of the three "locks" of the lifeline/thumb connection occurs when the lifeline of the trail hand is locked squarely and securely on the lead thumb to complete the grip. The second of the three "locks" of the lifeline/thumb connection occurs after the grip is completed and the trail foot is moved outward and away from the target by at least the width of one shoe when then the lifeline of the trail hand must be unlocked from the lead thumb by at least an inch without completely ungripping the club and then relocked on the lead thumb. The third of the three "locks" occurs when then, once again, the lifeline/thumb connection must be unlocked and relocked.

The lifeline/thumb connection may not be unlocked and relocked thereafter. If the lifeline/thumb connection is unlocked and relocked an additional time, the forearms will rotate the wrists, clubface and elbows to a different ball flight alignment and the straight ball flight alignment will no longer exist.

Disciplines Necessary to Perform the Trail Foot Out-N-Lock Technique™

One of the necessary disciplines to assemble and execute the TRAIL FOOT OUT-N-LOCK TECHNIQUE™ correctly is there must not be any clubface rotation during the gripping process. The clubface may not be allowed to rotate clockwise or counterclockwise during the time the lead hand is gripped on the club or during the time the trail hand is gripped on the club.

If there is any such rotation, you should disassemble the grip and repeat the procedure in accordance with the aforementioned instructions.

The clubface should be grounded in the middle of the stance when the TRAIL FOOT OUT-N-LOCK TECHNIQUE™ is performed. It is not necessary to center the sweet spot of the clubface directly behind the ball during the proceedings. The proceedings may be performed with the clubface placed in the near vicinity of the ball and, once completed, the sweet spot of the clubface then can be centered as near the back of the ball as possible.

The trail foot must be moved laterally outward and away from the target by at least the width of one shoe and until the clubface is rotated fully counterclockwise between the time the grip is completed and the lifeline/ thumb connection is unlocked and relocked twice.

Another discipline necessary to perform the TRAIL FOOT OUT-N-LOCK TECHNIQUE™ correctly is to ensure both elbows are disconnected from the rib cage during the entire proceedings. If either or both elbows are connected to the rib cage during any step in the proceedings to assemble and execute this technique, the forearms will rotate the elbows and clubface to establish a different straight ball flight alignment at the completion of the proceedings.

The SHOULDERS ONLY TEST™, ARMS-LIFT TEST™ and STRAIGHT-UP TEST™ must be conducted at the completion of the proceedings. Considering each step to complete the TRAIL FOOT OUT-N-LOCK TECHNIQUE™ must be performed precisely, it is easy to compromise one or more steps inadvertently in the process.

Once the three tests confirm the TRAIL FOOT OUT-N-LOCK TECHNIQUE™ has been assembled and executed correctly, the sweet spot of the clubface must be centered as near the back of the ball as possible (if not already so centered) and the shoulders simultaneously must be aligned squarely parallel with the shoulders, followed by the execution of a non-manipulative golf swing in order to fly the ball on a straight path in the direction of the target and on a straight path that parallels the shoulder line.

Recommended Practice Routines When Using the Trail Foot Out-N-Lock Technique™ in Combination with the Arrow Alignment Technique™

Prior to using the TRAIL FOOT OUT-N-LOCK TECHNIQUE™ in actual play, you should first engage in some meaningful practice sessions.

You should always select a safe and reasonably flat surface for your practice sessions.

Also, you should follow the steps below in your practice routine when using the TRAIL FOOT OUT-N-LOCK TECHNIQUE™.

STEP 1: Place a ball on the surface of your practice area. Select a specific target as well as identify your intended target line.

STEP 2: Ground the sole of your clubface either directly behind your ball or in the near vicinity of your ball.

STEP 3: Perform the steps to complete the TRAIL FOOT OUT-N-LOCK TECHNIQUE™ as instructed throughout this chapter. Do not allow your clubface to rotate from the time your lead hand is gripped on the club

until your grip is completed. Remember to move your trail foot outward and away from the target by at least the width of one shoe only after your grip is completed but before your lifeline/thumb connection is unlocked and relocked twice.

STEP 4: Once the proceedings are completed, conduct the SHOULDERS ONLY TEST™, ARMS-LIFT TEST™ and STRAIGHT-UP TEST™ to determine whether the technique has been performed correctly. If there is any clubface rotation during the three tests, disassemble the grip and repeat the steps precisely until the three tests confirm the technique has been performed correctly and a straight ball flight alignment has been established and locked-in.

STEP 5: Center the sweet spot of your clubface as near the back of your ball as possible (if not already so centered) and assume a comfortable stance and posture to your ball. Align your shoulders parallel with your intended target to the best of your ability.

STEP 6: Conduct the ARROW ALIGNMENT TECHNIQUE™ and adjust your stance, if necessary, until your alignment arrow points directly at your target when you turn your head and trail eye in the direction of your target <u>as far as possible</u> while immobilizing all other parts of your body.

STEP 7: Ensure the sweet spot of your clubface has remained as near the back of your ball as possible and then execute a non-manipulative golf swing.

If the above steps are performed correctly, your ball should fly on a straight path in the direction of your target.

During your practice sessions, you should begin with your most lofted club and practice with each next most lofted club in succession thereafter until you have practiced with each club in your set. You should begin with a simple wrist swing with each club, followed by a ½ swing, on to a ¾ swing and conclude with a full swing.

SUMMARY POINTS

1. The TRAIL FOOT OUT-N-LOCK TECHNIQUE™ is compatible with all four conventional styles of grip.

2. The first order of business is to ground the sole of the clubface in the middle of the stance.

3. The lead hand must be gripped on the club in a conventional (diagonal) manner. The clubface may not be allowed to rotate during the time the lead hand is gripped on the club.

4. The trail hand then must be gripped on the club either in the form of an original Vardon overlap, modified Vardon overlap, traditional interlock or regular baseball (ten-fingers) style of grip.

5. The clubface may not be allowed to move during the time the trail hand is gripped on the club or between the time the lead and trail hands are gripped on the club.

6. The grip is completed by locking the lifeline of the trail hand squarely and securely on the lead thumb. This is the first of the three "locks" of the lifeline/thumb connection that is necessary to complete the TRAIL FOOT OUT-N-LOCK TECHNIQUE™.

7. Once the grip is completed, the trail foot must be moved outward and away from the target by at least the width of one shoe.

8. **Once the trail foot is moved outward and away from the target by at least the width of one shoe, the lifeline of the trail hand then must be unlocked from the lead thumb by at least an inch without completely ungripping the club and then re-locked on the lead thumb. This is the second of the two "locks" of the lifeline/thumb connection that is necessary to assemble and execute the TRAIL FOOT OUT-N-LOCK TECHNIQUE™.**

9. **Then, once again, the lifeline of the trail hand must be unlocked from the lead thumb by at least an inch without ungripping the club and then, once again, relocked on the lead thumb. This is the third "lock" of the lifeline/thumb connection that is necessary to perform the TRAIL FOOT OUT-N-LOCK TECHNIQUE™.**

10. **Once the proceedings are completed, the SHOULDERS ONLY TEST™, ARMS-LIFT TEST™ and STRAIGHT-UP TEST™ must be conducted to determine if the technique was performed correctly and whether a straight ball flight alignment has been established and locked-in. If not, the grip should be disassembled and the procedure repeated until the three tests confirm such.**

11. **The ARROW ALIGNMENT TECHNIQUE™ should be conducted to align the shoulders squarely parallel with the intended target line when using the TRAIL FOOT OUT-N-LOCK TECHNIQUE™.**

CHAPTER 26

INTRODUCTION OF THE LEAD FOOT IN-N-LOCK TECHNIQUE™

The LEAD FOOT IN-N-LOCK TECHNIQUE™ requires the lead foot to be moved laterally inward and away from the target by at least the width of one shoe and until the clubface rotates fully counterclockwise after a conventional grip is completed but before a double locking of the lifeline/thumb connection.

The LEAD FOOT IN-N-LOCK TECHNIQUE™ is compatible with either an original Vardon overlap, modified Vardon overlap, traditional interlock or regular baseball (ten-fingers) style of grip.

The clubface must not be allowed to rotate clockwise or counterclockwise during the time the lead hand is gripped on the club, during the time the trail hand is gripped on the club or between the time the lead and trail hands are gripped on the club.

How to Assemble and Execute the Lead Foot In-N-Lock Technique™

First, the sole of the clubface should be grounded in the middle of the stance and remain grounded throughout the proceedings to complete the LEAD FOOT IN-N-LOCK TECHNIQUE™.

Second, the lead hand should he gripped on the club in a conventional (diagonal) manner.

Third, the trail hand then must be gripped on the club either in the form of an original Vardon overlap, modified Vardon overlap, traditional interlock or regular baseball (ten-fingers) style of grip. The grip must be completed by locking the lifeline of the trail hand squarely and securely on the lead thumb.

Fourth, once the grip is completed, the lead foot must be moved laterally inward and away from the target by at least the width of one shoe and until the clubface is rotated fully counterclockwise.

Fifth, once the lead foot is moved inward in such manner, the lifeline of the trail hand must be unlocked by at least an inch from the lead thumb without completely ungripping the club and then relocked on the lead thumb. Then, once again, the lifeline/thumb connection must be unlocked and relocked in the same manner. The lead foot then may be moved back to its original position. (Figure 26-1).

Sixth, once the proceedings are completed, the SHOULDERS ONLY TEST™, ARMS-LIFT TEST™ and STRAIGHT-UP TEST™ must be conducted to determine whether a straight ball flight alignment has been established and locked-in. If not confirmed, the procedure should be repeated until a straight ball flight alignment is confirmed as established and locked-in by the three tests.

Why the Lead Foot In-N-Lock Technique™ Works

The LEAD FOOT IN-N-LOCK TECHNIQUE™ works because once the grip is completed and then the lead foot is moved inward and away from the target by at least the width of one shoe, the forearms will rotate the elbows to a parallel alignment with the shoulders to create an on-line swing path of the clubface

When the elbows are rotated to a parallel alignment with the shoulders to create an

Figure 26-1

STEP 1: The first essential step in assembling and executing the LEAD FOOT IN-N-LOCK TECHNIQUE™ is to ground the clubface in the middle of the stance and then assume a conventional grip on the club.

STEP 2: Then the lead foot must be moved laterally inward and away from the target by at least the width of one shoe and until the clubface rotates fully counterclockwise.

STEP 3: While the lead foot remains in such position, the lifeline of the trail hand must be unlocked from the lead thumb without ungripping the club.

STEP 4: Then, while the lead foot continues to remain in such position with the clubface rotated fully counterclockwise, the lifeline of the trail hand must be relocked squarely and securely on the lead thumb.

STEP 5: Then, once again, the lifeline of the trail hand must be unlocked from the lead thumb by at least an inch without ungripping the club while the lead foot remains in such position with the clubface rotated fully counterclockwise.

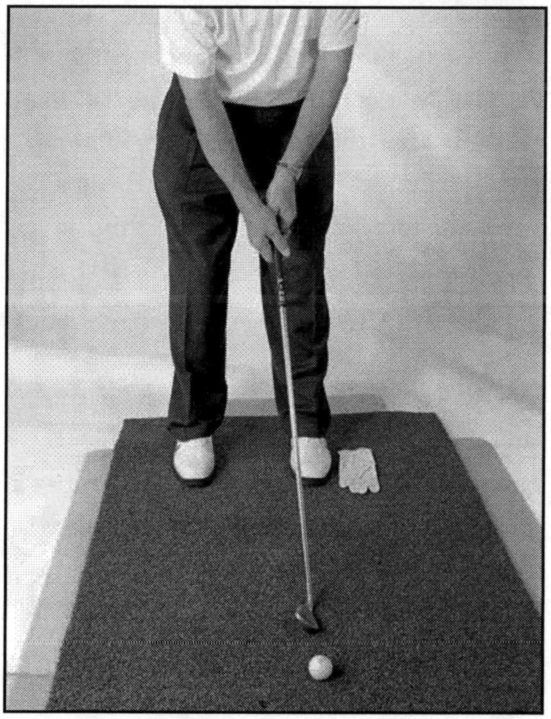

STEP 6: Then, once again, the lifeline of the trail hand must be relocked squarely and securely on the lead thumb while the lead foot remains in such position with the clubface rotated fully counterclockwise. *(The lead foot then may be moved back to its original position.)*

on-line swing path of the clubface the wrists correspondingly will rotate the clubface to a square alignment, all of which will establish a straight ball flight alignment.

However, the straight ball flight alignment will not be locked-in at such point. In order to lock-in the straight ball flight alignment, the lifeline/thumb connection then must be unlocked and relocked twice but no more thereafter.

The LEAD FOOT IN-N-LOCK TECHNIQUE™ requires a total of three "locks" of the lifeline/thumb connection. The first of the three "locks" of the lifeline/thumb connection that is required to complete the LEAD FOOT IN-N-LOCK TECHNIQUE™ occurs when the lifeline of the trail hand is locked on the lead thumb to complete the grip. The second of the three "locks" occurs after the lead foot is moved inward and away from the target by at least the width of one shoe when then the lifeline of the trail hand is unlocked from the lead thumb by at least an inch without completely ungripping the club and then relocked on the lead thumb. The third of the three "locks" occurs when then, once again, the lifeline of the trail hand is unlocked from the lead thumb by at least an inch without completely ungripping the club and then the lifeline of the trail hand once again is relocked on the lead thumb.

Disciplines Necessary to Perform the Lead Foot In-N-Lock Technique™

One of the most important disciplines required to perform the LEAD FOOT IN-N-LOCK TECHNIQUE™ is to move the lead foot inward and away from the target by at least the width of one shoe after a conventional style of grip is assembled on a club but before the lifeline/thumb connection is unlocked and relocked twice to lock-in the straight ball flight alignment.

If the lead foot is moved inward and away in such manner only before the lead hand is gripped on the club, such maneuver will not cause the forearms to rotate the elbows to a parallel alignment with the shoulders nor the wrists and clubface to a square alignment. If the lead foot is moved inward in such manner only after the grip is completed and the lifeline/thumb is unlocked and relocked twice, the forearms will not rotate the wrists, clubface and elbows to establish a straight ball flight alignment.

Therefore, the lead foot must be moved laterally inward and away from the target by at least the width of one shoe and until the clubface rotates fully counterclockwise only after the grip is completed but before the lifeline/thumb connection is unlocked and relocked twice. The lifeline/thumb connection may not be unlocked and relocked thereafter.

If the lifeline/thumb connection is unlocked and relocked an additional time, the forearms will not rotate the wrists, clubface and elbows to establish a straight ball flight alignment.

Another discipline is the sole of the clubface must be grounded throughout the proceedings to complete the LEAD FOOT IN-N-LOCK TECHNIQUE™. The sole of the clubface does not need to be grounded directly behind the ball during the proceedings. It can be grounded in the near vicinity of the ball and once the proceedings are completed and a locked-in straight ball flight alignment is confirmed, the sweet spot of the clubface then can be centered as near the back of the ball as possible.

An additional discipline is there can be no clubface rotation, either clockwise or counterclockwise, during the gripping process. If the clubface is allowed to rotate during the time the lead hand is being gripped on the club, during the time the trail hand is being gripped on the club or between the time the lead and trail hands are gripped on the club, the forearms will not rotate the wrists, clubface and elbows to establish a straight ball flight alignment at the completion of the proceedings.

The elbows must be disconnected from the rib cage during the proceedings. If either or both elbows are connected to the elbows at any time in the proceedings, the forearms will rotate the wrists, clubface and elbows to a different ball flight alignment.

A standard discipline relating to all the LOCKED-IN TECHNIQUES™ addressed in this book, including the LEAD FOOT IN-N-LOCK TECHNIQUE™, is to conduct the SHOULDERS ONLY TEST™, ARMS-LIFT TEST™ and STRAIGHT-UP TEST™ at the completion of the proceedings to determine if the technique was performed correctly and, in turn, whether a straight ball flight alignment has been established and locked-in. If there is any clubface rotation during any of the three tests, the proceedings should be abandoned and the procedure repeated until a properly assembled and executed technique is confirmed.

Once the three tests confirm a properly assembled and executed LEAD FOOT IN-N-LOCK TECHNIQUE™ and a straight ball flight alignment has been established and locked-in, the sweet spot of the clubface must be centered as near the back of the ball as possible (if not already so centered) and the shoulders simultaneously must be aligned squarely parallel with the intended target line, followed by the execution of a non-manipulative golf swing.

Recommended Practice Routines When Using the Lead Foot In-N-Lock Technique™ in Combination with the Arrow Alignment Technique™

Before using the LEAD FOOT IN-N-LOCK TECHNIQUE™, you should engage in some meaningful practice sessions. In each of your practice sessions, you should locate a safe and reasonably flat practice surface.

You also should conduct the ARROW ALIGNMENT TECHNIQUE™ to align your shoulders squarely parallel with your intended target line when using the LEAD FOOT IN-N-LOCK TECHNIQUE™.

Here are the steps you should follow during your practice sessions:

STEP 1: **Place a ball on the surface of your hitting area. Identify your target as well as your intended target line.**

STEP 2: **Ground the sole of your clubface and keep it grounded throughout the proceedings. Whether the sole of the clubface is grounded directly behind your ball or in its near vicinity, it should be grounded in the middle of the stance during the proceedings.**

STEP 3: **Perform the steps to complete the LEAD FOOT IN-N-LOCK TECHNIQUE™, as instructed throughout this chapter. Remember to complete your grip by locking the lifeline of your trail hand squarely and firmly on your lead thumb. Remember also to move your lead foot laterally inward and away from the target by at least the width of one shoe and until your clubface rotates fully counterclockwise once your grip is completed and then unlock and relock your lifeline/thumb connection twice but no more thereafter.**

STEP 4: **Conduct the SHOULDERS ONLY TEST™, ARMS-LIFT TEST™ and STRAIGHT-UP TEST™ and repeat the proceedings, if necessary, until the three tests confirm the technique was assembled and executed correctly and a straight ball flight alignment has been established and locked-in.**

STEP 5: **Once the three tests confirm a straight ball flight alignment has been established and locked-in, center the sweet spot of your clubface as near the back of your ball as possible (if not already so centered). Assume a comfortable posture and stance to your ball and align your shoulders parallel with your intended target line to the best of your ability.**

STEP 6: **Conduct the ARROW ALIGNMENT TECHNIQUE™ and adjust your stance, if necessary, until your alignment arrow points directly at your target when you turn your head and trail eye in the direction of your**

target as far as possible while immobilizing all other parts of your body.

STEP 7: Ensure the sweet spot of your clubface has remained centered as near the back of your ball as possible and then execute a non-manipulative golf swing.

You should begin with your most lofted club and practice with each next most lofted club in succession thereafter until you have practiced with each club in your set. You should begin with a simple wrist swing with each club, followed by a ½ swing, on to a ¾ swing and conclude with a full swing.

SUMMARY POINTS

1. **The LEAD FOOT IN-N-LOCK TECHNIQUE™ requires the lead foot to be moved laterally inward and away from the target by at least the width of one shoe after a conventional style of grip is assembled on a club.**

2. **The lead hand must be gripped on the club in a conventional (diagonal) manner and there must not be any clubface rotation allowed during the gripping process.**

3. **The trail hand must be gripped on the club in the form of an original Vardon overlap, modified Vardon overlap, traditional interlock or regular baseball (ten-fingers) style of grip.**

4. **There also must not be any clubface rotation allowed – either clockwise or counterclockwise – during the time the trail hand is gripped on the club or between the time the lead hand and trail hand are gripped on the club.**

5. **The grip is completed by locking the lifeline of the trail hand squarely and securely on the lead thumb. This constitutes the first of the three "locks" of the lifeline/thumb connection that is necessary to complete the LEAD FOOT IN-N-LOCK TECHNIQUE™.**

6. **The lead foot must be moved laterally inward and away from the target by at least the width of one shoe once the grip is completed and then the lifeline/thumb connection must be unlocked and relocked twice but no more thereafter. This**

constitutes the second and third of the three "locks" of the lifeline/thumb connection that are necessary to complete the LEAD FOOT IN-N-LOCK TECHNIQUE™.

7. **Once the proceedings are completed, the SHOULDERS ONLY TEST™, ARMS-LIFT TEST™ and STRAIGHT-UP TEST™ must be conducted to determine whether the technique was performed correctly and whether a straight ball flight alignment has been established and locked-in. If not, the proceedings should be repeated until such is confirmed.**

8. **The ARROW ALIGNMENT TECHNIQUE™ should be conducted to align the shoulders squarely parallel with the intended target line when using the LEAD FOOT IN-N-LOCK TECHNIQUE™.**

CHAPTER 27

INTRODUCTION OF THE TRAIL FOOT IN-N-LOCK TECHNIQUE™

The TRAIL FOOT IN-N-LOCK TECHNIQUE™ requires the trail foot to be moved inward laterally toward the target by at least the width of one shoe and until the clubface rotates fully clockwise after a conventional grip is completed but before a single locking of the lifeline/thumb connection.

The TRAIL FOOT IN-N-LOCK TECHNIQUE™ is compatible with either an original Vardon overlap, modified Vardon overlap, traditional interlock or regular baseball (ten-fingers) style of grip.

The clubface must not be allowed to rotate clockwise or counterclockwise during the time the lead hand is gripped on the club, during the time the trail hand is gripped on the club or between the time the lead and trail hand are gripped on the club.

How to Assemble and Execute the Trail Foot In-N-Lock Technique™

First, the sole of the clubface should be grounded in the middle of the stance and remain grounded throughout the proceedings.

Second, the lead hand should he gripped on the club in a conventional (diagonal) manner.

Third, the trail hand then must be gripped on the club either in the form of an original Vardon overlap, modified Vardon overlap, traditional interlock or regular baseball (ten-fingers) style of grip. The grip must be completed by locking the lifeline of the trail hand squarely and securely on the lead thumb.

Fourth, once the grip is completed, the trail foot must be moved laterally toward the target by at least the width of one shoe and until the clubface rotates fully clockwise.

Fifth, once the trail foot is moved inward in such manner, the lifeline of the trail hand must be unlocked by at least an inch from the lead thumb without completely ungripping the club and then relocked on the lead thumb. The trail foot then may be moved back to its original position. (Figure 27-1).

Sixth, once the proceedings are completed, the SHOULDERS ONLY TEST™, ARMS-LIFT TEST™ and STRAIGHT-UP TEST™ must be conducted to determine whether a straight ball flight alignment has been established and locked-in. If not confirmed, the procedure should be repeated until a straight ball flight alignment is confirmed as established and locked-in by the three tests.

Why the Trail Foot In-N-Lock Technique™ Works

The TRAIL FOOT IN-N-LOCK TECHNIQUE™ works because once the grip is completed and then the trail foot is moved laterally inward toward the target by at least the width of one shoe and until the clubface rotates fully clockwise, the forearms will rotate the elbows to a parallel alignment with the shoulders to create an on-line swing path of the clubface.

When the elbows are rotated to a parallel alignment with the shoulders to create an on-line swing path of the clubface the wrists correspondingly will rotate the clubface to a square alignment, all of which will establish a straight ball flight alignment.

Figure 27-1

STEP 1: The first essential step to assemble and execute the TRAIL FOOT IN-N-LOCK TECHNIQUE™ is to ground the clubface in the middle of the stance and then assume a conventional grip on the club.

STEP 2: Then the trail foot must be moved laterally inward toward the target by at least the width of one shoe and until the clubface rotates fully clockwise.

STEP 3: Then, while the trail foot remains in such position, the lifeline of the trail hand must be unlocked from the lead thumb by at least an inch without completely ungripping the club.

STEP 4: Then the lifeline of the trail hand must be relocked squarely and securely on the lead thumb. *(The trail foot then may be moved back to its original position.)*

However, the straight ball flight alignment will not be locked-in at such point. In order to lock-in the straight ball flight alignment, the lifeline/thumb connection then must be unlocked and relocked once. It may not be unlocked and relocked thereafter.

The TRAIL FOOT IN-N-LOCK TECHNIQUE™ requires a total of two"locks" of the lifeline/thumb connection. The first of the two "locks" of the lifeline/thumb connection that is required to complete the TRAIL FOOT IN-N-LOCK TECHNIQUE™ occurs when the lifeline of the trail hand is locked on the lead thumb to complete the grip. The second of the two "locks" occurs after the trail foot is moved laterally inward toward the target by at least the width of one shoe when then the lifeline of the trail hand is unlocked from the lead thumb by at least an inch without completely ungripping the club and then relocked on the lead thumb.

Disciplines Necessary to Perform the Trail Foot In-N-Lock Technique™

One of the most important disciplines required to perform the TRAIL FOOT IN-N-LOCK TECHNIQUE™ is to move the trail foot laterally inward toward the target by at least the width of one shoe after a conventional style of grip is assembled on a club but before the lifeline/thumb connection is unlocked and relocked once.

If the trail foot is moved inward in such manner only before the lead hand is gripped on the club, such maneuver will not cause the forearms to rotate the elbows to a parallel alignment with the shoulders nor the wrists and clubface to a square alignment. If the trail foot is moved inward in such manner only after the grip is completed and the lifeline/thumb is unlocked and relocked once, the forearms will not rotate the wrists, clubface and elbows to establish a straight ball flight alignment.

Therefore, the trail foot must be moved inward in such manner only after the grip is completed but before the lifeline/thumb connection is unlocked and relocked. The lifeline/thumb connection must be unlocked and relocked only once and no more thereafter. If the lifeline/thumb connection is unlocked and relocked an additional time, the forearms will not rotate the wrists, clubface and elbows to establish a straight ball flight alignment.

Another discipline is the sole of the clubface must be grounded throughout the proceedings. However, the sole of the clubface does not need to be grounded directly behind the ball during the proceedings. It may be grounded in the near vicinity of the ball and once the proceedings are completed and a locked-in straight ball flight alignment is confirmed, the sweet spot of the clubface then can be centered as near the back of the ball as possible.

An additional discipline is there must not be any clubface rotation, either clockwise or counterclockwise, during the gripping process. If the clubface is allowed to rotate during the time the lead hand is gripped on the club, during the time the trail hand is gripped on the club or between the time the lead and trail hand are gripped on the club, the forearms will not rotate the wrists, clubface and elbows to establish a straight ball flight alignment at the completion of the proceedings.

The elbows must be disconnected from the rib cage during the proceedings. If either or both elbows are connected to the elbows at any time during the proceedings, the forearms will rotate the wrists, clubface and elbows to a different ball flight alignment.

The SHOULDERS ONLY TEST™, ARMS-LIFT TEST™ and STRAIGHT-UP TEST™ must be conducted at the completion of the proceedings to determine if the technique was performed correctly and, in turn, whether a straight ball flight alignment has been established and locked-in. If there is any clubface rotation during any of the three tests, the grip should be disassembled and the procedure repeated until a properly performed technique is confirmed.

Once the three tests confirm a properly assembled and executed TRAIL FOOT IN-N-LOCK TECHNIQUE™ and a straight ball flight alignment has been established and locked-in, the sweet spot of the clubface must be centered as near the back of the ball as possible (if not already so centered) and the shoulders simultaneously must be aligned squarely parallel with the intended target line, followed by the execution of a non-manipulative golf swing.

Recommended Practice Routines When Using the Trail Foot In-N-Lock Technique™ in Combination with the Arrow Alignment Technique™

Before using the TRAIL FOOT IN-N-LOCK TECHNIQUE™ in actual play, you should engage in some meaningful practice sessions. In each of your practice sessions, you should locate a safe and reasonably flat practice surface.

You should conduct the ARROW ALIGNMENT TECHNIQUE™ to align your shoulders squarely parallel with your intended target line when using the TRAIL FOOT IN-N-LOCK TECHNIQUE™.

You also should follow these steps during your practice sessions:

STEP 1: Place a ball on the surface of your hitting area. Identify your target as well as your intended target line.

STEP 2: Ground the sole of your clubface and keep it grounded throughout the proceedings. Whether the sole of your clubface is grounded directly behind your ball or in its near vicinity, it should be grounded in the middle of your stance during the proceedings.

STEP 3: Perform the steps to complete the TRAIL FOOT IN-N-LOCK TECHNIQUE™, as instructed throughout this chapter. Remember to complete your grip by locking the lifeline of the trail hand squarely and firmly on your lead thumb. Remember also to move your trail foot inward toward the target by at least the width of one shoe once your grip is completed and then unlock and relock your lifeline/thumb connection once.

STEP 4: Conduct the SHOULDERS ONLY TEST™, ARMS-LIFT TEST™ and STRAIGHT-UP TEST™ and repeat the proceedings, if necessary, until the three tests confirm the TRAIL FOOT IN-N-LOCK TECHNIQUE™ was assembled and executed correctly and a straight ball flight alignment has been established and locked-in.

STEP 5: Once the three tests confirm a straight ball flight alignment has been established and locked-in, center the sweet spot of your clubface as near the back of your ball as possible (if not already so centered). Assume a comfortable posture and stance to your ball and align your shoulders parallel with your intended target line to the best of your ability.

STEP 6: Conduct the ARROW ALIGNMENT TECHNIQUE™ and adjust your stance, if necessary, until your alignment arrow points directly at your target when you turn your head and trail eye in the direction of your target <u>as far as possible</u> while immobilizing all other parts of your body.

STEP 7: Ensure the sweet spot of your clubface has remained centered as near the back of your ball as possible and then execute a non-manipulative golf swing.

You should begin with your most lofted club and practice with each next most lofted club in succession thereafter until you have practiced with each club in your set. You should begin with a simple wrist swing with each club, followed by a ½ swing, on to a ¾ swing and conclude with a full swing.

SUMMARY POINTS

1. The TRAIL FOOT IN-N-LOCK TECHNIQUE™ requires the trail foot to be moved inward toward the target by at least the width of one shoe after a conventional style of grip is assembled on a club.

2. The lead hand must be gripped on the club in a conventional (diagonal) manner and there must not be any clubface rotation allowed during the gripping process.

3. The trail hand must be gripped on the club in the form of an original Vardon overlap, modified Vardon overlap, traditional interlock or regular baseball (ten-fingers) style of grip.

4. There also must not be any clubface rotation allowed – either clockwise or counterclockwise – during the time the trail hand is gripped on the club or between the time the lead hand and trail hand are gripped on the club.

5. The grip is completed by locking the lifeline of the trail hand squarely and securely on the lead thumb. This constitutes the first of the two "locks" of the lifeline/thumb connection that is necessary to complete the TRAIL FOOT IN-N-LOCK TECHNIQUE™.

6. The trail foot must be moved inward toward the target by at least the width of one shoe once the grip is completed and then the lifeline/thumb connection must be unlocked and relocked once but no more thereafter. This constitutes the

second of the two "locks" of the lifeline/thumb connection that is necessary to complete the TRAIL FOOT IN-N-LOCK TECHNIQUE™.

7. **Once the proceedings are completed, the SHOULDERS ONLY TEST™, ARMS-LIFT TEST™ and STRAIGHT-UP TEST™ must be conducted to determine whether the technique was performed correctly and whether a straight ball flight alignment has been established and locked-in. If not confirmed, the proceedings should be repeated until such is confirmed.**

8. **The ARROW ALIGNMENT TECHNIQUE™ should be conducted to align the shoulders squarely parallel with the intended target line when using the TRAIL FOOT IN-N-LOCK TECHNIQUE™.**

CHAPTER 28

INTRODUCTION OF THE LEAD FOOT BACK-N-LOCK TECHNIQUE™

The LEAD FOOT BACK-N-LOCK TECHNIQUE™ requires the sole of the clubface to be grounded throughout the procedure.

It also requires the lead foot to be moved back from the initial stance line by at least the length of one shoe after a conventional style of grip is assumed on a club.

The LEAD FOOT BACK-N-LOCK TECHNIQUE™ is compatible with the original Vardon overlap, modified Vardon overlap, traditional interlock and regular baseball (ten-finger) styles of grip.

How to Assemble the Lead Foot Back-N-Lock Technique™

First, the clubface should be grounded and remain grounded throughout the proceedings. The clubface does not necessarily need to be grounded directly behind the ball during the proceedings to assemble and execute the LEAD FOOT BACK-N-LOCK TECHNIQUE™. It may be grounded near its vicinity during the procedure and, once the proceedings are completed, the sweet spot of the clubface then may be centered as near the back of the ball as possible.

Second, the lead hand must be gripped on a club in a conventional (diagonal) manner without allowing any clubface rotation during such time.

Third, the trail hand then must be gripped on the club either in the form of an original Vardon overlap, modified Vardon overlap, traditional interlock or regular baseball (ten-fingers) style of grip without allowing the clubface to rotate clockwise or counterclockwise during the gripping process. The lifeline of the trail hand must be locked squarely and securely on the lead thumb to complete the grip.

Fourth, then the lead foot must be moved back from the initial stance line by at least the length of one shoe.

Fifth, once the lead foot is moved back from the initial stance line by at least the length of one shoe, the lifeline of the trail hand must be unlocked from the lead thumb by at least an inch without completely ungripping the club and then the trail lifeline must be relocked on the lead thumb. The lead foot then may be moved back to its original position. (Figure 28-1).

Sixth, at the completion of the proceedings, the SHOULDERS ONLY TEST™, ARMS-LIFT TEST™, and STRAIGHT-UP TEST™ must be conducted to determine whether the technique has established and locked-in a straight ball flight alignment. If there is any clubface rotation during any of the three tests, the grip should be disassembled and the procedure repeated until the three tests confirm a straight ball flight alignment has been established and locked-in.

Why the Lead Foot Back-N-Lock Technique™ Works

When the lead foot is moved back from the initial stance line by at least the length of one shoe after a conventional style of grip is formed on a club, the forearms will rotate the elbows to a parallel alignment with the shoulders to create an on-line swing path of the clubface. In turn, the wrists correspondingly will rotate the clubface to a square alignment, all of which will establish a straight ball flight alignment.

Figure 28-1

STEP 1: The first essential step to assemble and execute the LEAD FOOT BACK-N-LOCK TECHNIQUE™ is to ground the clubface in the middle of the stance and then assume a conventional style of grip on the club.

STEP 2: Then move the lead foot back from the stance line by at least the length of one shoe.

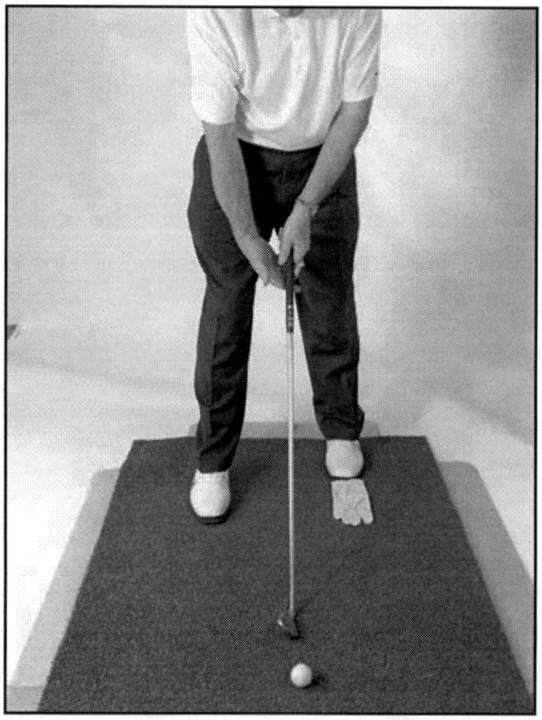

STEP 3: While the lead foot is moved back from the stance line by at least the length of one shoe, unlock the lifeline of the trail hand from the lead thumb by at least an inch without ungripping the club.

STEP 4: Then relock the lifeline of the trail hand squarely and securely on the lead thumb while the lead foot remains in such position. *(The lead foot then may be moved forward to its original position.)*

When then the lifeline/thumb connection is unlocked and relocked, the straight ball flight alignment will be locked-in.

The LEAD FOOT BACK-N-LOCK TECHNIQUE™ requires a total of two "locks" of the lifeline/thumb connection.

The first of the two "locks" of the lifeline/thumb connection that is required to assemble and execute the LEAD FOOT BACK-N-LOCK TECHNIQUE™ occurs when the lifeline of the trail hand is locked squarely and securely on the lead thumb to complete the grip. The second of the two "locks" of the lifeline/thumb connection occurs after the lead foot is moved back from the initial stance line by at least the length of one shoe when then the lifeline of the trail hand is unlocked from the trail thumb by at least an inch without completely ungripping the club and then the lifeline of the trail hand is relocked on trail thumb.

Disciplines Required to Assemble the Lead Foot Back-N-Lock Technique™

The first discipline is the sole of the clubface must be grounded throughout the proceedings. Preferably, the sole of the clubface should be grounded in the middle of the stance during the proceedings.

Another discipline associated with the assemblage and execution of the LEAD FOOT BACK-N-LOCK TECHNIQUE™ is the lead hand must be assembled on the club in a conventional (diagonal) manner. If the lead hand assumes a "fingers-only" type of grip, the forearms will not rotate the elbows and clubface to establish a straight ball flight alignment when the lead foot is moved back from the initial stance line.

Neither elbow may be connected to the rib cage during the proceedings. If either or both elbows are connected to the rib cage during the proceedings the forearms will not rotate the wrists, clubface and elbows to establish a straight ball flight alignment at the completion of the proceedings.

An additional discipline is the lifeline/thumb connection must be unlocked and relocked only once after the lead foot is moved back from the initial stance line – but no more thereafter. If the lifeline/thumb connection is unlocked and relocked once more thereafter the forearms will not rotate the wrists, clubface and elbows to establish a straight ball flight alignment at the completion of the proceedings.

Another discipline is once the proceedings are completed, the SHOULDERS ONLY TEST™, ARMS-LIFT TEST™ and STRAIGHT-UP TEST™ must be conducted to determine if the technique has been properly assembled and executed. If there is any counterclockwise or clockwise rotation of the clubface during any of the three tests, the grip should be disassembled and the procedure repeated until a properly assembled and executed LEAD FOOT BACK-N-LOCK TECHNIQUE™ is confirmed.

Establishing and locking-in a straight ball flight alignment is just part of what must be achieved during the pre-swing procedure if the objective is to flight the ball on a straight path to a specific target. Once a locked-in straight ball flight alignment has been confirmed, the sweet spot of the clubface then must be centered as near the back of the ball as possible (if not already so centered) and the shoulders simultaneously must be aligned squarely parallel with the intended target line, followed by a non-manipulative golf swing.

The easiest and most reliable way to align the shoulders squarely parallel with the intended target line during the pre-swing routine is to utilize the ARROW ALIGNMENT TECHNIQUE™.

Recommended Practice Routines When Using the Lead Foot Back-N-Lock Technique™ in Combination with the Arrow Alignment Technique™

You should always select a safe and relatively flat hitting area when using a combination of the LEAD FOOT BACK-N-LOCK TECHNIQUE™ and the ARROW ALIGNMENT TECHNIQUE™ in your practice routines.

Here are the steps recommended during your practice sessions:

STEP 1: Place a ball on the surface of your practice area. Identify a narrow and specific target. Also identify your intended target line.

STEP 2: Ground the sole of your clubface in the middle of your stance and keep it grounded throughout the proceedings. Remember it does not need to be grounded directly behind your ball when assembling and executing the LEAD FOOT BACK-N-LOCK TECHNIQUE™. It may be grounded in the vicinity of the ball and then the sweet spot of the clubface later can be centered as near the back of the ball as possible once the proceedings are completed.

STEP 3: Assemble and execute the LEAD FOOT BACK-N-LOCK TECHNIQUE™ in accordance with the instructions in this chapter. Remember to move the lead foot back from the initial stance line by at least the length of one shoe after assuming a conventional style of grip on the club. Then the lifeline/thumb connection must be unlocked and relocked once but no more thereafter.

STEP 4: Conduct the SHOULDERS ONLY TEST™, ARMS-LIFT TEST™ and the STRAIGHT-UP TEST™ once the proceedings are completed. If there is any clubface rotation, either clockwise or counterclockwise during any of the tests, disassemble the grip and repeat the procedure until the three tests confirm the technique was assembled and executed correctly and a straight ball flight alignment has been established and locked-in.

STEP 5: Center the sweet spot of your clubface as near the back of your ball as possible (if not already so centered) and then assume a comfortable posture and stance to the ball. Align your shoulders squarely parallel with your intended target line to the best of your ability.

STEP 6: Conduct the ARROW ALIGNMENT TECHNIQUE™ and adjust your stance, if necessary, until your alignment arrow points directly at your target when you turn your head and trail eye in the direction of your target as far as possible. Remember to immobilize all parts of your body except your head and trail eye when conducting the ARROW ALIGNMENT TECHNIQUE™.

STEP 7: Ensure the sweet spot of your clubface has remained centered as near the back of your ball as possible and then execute a non-manipulative golf swing.

You should begin each practice session with your most lofted club and then with each next most lofted club thereafter until you have practiced with each club in your set. With each respective club, you should begin with a wrist swing, then with a ½ swing, on to a ¾ swing and conclude with a full swing.

SUMMARY POINTS

1. The LEAD FOOT BACK-N-LOCK TECHNIQUE™ requires the lead foot to be moved back from the initial stance line by at least the length of one shoe after a conventional style of grip is assembled on a club.

2. It requires the lead hand to be gripped on a club in a conventional (diagonal) manner. There must not be any clubface rotation while the lead hand is being gripped on a club.

3. It then requires either an original Vardon overlap, modified Vardon overlap, traditional interlock or regular baseball (ten-fingers) style of grip be formed on a club with the trail hand without allowing any clubface rotation during the process.

4. The grip must be completed by locking the lifeline of the trail hand squarely and securely on the lead thumb.

5. After a conventional style of grip is assembled on a club, the lead foot must be moved back from the initial stance line by at least the length of the one shoe.

6. Once the lead foot is moved back in such manner, the lifeline of the trail hand must be unlocked from the lead thumb by at least an inch and then relocked on the lead thumb. The lifeline/thumb connection may not be unlocked and relocked thereafter.

7. The clubface must be grounded in the middle of the stance during the proceedings.

8. The LEAD FOOT BACK-N-LOCK TECHNIQUE™ is compatible with all four conventional styles of grip.

9. Once the proceedings are completed, the SHOULDERS ONLY TEST™, ARMS-LIFT TEST™ and STRAIGHT-UP TEST™ must be conducted to determine if the technique has been assembled and executed correctly. If not, the grip should be disassembled and the procedure repeated until so confirmed.

10. The LEAD FOOT BACK-N-LOCK TECHNIQUE™ should be used in combination with the ARROW ALIGNMENT TECHNIQUE™ to ensure the shoulders are aligned squarely parallel with the intended target line at the completion of the pre-swing proceedings.

CHAPTER 29

INTRODUCTION OF THE TRAIL FOOT BACK-N-LOCK TECHNIQUE™

The TRAIL FOOT BACK-N-LOCK TECHNIQUE™ requires the sole of the clubface to be grounded throughout the procedure.

It also requires the trail foot to be moved back from the initial stance line by at least the length of one shoe after a conventional style of grip is assumed on a club.

The TRAIL FOOT BACK-N-LOCK TECHNIQUE™ is compatible with the original Vardon overlap, modified Vardon overlap, traditional interlock and regular baseball (ten-finger) styles of grip.

How to Assemble the Trail Foot Back-N-Lock Technique™

First, the clubface should be grounded and remain grounded throughout the proceedings. The clubface does not necessarily need to be grounded directly behind the ball during the proceedings to assemble and execute the TRAIL FOOT BACK-N-LOCK TECHNIQUE™. It may be grounded near its vicinity during the procedure and, once the proceedings are completed, the sweet spot of the clubface then may be centered as near the back of the ball as possible.

Second, the lead hand must be gripped on a club in a conventional (diagonal) manner without allowing any clubface rotation during such time.

Third, the trail hand then must be gripped on the club either in the form of an original Vardon overlap, modified Vardon overlap, traditional interlock or regular baseball (ten-fingers) style of grip without allowing the clubface to rotate clockwise or counterclockwise during the gripping process or between the time the lead hand and trail hand are gripped on the club.

The lifeline of the trail hand must be locked squarely and securely on the lead thumb to complete the grip.

Fourth, then the trail foot must be moved back from the initial stance line by the length of one shoe.

Fifth, once the trail foot is moved back from the initial stance line by at least the length of one shoe, the lifeline of the trail hand must be unlocked from the lead thumb by at least an inch without completely ungripping the club and then the trail lifeline must be relocked on the lead thumb. Then, once again, the lifeline/thumb connection must be unlocked and relocked in the same manner. The trail foot then may be moved forward to its original position. (Figure 29-1).

Sixth, at the completion of the proceedings, the SHOULDERS ONLY TEST™, ARMS-LIFT TEST™, and STRAIGHT-UP TEST™ must be conducted to determine whether the technique has established and locked-in a straight ball flight alignment. If there is any clubface rotation during any of the three tests, the grip should be disassembled and the procedure repeated until the tests confirm a straight ball flight alignment has been established and locked-in.

Why the Trail Foot Back-N-Lock Technique™ Works

When the trail foot is moved back from the initial stance line by at least the length of one shoe after a conventional style of grip

Figure 29-1

STEP 1: The first essential step to assemble and execute the TRAIL FOOT BACK-N-LOCK TECHNIQUE™ is to ground the clubface in the middle of the stance and then assume a conventional style of grip on the club.

STEP 2: Then move the trail foot back from the stance line by at least the length of one shoe.

STEP 3: Then unlock the lifeline of the trail hand from the lead thumb by at least one inch without completely ungripping the club while the trail foot is moved back from the stance line.

STEP 4: While the trail foot remains in such position, relock the lifeline of the trail hand squarely and securely on the lead thumb.

STEP 5: Then, once again, unlock the lifeline of the trail hand from the lead thumb by at least an inch without completely ungripping the club while the trail foot remains in such position.

STEP 6: Then, once again, relock the lifeline of the trail hand squarely and securely on the lead thumb while the trail foot remains in such position. *(Then the trail foot may be moved forward to its original position.)*

is formed on a club, the forearms will rotate the elbows to a parallel alignment with the shoulders to create an on-line swing path of the clubface. In turn, the wrists correspondingly will rotate the clubface to a square alignment, all of which will establish a straight ball flight alignment.

When then the lifeline/thumb connection is unlocked and relocked twice the straight ball flight alignment will be locked-in.

The TRAIL FOOT BACK-N-LOCK TECHNIQUE™ requires a total of three "locks" of the lifeline/thumb connection.

The first of the three "locks" of the lifeline/thumb connection that is required to assemble and execute the TRAIL FOOT BACK-N-LOCK TECHNIQUE™ occurs when the lifeline of the trail hand is locked squarely and securely on the lead thumb to complete the grip. The second of the three "locks" of the lifeline/thumb connection occurs after the trail foot is moved back from the initial stance line by at least the length of one shoe when then the lifeline of the trail hand is unlocked from the trail thumb by at least an inch without completely ungripping the club and then the lifeline of the trail hand is relocked on trail thumb. The third of the three "locks" occurs when then, once again, the lifeline/thumb connection is unlocked and relocked in the same manner.

Disciplines Required to Assemble the Trail Foot Back-N-Lock Technique™

The first discipline is the sole of the clubface must be grounded throughout the proceedings when assembling the TRAIL FOOT BACK-N-LOCK TECHNIQUE™.

Another discipline associated with the assemblage and execution of the TRAIL FOOT BACK-N-LOCK TECHNIQUE™ is the lead hand must be assembled on the club in a conventional (diagonal) manner. If the lead hand assumes a "fingers-only" type of grip, the forearms will not rotate the wrists, clubface and elbows to establish a straight ball flight alignment at the completion of the proceedings.

Neither elbow may be connected to the rib cage during the proceedings to assemble and execute the TRAIL FOOT BACK-N-LOCK TECHNIQUE™. If either or both elbows are connected to the rib cage during the proceedings the forearms will not rotate the wrists, clubface and elbows to establish a straight ball flight alignment at the completion of the proceedings.

An additional discipline is the lifeline/thumb connection must be unlocked and relocked twice after the trail foot is moved back from the initial stance line. If the lifeline/thumb connection is unlocked and relocked once more thereafter the forearms will not rotate the wrists, clubface and elbows to establish a straight ball flight alignment at the completion of the proceedings.

Another discipline is once the proceedings are completed, the SHOULDERS ONLY TEST™, ARMS-LIFT TEST™ and STRAIGHT-UP TEST™ must be conducted to determine if the technique was properly assembled and executed. If there is any counterclockwise or clockwise rotation of the clubface during any of the three tests, the grip should be disassembled and the procedure repeated until a properly assembled and executed TRAIL FOOT BACK-N-LOCK TECHNIQUE™ is confirmed.

Establishing and locking-in a straight ball flight alignment is just part of what must be achieved during the pre-swing procedure if the objective is to flight the ball on a straight path to a specific target. Once a locked-in straight ball flight alignment has been confirmed, the sweet spot of the clubface then must be centered as near the back of the ball as possible (if not already so centered) and the shoulders simultaneously must be aligned squarely parallel with the intended target line, followed by a non-manipulative golf swing.

The easiest and most reliable way to align the shoulders squarely parallel with the intended target line during the pre-swing routine is to utilize the ARROW ALIGNMENT TECHNIQUE™.

Recommended Practice Routines When Using the Trail Foot Back-N-Lock Technique™ in Combination with the Arrow Alignment Technique™

You should always select a safe and relatively flat hitting area when using a combination of the TRAIL FOOT BACK-N-LOCK TECHNIQUE™ and the ARROW ALIGNMENT TECHNIQUE™ in your practice routines.

Here are the steps recommended during your practice sessions:

STEP 1: Place a ball on the surface of your practice area. Identify a narrow and specific target. Also identify your intended target line.

STEP 2: Ground the sole of your clubface in the middle of your stance and keep it grounded throughout the proceedings.

STEP 3: Assemble and execute the TRAIL FOOT BACK-N-LOCK TECHNIQUE™ in accordance with the instructions in this chapter. Remember to move the trail foot back from your initial stance line by

at least the length of one shoe after assuming a conventional style of grip on the club. Once your trail foot has been moved back from the original stance line by such distance, remember to unlock and relock your lifeline/thumb connection twice – but no more thereafter.

STEP 4: **Conduct the SHOULDERS ONLY TEST™, ARMS-LIFT TEST™ and the STRAIGHT-UP TEST™ once the proceedings are completed. If there is any clubface rotation, either clockwise or counterclockwise during any of the tests, disassemble the grip and repeat the procedure until the three tests confirm the technique has been assembled and executed correctly and a straight ball flight alignment has been established and locked-in.**

STEP 5: **Center the sweet spot of your clubface as near the back of your ball as possible (if not already so centered) and then assume a comfortable posture and stance to the ball. Align your shoulders squarely parallel with your intended target line to the best of your ability.**

STEP 6: **Conduct the ARROW ALIGNMENT TECHNIQUE™ and adjust your stance, if necessary, until your alignment arrow points directly at your target when you turn your head and trail eye in the direction of your target as far as possible. Remember to immobilize all parts of your body except your head and trail eye when conducting the ARROW ALIGNMENT TECHNIQUE™.**

STEP 7: **Ensure the sweet spot of your clubface has remained centered as near the back of your ball as possible and then execute a non-manipulative golf swing.**

You should begin each practice session with your most lofted club and then with each next most lofted club thereafter until you have practiced with each club in your set. With each respective club, you should begin with a wrist swing, then with a ½ swing, on to a ¾ swing and conclude with a full swing.

SUMMARY POINTS

1. **The TRAIL FOOT BACK-N-LOCK TECHNIQUE™ requires the trail foot to be moved back from the initial stance line by at least the length of one shoe after a conventional style of grip is assembled on a club.**

2. **The TRAIL FOOT BACK-N-LOCK TECHNIQUE™ requires the lead hand to be gripped on a club in a conventional (diagonal) manner. There must not be any clubface rotation while the lead hand is being gripped on a club.**

3. **The technique then requires either an original Vardon overlap, modified Vardon overlap, traditional interlock or regular baseball (ten-fingers) style of grip to be formed on a club with the trail hand without allowing any clubface rotation during the process.**

4. **The grip must be completed by locking the lifeline of the trail hand squarely and securely on the lead thumb.**

5. **After a conventional style of grip is assembled on a club, the trail foot must be moved back from the initial stance line by at least the length of the one shoe.**

6. **Once the trail foot is moved back in such manner, the lifeline of the trail hand must be unlocked from the lead thumb by at least an inch and then relocked on the lead thumb. Then, once again, the lifeline/thumb connection must be unlocked and relocked in the same manner.**

7. **The clubface must be grounded in the middle of the stance during the proceedings.**

8. **The TRAIL FOOT BACK-N-LOCK TECHNIQUE™ is compatible with all four conventional styles of grip.**

9. **Once the proceedings are completed, the SHOULDERS ONLY TEST™, ARMS-LIFT TEST™ and STRAIGHT-UP TEST™ must be conducted to determine if the technique has been assembled and executed correctly. If not, the grip should be disassembled and the procedure repeated until so confirmed.**

10. **The TRAIL LEAD FOOT BACK-N-LOCK TECHNIQUE™ should be used in combination with the ARROW ALIGNMENT TECHNIQUE™ to ensure the shoulders are aligned squarely parallel with the intended target line at the completion of the pre-swing proceedings.**

CHAPTER 30

INTRODUCTION OF THE LEAD FOOT FORWARD-N-LOCK TECHNIQUE™

The LEAD FOOT FORWARD-N-LOCK TECHNIQUE™ requires the lead foot to be moved forward of the initial stance line by at least the length of one shoe after a conventional style of grip is formed on a club.

It requires the sole of the clubface to be grounded during the entire proceedings. After the lead foot is moved forward of the initial stance line by at least the length of one shoe, it then requires the lifeline/thumb connection to be unlocked and re-locked twice.

The LEAD FOOT FORWARD-N-LOCK TECHNIQUE™ is compatible with all four conventional styles of grip whether that of an original Vardon overlap, modified Vardon overlap, traditional interlock or regular baseball (ten-fingers) style of grip.

How to Assemble and Execute the Lead Foot Forward-N-Lock Technique™

First, the sole of the clubface should be grounded in the middle of the stance and remain grounded throughout the proceedings. The sole of the clubface does not need to be grounded directly behind the ball during the procedure. It may be grounded in the near vicinity of the ball and once the proceedings are completed, the sweet spot of the clubface then can be centered as near the back of the ball as possible.

Second, the lead hand must be assembled on the club in a conventional (diagonal) manner. The clubface may not be allowed to rotate during this gripping process.

Third, the trail hand then must be assembled on the club either in the form of an original Vardon overlap, modified Vardon overlap, traditional interlock or regular baseball (ten-fingers) style of grip. There should be no clubface rotation allowed during the time the trail hand is gripped on the club or between the time the lead and trail hands are gripped on the club.

The lifeline of the trail hand must be locked squarely and securely on the lead thumb to complete the grip.

Fourth, after the hands are gripped on the club in a conventional manner, the lead foot must be moved forward of the initial stance line by at least the length of one shoe.

Fifth, once the lead foot is moved forward of the initial stance line by at least the length of one shoe, the lifeline of the trail hand then must be unlocked from the lead thumb by at least an inch without completely ungripping the club. The lifeline then must be relocked squarely and securely on the lead thumb. Then, once again, the lifeline/thumb connection must be unlocked and relocked in the same manner. The lead foot then may be moved back to its original position. (Figure 30-1).

Sixth, once the proceedings are completed the SHOULDERS ONLY TEST™, ARMS-LIFT TEST™, and the STRAIGHT-UP TEST™ must be conducted to determine whether the technique was properly assembled and executed.

Why the Lead Foot Forward-N-Lock Technique™ Works

When the lead foot is moved forward of the initial stance line by at least the length of one

Figure 30-1

STEP 1: The first essential step in assembling and executing the LEAD FOOT FORWARD-N-LOCK TECHNIQUE™ is to ground the clubface in the middle of the stance and assume a conventional style of grip on the club.

STEP 2: Then the lead foot must be moved forward of the stance line by at least the length of one shoe.

STEP 3: While the lead foot is moved forward of the stance line in such manner, the lifeline of the trail hand must be unlocked from the lead thumb by at least an inch without completely ungripping the club.

STEP 4: Then the lifeline of the trail hand must be relocked squarely and securely on the lead thumb while the lead foot remains in such position.

STEP 5: Once again the lifeline of the trail hand must be unlocked from the lead thumb by at least an inch without completely ungripping the club while the lead foot remains in such position.

STEP 6: Then, once again, the lifeline of the trail hand must be relocked squarely and securely on the lead thumb while the lead foot remains in such position. *(Then the lead foot may be moved back to its original position.)*

shoe after a conventional grip is formed on a club, the forearms will rotate the elbows to a parallel alignment with the shoulders to create an on-line swing path of the clubface.

When the elbows are aligned squarely parallel with the shoulders the wrists correspondingly will rotate the clubface to a square alignment. In turn, a straight ball flight alignment will be established.

However, the straight ball flight alignment will not be locked-in at this point.

In order to lock-in the straight ball flight alignment the lifeline of the trail hand then must be unlocked from the lead thumb by at least an inch without completely ungripping the club and then the lifeline must be relocked on the lead thumb.

Then, once again, the lifeline of the trail hand must be unlocked from the lead thumb by at least an inch without completely ungripping the club and then, once again, the lifeline of the trail hand must be relocked on the lead thumb.

Disciplines Necessary to Assemble and Execute the Lead Foot Forward-N-Lock Technique™

One of the most important disciplines relating to the LEAD FOOT FORWARD-N-LOCK TECHNIQUE™ is both elbows must be disconnected from the rib cage during the entire proceedings. If either elbow is connected to the rib cage during the proceedings the forearms will not rotate the wrists, clubface and elbows to establish a straight ball flight alignment at the completion of the proceedings.

Another discipline is the only clubface rotation allowed during the proceedings is the clockwise rotation caused by moving the lead foot forward of the initial stance line by at least the length of one shoe after assuming a conventional grip on the club. If the clubface rotates during the time the lead hand is assembled on the club, the procedure will be compromised. If the clubface rotates during the time the trail hand is assembled on the club or between the time the lead and trail hand are gripped on the club, the procedure likewise will be compromised.

A most critical discipline is the lifeline/thumb connection must be unlocked and relocked twice after the lead foot is moved forward of the initial stance line by at least the length of one shoe. If unlocked and relocked an additional time thereafter the forearms will rotate the wrists, clubface and elbows to establish a different ball flight alignment.

The lead foot must be moved forward of the initial stance line only after a conventional grip is formed on the club. If moved forward of the initial stance line before a conventional grip is formed on a club, the forearms will not rotate the elbows to a parallel alignment with the shoulders nor the wrists and clubface to a square alignment.

If the lead foot is moved forward of the initial stance line only after the lifeline/thumb connection is unlocked and relocked twice, the forearms will not rotate the wrists, clubface and elbows to establish a straight ball flight alignment.

The SHOULDERS ONLY TEST™, ARMS-LIFT TEST™ and STRAIGHT-UP TEST™ must be conducted at the completion the proceedings. If during any of the three tests the clubface rotates counterclockwise or clockwise, it would be necessary to disassemble the grip and repeat the procedure until the three tests confirm the technique has been assembled and executed correctly and a straight ball flight alignment has been established and locked-in.

Establishing and locking-in a straight ball flight alignment is only a part of the pre-swing requirements. If the objective is to flight a ball in the direction of a specific target, then once a straight ball flight alignment has been established and locked-in, the sweet spot of the clubface must be centered as near the back of the ball as possible (if not already so centered) and the shoulders simultaneously must be aligned squarely parallel with the intended target line, followed by a non-manipulative golf swing.

You should engage in some meaningful practice sessions while using the LEAD FOOT FORWARD-N-LOCK TECHNIQUE™ before using it in actual play.

Recommended Practice Routines When Using the Lead Foot Forward-N-Lock Technique™ in Combination with the Arrow Alignment Technique™

When practicing with the LEAD FOOT FORWARD-N-LOCK TECHNIQUE™ you should locate a safe and relatively flat practice area.

You also should follow the steps below in each of your practice sessions:

STEP 1: Place a ball on the surface of your practice area. Identify a narrow and specific target. Also identify your intended target line.

STEP 2: Ground the sole of your clubface in the middle of your stance and keep it grounded during the entire proceedings. It can be grounded either directly behind the ball or in the near vicinity of the ball. If grounded in the near vicinity of the ball,

once the proceedings are completed the sweet spot of the clubface then can be centered as near the back of the ball as possible.

STEP 3: Assemble and execute the LEAD FOOT FORWARD-N-LOCK TECHNIQUE™ in accordance with the instructions discussed in this chapter. Remember to unlock and relock your lifeline/thumb connection twice after moving your lead foot forward of the initial stance line by at least the length of one shoe.

STEP 4: Conduct the SHOULDERS ONLY TEST™, ARMS-LIFT TEST™ and STRAIGHT-UP TEST™ at the completion of the proceedings. If a locked-in straight ball flight alignment is not confirmed, repeat the procedure until it is confirmed.

STEP 5: Once a straight ball flight has been confirmed as established and locked-in, center the sweet spot of your clubface as near the back of your ball as possible (if not already so centered) and assume a comfortable stance and posture to the ball. Align your shoulders squarely parallel with your intended target line to the best of your ability.

STEP 6: Conduct the ARROW ALIGNMENT TECHNIQUE™ and adjust your stance, if necessary, until your alignment arrow points directly at your target when you turn your head and trail eye in the direction of your target <u>as far as possible</u> while immobilizing all other parts of your body.

STEP 7: Ensure the sweet spot of your clubface has remained centered as near the back of your ball as possible and then execute a non-manipulative golf swing.

As suggested previously, you should begin each practice session with your most lofted club and then with each next most lofted club thereafter until you have practiced with each club in your set. With each respective club you should begin with a wrist swing, then with a ½ swing, onto a ¾ swing and conclude with a full swing.

SUMMARY POINTS

1. **The LEAD FOOT FORWARD-N-LOCK TECHNIQUE™ requires the lead foot to be moved forward of the initial stance line by at least the length of one shoe after a conventional style of grip is formed on a club.**

2. **The clubface should be grounded during the entire proceedings.**

3. **The lead hand then must be gripped on a club in a conventional (diagonal) manner without allowing the clubface to rotate during the process.**

4. **The trail hand then must be formed on the club in a conventional manner.**

5. **The lead foot then must be moved forward of the initial stance line by at least the length of one shoe after the conventional grip is assembled on the club.**

6. **Once the lead foot has been moved forward of the initial stance line by at least the length of one shoe, the lifeline/thumb connection must be unlocked and relocked twice to lock-in the straight ball flight alignment.**

7. **The clubface may not be allowed to rotate during the entire proceedings except for the rotation that is caused in response to the lead foot being moved forward of the initial stance line.**

8. **Another important discipline is both elbows must be disconnected from the rib cage during the entire proceedings.**

9. **The SHOULDERS ONLY TEST™, ARMS-LIFT TEST™ and the STRAIGHT-UP TEST™ must be conducted at the completion of the proceedings. If the clubface rotates either counter-clockwise or clockwise during any of the three tests, the grip must be disassembled and the procedure repeated until a locked-in straight ball flight alignment is confirmed.**

10. **The LEAD FOOT FORWARD-N-LOCK TECHNIQUE™ should be used in combination with the ARROW ALIGNMENT TECHNIQUE™ to align the shoulders squarely parallel with the intended target line as the last step in the pre-swing proceedings.**

CHAPTER 31

INTRODUCTION OF THE TRAIL FOOT FORWARD-N-LOCK TECHNIQUE™

The TRAIL FOOT FORWARD-N-LOCK TECHNIQUE™ requires the trail foot to be moved forward of the initial stance line by at least the length of one shoe after a conventional style of grip is formed on a club.

It requires the sole of the clubface to be grounded during the entire proceedings. After the trail foot is moved forward of the initial stance line by at least the length of one shoe, it then requires the lifeline/thumb connection to be unlocked and re-locked once.

The TRAIL FOOT FORWARD-N-LOCK TECHNIQUE™ is compatible with all four conventional styles of grip whether that of an original Vardon overlap, modified Vardon overlap, traditional interlock or regular baseball (ten-fingers) style of grip.

How to Assemble and Execute the Trail Foot Forward-N-Lock Technique™

First, the sole of the clubface should be grounded in the middle of the stance and remain grounded throughout the proceedings. The sole of the clubface does not need to be grounded directly behind the ball during the procedure. It may be grounded in the near vicinity of the ball and once the proceedings are completed, the sweet spot of the clubface then can be centered as near the back of the ball as possible.

Second, the lead hand must be assembled on the club in a conventional (diagonal) manner. The clubface may not be allowed to rotate during this gripping process.

Third, the trail hand then should be assembled on the club either in the form of an original Vardon overlap, modified Vardon overlap, traditional interlock or regular baseball (ten-fingers) style of grip. There should be no clubface rotation allowed during the time the trail hand is gripped on the club or between the time the lead and trail hands are gripped on the club.

The lifeline of the trail hand must be locked squarely and securely on the lead thumb to complete the grip.

Fourth, after the hands are gripped on the club in a conventional manner, the trail foot must be moved forward of the initial stance line by at least the length of one shoe.

Fifth, once the trail foot is moved forward of the initial stance line by at least the length of one shoe, the lifeline of the trail hand then must be unlocked from the lead thumb by at least an inch without completely ungripping the club. The lifeline then must be relocked squarely and securely on the lead thumb. The trail foot then may be moved back to its original position. (Figure 31-1).

Sixth, once the proceedings are completed the SHOULDERS ONLY TEST™, ARMS-LIFT TEST™, and the STRAIGHT-UP TEST™ must be conducted to determine whether the technique was properly assembled and executed.

Why the Trail Foot Forward-N-Lock Technique™ Works

When the trail foot is moved forward of the initial stance line by at least the length of one

Figure 31-1

STEP 1: The first essential step in assembling and executing the TRAIL FOOT FORWARD-N-LOCK TECHNIQUE™ is to ground the clubface in the middle of the stance and then assume a conventional style of grip on the club.

STEP 2: Then move the trail foot forward of the stance line by at least the length of one shoe.

STEP 3: Then, with the trail foot moved forward of the stance line in such a manner, unlock the lifeline of the trail hand from the lead thumb by at least an inch without completely ungripping the club.

STEP 4: Then relock the lifeline of the trail hand squarely and securely on the lead thumb as the trail foot remains in such position. *(Then the trail foot then may be moved back to its original position.)*

shoe after a conventional grip is formed on a club, the forearms will rotate the elbows to a parallel alignment with the shoulders to create an on-line swing path of the clubface.

When the elbows are aligned squarely parallel with the shoulders the wrists correspondingly will rotate the clubface to a square alignment. In turn, a straight ball flight alignment will be established.

However, the straight ball flight alignment will not be locked-in at this point.

In order to lock-in the straight ball flight alignment the lifeline of the trail hand then must be unlocked from the lead thumb by at least an inch without completely ungripping the club and then the lifeline must be relocked on the lead thumb.

Disciplines Necessary to Assemble and Execute the Trail Foot Forward-N-Lock Technique™

One of the most important disciplines relating to the TRAIL FOOT FORWARD-N-LOCK TECHNIQUE™ is both elbows must be disconnected from the rib cage during the entire proceedings. If either elbow is connected to the rib cage during the proceedings the forearms will not rotate the wrists, clubface and elbows to establish a straight ball flight alignment at the completion of the proceedings.

Another discipline is the only clubface rotation allowed during the proceedings is the clockwise rotation caused by moving the trail foot forward of the initial stance line by at least the length of one shoe after assuming a conventional grip on the club. If the clubface rotates during the time the lead hand is assembled on the club, the procedure will be compromised. If the clubface rotates during the time the trail hand is assembled on the club or between the time the lead and trail hand are gripped on the club, the procedure likewise will be compromised.

A most critical discipline is the lifeline/thumb connection must be unlocked and relocked once after the trail foot is moved forward of the initial stance line by at least the length of one shoe. If unlocked and relocked an additional time thereafter the forearms will rotate the wrists, clubface and elbows to establish a different ball flight alignment.

The trail foot must be moved forward of the initial stance line only after a conventional grip is formed on the club. If moved forward of the initial stance line before a conventional grip is formed on a club, the forearms will not rotate the elbows to a parallel alignment with the shoulders nor the wrists and clubface to a square alignment.

If the trail foot is moved forward of the initial stance line only after the lifeline/thumb connection is unlocked and relocked once, the forearms will not rotate the wrists, clubface and elbows to establish a straight ball flight alignment.

The SHOULDERS ONLY TEST™, ARMS-LIFT TEST™ and STRAIGHT-UP TEST™ must be conducted at the completion the proceedings. If during any of the three tests the clubface rotates counterclockwise or clockwise, it would be necessary to disassemble the grip and repeat the procedure until the three tests confirm the technique has been assembled and executed correctly and a straight ball flight alignment has been established and locked-in.

Establishing and locking-in a straight ball flight alignment is only a part of the preswing requirements. If the objective is to flight a ball in the direction of a specific target, then once a straight ball flight alignment has been established and locked-in, the sweet spot of the clubface must be centered as near the back of the ball as possible (if not already so centered) and the shoulders simultaneously must be aligned squarely parallel with the intended target line, followed by a non-manipulative golf swing.

You should engage in some meaningful practice sessions while using the TRAIL FOOT FORWARD-N-LOCK TECHNIQUE™ before using it in actual play.

Recommended Practice Routines When Using the Trail Foot Forward-N-Lock Technique™ in Combination with the Arrow Alignment Technique™

When practicing with the TRAIL FOOT FORWARD-N-LOCK TECHNIQUE™ you should locate a safe and relatively flat practice area.

You also should follow the steps below in each of your practice sessions:

STEP 1: Place a ball on the surface of your practice area. Identify a narrow and specific target. Also identify your intended target line.

STEP 2: Ground the sole of your clubface in the middle of your stance and keep it grounded during the entire proceedings. It can be grounded either directly behind the ball or in the near vicinity of the ball. If grounded in the near vicinity of the ball, once the proceedings are completed the sweet spot of the clubface then can be centered as near the back of the ball as possible.

STEP 3: Assemble and execute the TRAIL FOOT FORWARD-N-LOCK TECHNIQUE™ in accordance with the instructions discussed in this chapter. Remember to unlock and re-

lock your lifeline/thumb connection once after moving your trail foot forward of the initial stance line by at least the length of one shoe.

STEP 4: Conduct the SHOULDERS ONLY TEST™, ARMS-LIFT TEST™ and STRAIGHT-UP TEST™ at the completion of the proceedings. If a locked-in straight ball flight alignment is not confirmed, repeat the procedure until it is confirmed.

STEP 5: Once a straight ball flight has been confirmed as established and locked-in, center the sweet spot of your clubface as near the back of your ball as possible (if not already so centered) and assume a comfortable stance and posture to the ball. Align your shoulders squarely parallel with your intended target line to the best of your ability.

STEP 6: Conduct the ARROW ALIGNMENT TECHNIQUE™ and adjust your stance, if necessary, until your alignment arrow points directly at your target when you turn your head and trail eye in the direction of your target as far as possible while immobilizing all other parts of your body.

STEP 7: Ensure the sweet spot of your clubface has remained centered as near the back of your ball as possible and then execute a non-manipulative golf swing.

As suggested previously, you should begin each practice session with your most lofted club and then with each next most lofted club thereafter until you have practiced with each club in your set. With each respective club you should begin with a wrist swing, then with a ½ swing, on to a ¾ swing and conclude with a full swing.

SUMMARY POINTS

1. **The TRAIL FOOT FORWARD-N-LOCK TECHNIQUE™ requires the trail foot to be moved forward of the initial stance line by at least the length of one shoe after a conventional style of grip is formed on a club.**

2. **The clubface should be grounded during the entire proceedings to assemble and execute the TRAIL FOOT FORWARD-N-LOCK TECHNIQUE™.**

3. **The lead hand then must be gripped on a club in a conventional (diagonal) manner without allowing the clubface to rotate during the process.**

4. **The trail hand then must be formed on the club in a conventional manner.**

5. **The trail foot then must be moved forward of the initial stance line by at least the length of one shoe.**

6. **Once the trail foot has been moved forward of the initial stance line by at least the length of one shoe, the lifeline/thumb connection must be unlocked and relocked once to lock-in the straight ball flight alignment.**

7. **The clubface may not be allowed to rotate during the entire proceedings except for the rotation caused in response to the trail foot being moved forward of the initial stance line.**

8. **Another important discipline is both elbows must be disconnected from the rib cage during the entire proceedings.**

9. **The SHOULDERS ONLY TEST™, ARMS-LIFT TEST™ and the STRAIGHT-UP TEST™ must be conducted at the completion of the proceedings. If the clubface rotates either counterclockwise or clockwise during any of the three tests, the grip must be disassembled and the procedure repeated until a locked-in straight ball flight alignment is confirmed.**

10. **The TRAIL FOOT FORWARD-N-LOCK TECHNIQUE™ should be used in combination with the ARROW ALIGNMENT TECHNIQUE™ to align the shoulders squarely parallel with the intended target line as the last step in the pre-swing proceedings.**

CHAPTER 32

INTRODUCTION OF THE KNEES DOWN-N-LOCK TECHNIQUE™

The KNEES DOWN-N-LOCK TECHNIQUE™ requires the clubface to be grounded, the shoulders stabilized, the arms, wrists and hands relaxed and the knees to be flexed downward by at least three inches after a conventional style of grip is formed on a club.

When the knees are flexed downward by at least three inches after a conventional style of grip is formed on a club, the forearms will rotate the wrists, clubface and elbows to establish a straight ball flight alignment.

The KNEES DOWN-N-LOCK TECHNIQUE™ is compatible with all four conventional styles of grip whether that of an original or modified Vardon overlap, traditional interlock or regular baseball (ten-fingers) type of grip.

How to Assemble and Execute the Knees Down-N-Lock Technique™

First, ground the sole of your clubface either directly behind your ball or in the near vicinity of your ball. It does not necessarily need to be grounded directly behind your ball during the proceedings. It may be grounded elsewhere and once the technique properly is assembled and executed, the sweet spot of the clubface then can be transferred and centered as near the back of the ball as possible.

Preferably, the sole of the clubface should be grounded in the middle of the stance.

Second, the lead hand must be gripped on the club in a conventional (diagonal) manner. The clubface may not be allowed to move or rotate during the gripping process.

Third, the trail hand must be gripped on the club either in the form of an original Vardon overlap, modified Vardon overlap, traditional interlock or regular baseball (ten-fingers) style of grip. The clubface may not be allowed to rotate clockwise or counterclockwise during the time the trail hand is gripped on the club or between the time the lead and trail hands are gripped on the club.

The lifeline of the trail hand must be locked squarely and securely on the lead thumb to complete the grip. This is the first of a total of three "locks" of the lifeline/thumb connection that is necessary to assemble and execute the KNEES DOWN-N-LOCK TECHNIQUE™.

Fourth, the most critical part of the procedure is to stabilize the shoulders, keep the arms, wrists and hands relaxed and then flex the knees downward by at least three inches – until the clubface stops rotating clockwise.

Fifth, once the knees are flexed downward in such manner after assuming a conventional style of grip on the club, the lifeline of the trail thumb must be unlocked from the lead thumb by at least an inch without completely ungripping the club and then the lifeline of the trail hand must be relocked on the lead thumb.

Sixth, then once again the lifeline of the trail hand must be unlocked from the lead thumb by at least an inch without completely ungripping the club and then, once again, the trail lifeline must be relocked on the lead thumb. The knees then should be flexed upward to their original position. (Figure 32-1).

Figure 32-1

STEP 1: The first essential step to assemble and execute the KNEES DOWN-N-LOCK TECHNIQUE™ is to ground the clubface in the middle of the stance and then assume a conventional style of grip on the club.

STEP 2: Then the knees must be flexed downward by at least three inches and held in such position until the proceedings are completed.

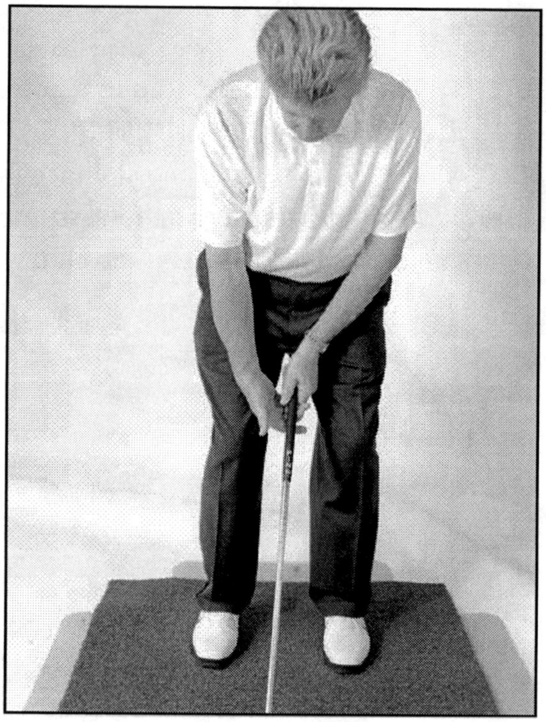

STEP 3: Then the lifeline of the trail hand must be unlocked from the lead thumb by at least an inch without completely ungripping the club with the knees flexed down by at least three inches.

STEP 4: The lifeline of the trail hand then must be relocked squarely and securely on the lead thumb with the knees flexed down by at least three inches.

STEP 5: Then, once again, the lifeline of the trail hand must be unlocked from the lead thumb by at least an inch without completely ungripping the club with the knees flexed down in such a manner.

STEP 6: Then, once again, the lifeline of the trail hand must be relocked squarely and securely on the lead thumb with the knees flexed down in such a manner. *(Then the knees may be flexed upward to their original position.)*

Seventh, once the proceedings are completed, the SHOULDERS ONLY TEST™, ARMS-LIFT TEST™ and STRAIGHT-UP TEST™ must be conducted to determine whether the technique was assembled and executed correctly and, consequently, whether a straight ball flight alignment has been established and locked-in. If not, the grip should be disassembled and the procedure repeated until the three tests confirm a properly assembled and executed KNEES DOWN-N-LOCK TECHNIQUE™.

Why the Knees Down-N-Lock Technique™ Works

The KNEES DOWN-N-LOCK TECHNIQUE™ works because when the knees are flexed downward by at least three inches after assuming a conventional style of grip on a club, the forearms will rotate the elbows to a parallel alignment with the shoulders to create an on-line swing path.

When the elbows are rotated to a parallel alignment with the shoulders to create an on-line swing path of the clubface the wrists correspondingly will rotate the clubface to a square alignment, all of which will establish a straight ball flight alignment.

However, the straight ball flight alignment will not be locked-in at this point.

In order to lock-in the straight ball flight alignment, the lifeline/thumb connection then must be unlocked and relocked twice – but no more thereafter.

Disciplines Required to Assemble the Knees Down-N-Lock Technique™

The first discipline, as discussed earlier, is to keep the sole of the clubface grounded in the middle of the stance throughout the proceedings.

There may be no clubface rotation allowed during the proceedings except for the clockwise rotation of the clubface in response to the flexing of the knees downward after a conventional style of grip is formed on a club.

Although flexing the knees downward by at least three inches after forming a conventional style of grip on a club appears to be a simple maneuver, it should not be done in a lackadaisical or cavalier manner.

The knees must be flexed downward in a balanced manner without too much weight placed on either the balls or heels of the feet.

Flexing the knees downward before gripping the club will not cause the forearms to rotate the wrists, clubface and elbows to establish a straight ball flight alignment. Flexing the knees downward only after the lifeline/thumb connection is unlocked and relocked twice will not rotate the wrists, clubface and elbows to establish a straight ball flight alignment.

The only time to flex the knees downward is after a conventional grip is assumed on the club but before the lifeline/thumb connection is unlocked and relocked twice.

The shoulders should be stabilized and the arms, wrists and hands should remain passive and only move in response to the downward movement of the knees.

The lifeline/thumb connection must be unlocked and relocked twice after the knees are flexed downward but no more thereafter. If unlocked and relocked once more thereafter, the forearms will rotate the wrists, clubface and elbows to establish a different ball flight alignment.

Another important discipline relating to the KNEES DOWN-N-LOCK TECHNIQUE™ is the elbows must be disconnected from the rib cage during the entire proceedings. If either elbow is connected to the rib cage during the proceedings, the forearms will rotate the wrists, clubface and elbows to a different and much less desirable ball flight alignment at the completion of the proceedings.

The KNEES DOWN-N-LOCK TECHNIQUE™ requires a total of three "locks" of the lifeline/thumb connection.

The first of the three "locks" of the lifeline/thumb connection that is required to assemble and execute the KNEES DOWN-N-LOCK TECHNIQUE™ occurs when the lifeline of the trail hand is locked squarely and securely on the lead thumb to complete the grip.

The second of the three "locks" occurs after the knees are flexed downward by at least three inches when then the lifeline of the trail hand is unlocked from the lead thumb by at least an inch without completely ungripping the club and then relocked on the lead thumb.

The third of the three "locks" occurs when then, once again, the lifeline of the trail hand is unlocked from the lead thumb by at least an inch without completely ungripping the club and then, once again, the lifeline of the trail hand is relocked on the lead thumb.

Establishing and locking-in a straight ball flight alignment is just a part of the preswing requirements. In addition, the sweet spot of the clubface must be centered as near the back of the ball as possible and, simultaneously, the shoulders must be aligned squarely parallel with the intended target line at final address, followed by the execution of a non-manipulative golf swing if the objective is to hit a ball on a straight path in the direction of the target.

Recommended Practice Routines When Using the Knees Down-N-Lock Technique™ in Combination with the Arrow Alignment Technique™

You should find a safe and relatively flat practice area for your practice sessions. These are the steps you should follow in your practice routine when using the KNEES DOWN-N-LOCK TECHNIQUE™.

STEP 1: Place a ball on the surface of your practice area. Identify a narrow and specific target. Also identify your intended target line.

STEP 2: Ground the sole of your clubface in the middle of your stance and keep it grounded either directly behind your ball or in the near vicinity of your ball.

STEP 3: Assemble and execute the KNEES DOWN-N-LOCK TECHNIQUE™ as instructed in this chapter. Remember to flex your knees downward in a balanced manner by at least three inches after forming a conventional style of grip on your club. Then unlock and relock your lifeline/thumb connection twice but no more thereafter.

STEP 4: Conduct the SHOULDERS ONLY TEST™, ARMS-LIFT TEST™ and STRAIGHT-UP TEST™ once you have completed the proceedings. If your clubface rotates counterclockwise or clockwise during any of the three tests, disassemble your grip and repeat the procedure until there is no such clubface rotation during the tests.

STEP 5: Center the sweet spot of your clubface as near the back of your ball as possible(unless already so centered) and assume a comfortable posture and stance to the ball. Align your shoulders squarely parallel with your intended target line to the best of your ability.

STEP 6: Conduct the ARROW ALIGNMENT TECHNIQUE™ and adjust your stance, if necessary, until your alignment arrow points directly at your target when you turn your head and trail eye in the direction of your target as far as possible, while immobilizing all other parts of your body.

STEP 7: Ensure the sweet spot of your clubface has remained centered as near the back of the ball as possible and then execute a non-manipulative golf swing.

You should begin each practice session with your most lofted club and then with each next most lofted club thereafter until you have practiced with each club in your set. With each club you should begin with a wrist swing, then with a ½ swing, on to a ¾ swing and conclude with a full swing.

SUMMARY POINTS

1. The KNEES DOWN-N-LOCK TECHNIQUE™ requires a flexing of the knees downward by at least three inches after assuming a conventional style of grip on a club.

2. The sole of the clubface should be grounded during the entire proceedings.

3. The lead hand must be gripped on the club in a conventional (diagonal) manner.

4. The trail hand must be formed on the club in a conventional manner and the lifeline of the trail hand must be locked on the lead thumb to complete the grip.

5. The flexing down of the knees after a conventional style of grip is formed on a club should be the only active body movement during the proceedings. The shoulders should be stabilized and the arms, wrists and hands should remain inactive and passive and only move in response to the downward movement of the knees during the procedure.

6. The lifeline/thumb connection must be unlocked and relocked twice after the knees are flexed downward but no more thereafter.

7. If the lifeline/thumb connection is unlocked and relocked once more thereafter, the forearms will rotate the wrists, clubface and elbows to establish a different ball flight alignment.

8. The elbows must be disconnected from the rib cage during the entire proceedings. If either elbow is connected to the rib cage during the proceedings, the forearms will rotate the wrists, clubface and elbows to a different ball flight alignment at the completion of the proceedings.

9. The KNEES DOWN-N-LOCK TECHNIQUE™ works because when the knees are flexed downward by at least three inches after a conventional style of grip is assumed, the forearms will rotate the elbows to a parallel alignment with the shoulders and the wrists will rotate the clubface to a square alignment, all of which will establish a straight ball flight alignment. Then when the lifeline/thumb connection is unlocked and relocked twice, the straight ball flight alignment will be locked-in.

10. Once the proceedings are completed, the SHOULDERS ONLY TEST™, ARMS-LIFT TEST™ and STRAIGHT-UP TEST™ must be conducted and the procedure repeated, if necessary, until all three tests confirm the technique was assembled correctly and a straight ball flight alignment has been established and locked-in.

11. The ARROW ALIGNMENT TECHNIQUE™ should be conducted to align the shoulders parallel with the intended target line when using the KNEES DOWN-N-LOCK TECHNIQUE™.

CHAPTER 33

INTRODUCTION OF THE KNEES UP-N-LOCK TECHNIQUE™

The KNEES UP-N-LOCK TECHNIQUE™ also relies on a specific body movement after a conventional style of grip is assembled on a club in which there is no clubface rotation during the gripping process.

Instead of flexing the knees downward by at least three inches after a conventional style of grip is formed on a club, as is required in the KNEES DOWN-N-LOCK TECHNIQUE™, the knees must be flexed upward by at least three inches while keeping the clubface grounded, the arms, wrists and arms relaxed and passive and the shoulders stabilized after a conventional style of grip is formed on a club.

Once the knees are flexed upward by at least three inches while keeping the shoulders stabilized and the arms, wrists and hands relaxed, the lifeline of the trail hand must be unlocked from the lead thumb by at least an inch without ungripping the club and then the trail lifeline must be relocked on the lead thumb. The lifeline/thumb connection may not be unlocked and relocked thereafter.

The KNEES UP-N-N-LOCK TECHNIQUE™ is compatible with all four conventional styles of grip whether that of the original Vardon overlap, modified Vardon overlap, traditional interlock or the regular baseball (ten-fingers) type of grip.

How to Assemble the Knees Up-N-Lock Technique™

First, the sole of the clubface should be grounded and remain grounded during the proceedings. Preferably, it should be grounded in the middle of the stance during the proceedings although it does not necessarily need to be grounded directly behind the ball at such time.

Second, the club must be gripped with the lead hand in a conventional (diagonal) manner without allowing any clubface rotation during the gripping process. If there is any clubface rotation detected when the lead hand is gripped on the club, the grip should be disassembled and regripped with the lead hand.

Third, the trail hand then must be gripped on the club either in the form of an original Vardon overlap, modified Vardon overlap, traditional interlock or regular baseball (ten-fingers) style of grip. There may not be any clubface rotation allowed during the time the trail hand is gripped on the club or between the time the lead and trail hands are gripped on a club.

The lifeline of the trail hand must be locked squarely and securely on the lead hand to complete the grip.

Fourth, once both hands are gripped on the club properly, the knees must be flexed upward by at least three inches while the shoulders remain stabilized and all other body parts remain relaxed and passive.

Fifth, the lifeline of the trail hand then must be unlocked from the lead thumb by at least an inch without completely ungripping the club and then relocked on the lead thumb to secure and lock-in the straight ball flight alignment. The knees then may be flexed downward to their original position. (Figure 33-1).

Sixth, once the proceedings are completed, the SHOULDERS ONLY TEST™, ARMS-

Figure 33-1

STEP 1: The first essential step to assemble and execute the KNEES UP-N-LOCK TECHNIQUE™ is to ground the clubface in the middle of the stance and then assume a conventional style of grip on a club.

STEP 2: Then the knees must be flexed upward by at least three inches and held in such position until the proceedings are completed.

STEP 3: Then while holding the knees in such position, the lifeline of the trail hand must be unlocked from the lead thumb by at least an inch without completely ungripping the club.

STEP 4: Then the lifeline of the trail hand must be relocked squarely and securely on the lead thumb while the knees are held in such position. *(The knees then may be flexed downward to their original position.)*

LIFT TEST™ and STRAIGHT-UP TEST™ must be conducted to determine if the procedure has been assembled correctly.

Why The Knees Up-n-lock Technique™ Works

The KNEES UP-N-LOCK TECHNIQUE™ works because when the knees are flexed upward by at least three inches after a conventional style of grip is assumed on a club in which there is no clubface rotation during the gripping process, the forearms will rotate the elbows to a parallel alignment with the shoulders to create an on-line swing path of the clubface.

When the elbows are aligned parallel with the shoulders the wrists correspondingly will rotate the clubface to a square alignment, all of which will establish a straight ball flight alignment.

However, the straight alignment will not be locked-in at such point.

In order to lock-in the established straight ball flight alignment, the lifeline of the trail hand then must be unlocked from the lead thumb by at least an inch without ungripping the club and then relocked on the lead thumb. The lifeline/thumb connection may not be unlocked and relocked thereafter.

Disciplines Required to Assemble and Execute the Knees Up-N-Lock Technique™

The most critical discipline relating to this technique is the knees must be flexed upward by at least three inches after a conventional style of grip is formed on a club and held in such position until the lifeline/thumb connection is unlocked and relocked.

In order to flex the knees upward by at least three inches, the knees must have at least three inches of flex in them before a conventional grip is assumed. Thus, the knees need to be flexed downward appreciatively before the grip is assumed.

If the knees are flexed upward only before the hands are gripped on a club, the forearms will not rotate the wrists, clubface and elbows to establish a straight ball flight alignment at the completion of the proceedings. On the other hand, if the knees are flexed upward only after the lifeline/thumb connection is unlocked and relocked, the forearms likewise will not rotate the wrists, clubface and elbows to establish a straight ball flight alignment at the completion of the proceedings.

Another critical discipline is the unlocking and relocking of the lifeline/thumb connection after the grip is completed and the knees flexed upward by at least three inches. If the lifeline/thumb connection is not unlocked and relocked after the knees are flexed upward by at least three inches, a straight ball flight alignment will not be established and locked-in at the completion of the proceedings. If the lifeline/thumb connection is unlocked and relocked an additional time, the forearms will not rotate the wrists, clubface and elbows to establish a straight ball flight alignment at the completion of the proceedings.

The only clubface rotation allowed during the proceedings is that caused by flexing the knees upward.

If you prefer, you may flex your knees upward completely even to the extent of locking your knee joints between the time you assemble a conventional style of grip on your club and the time you unlock and relock your lifeline/thumb connection, assuming there is at least three inches of upward flex of the knees.

To do so should offset any shoulder movement that might creep into the procedure.

Another discipline relating to this technique is the elbows must remain disconnected from the rib cage throughout the proceedings.

An additional discipline is that a properly assembled conventional style of grip is imperative. As noted earlier, if your preferred style of grip is a modified Vardon overlap, you must fit the tip-end of your lead index finger snugly into the web between the little and ring fingers of your trail hand as you overlap your trail little finger on the groove atop the index and middle fingers of your lead hand.

Likewise, if you prefer a traditional interlock style of grip, you must ensure your lead index finger fits snugly into the web between the little and ring fingers of your trail hand.

If you have trouble assembling either of these properly, you should consider converting to an original Vardon overlap or regular baseball (ten-fingers) style of grip.

At the completion of the proceedings, the SHOULDERS ONLY TEST™, ARMS-LIFT TEST™ and STRAIGHT-UP TEST™ must be conducted. If there is any clubface rotation during the tests, the grip should be disassembled and the procedure repeated until there is no such clubface rotation when the three tests are conducted.

Once a straight ball flight alignment is confirmed as established and locked-in, the sweet spot of the clubface must be centered as near the back of the ball as possible (if not already so centered) and, simultaneously, the shoulders must be aligned squarely parallel with the intended target line as the last step in the pre-swing routine. All that will remain will be to execute a non-manipulative golf swing.

You should engage in some meaningful practice sessions when using the KNEES UP-N-LOCK TECHNIQUE™ in combination with the ARROW ALIGNMENT TECHNIQUE™ to align your shoulders squarely parallel with your intended target line before using them in actual play.

Recommended Practice Routines When Using the Knees Up-N-Lock Technique™ in Combination with the Arrow Alignment Technique™

You should locate a safe and relatively flat practice area. You should follow these steps when using the KNEES UP-N-LOCK TECHNIQUE™ in your practice sessions:

STEP 1: **Place a ball on the surface of your practice area. Identify a narrow and specific target. Also identify your intended target line.**

STEP 2: **Ground the sole of your clubface either directly behind your ball or in the near vicinity of your ball.**

STEP 3: **Assemble and execute the KNEES UP-N-LOCK TECHNIQUE™ as instructed throughout this chapter. Remember to flex your knees upward by at least three inches after gripping your club with both hands in a conventional manner and then unlock and relock your lifeline/thumb connection only once.**

STEP 4: **Confirm whether you have assembled and executed the procedure correctly by conducting the SHOULDERS ONLY TEST™, ARMS-LIFT TEST™ and STRAIGHT-UP TEST™. Repeat the procedure, if necessary, until the tests confirm the technique has been assembled and executed correctly.**

STEP 5: **Once confirmed, center the sweet spot of your clubface as near the back of the ball as possible (if not already so centered) and assume a comfortable posture and stance to the ball. Align your shoulders squarely parallel with your intended target line to the best of your ability.**

STEP 6: **Conduct the ARROW ALIGNMENT TECHNIQUE™ and adjust your stance, if necessary, until your alignment arrow points directly at your target when you turn your head and trail eye in the direction of your target as far as possible while immobilizing all other parts of your body.**

STEP 7: **Ensure the sweet spot of your clubface has remained centered as near the back of your ball as possible and then execute a non-manipulative golf swing.**

A steady head and planted feet during you backswing greatly will enhance your ability to execute a non-manipulative golf swing. A non-manipulative golf swing is one in which there is no intentional or inadvertent re-routing of the clubface alignment or its swing path during the golf swing.

You should begin each practice session with your most lofted club and then with each next most lofted club thereafter until you have practiced with each club in your set. With each club you should begin with a wrist swing, then with a ½ swing, on to a ¾ swing and conclude with a full swing.

SUMMARY POINTS

1. The KNEES UP-N-LOCK TECHNIQUE™ requires the knees to be flexed upward by at least three inches after both hands are gripped on a club in a conventional manner.

2. The sole of the clubface must be grounded in the middle of the stance throughout the proceedings to perform the KNEES UP-N-LOCK TECHNIQUE™.

3. The sole of the clubface does not necessarily need to be grounded directly behind the ball during the proceedings. It may be grounded near the vicinity of the ball and once the proceedings are completed, the sweet spot of the clubface then can be centered as near the back of the ball as possible.

4. The lead hand must be gripped on the club in a conventional (diagonal) manner without allowing any clubface rotation during the gripping process.

5. The trail hand then must be assembled on the club in a conventional manner. The grip must be completed by locking the lifeline of the trail hand firmly on the lead thumb. This constitutes the first of the two "locks" of the lifeline/thumb connection that is necessary to assemble and execute the KNEES UP-N-LOCK TECHNIQUE™.

6. Once the knees are flexed upward by at least three inches after assuming a conventional style of grip, the lifeline of the trail hand must be unlocked from the lead thumb by at

least an inch without completely ungripping the club and then relocked on the lead thumb. This constitutes the second of the two "locks" of the lifeline/thumb connection that is required to assemble and execute the KNEES UP-N-LOCK TECHNIQUE™.

7. **The elbows must be disconnected from the rib cage during the entire proceedings when assembling and executing the KNEES UP-N-LOCK TECHNIQUE™.**

8. **The shoulders must be stabilized and the arms, wrists and hands must remain relaxed and passive during the proceedings.**

9. **At the completion of the proceedings, the SHOULDERS ONLY TEST™, ARMS-LIFT TEST™ and STRAIGHT-UP TEST™ must be conducted and the procedure repeated, if necessary, until a correctly assembled and executed KNEES UP-N-LOCK TECHNIQUE™ is confirmed by the three tests.**

10. **The ARROW ALIGNMENT TECHNIQUE™ should be conducted to align the shoulders parallel with the intended target line when using the KNEES UP-N-LOCK TECHNIQUE™.**

CHAPTER 34

INTRODUCTION OF THE LATERAL DOWN-N-LOCK TECHNIQUE™

The LATERAL DOWN-N-LOCK TECHNIQUE™ requires the shoulders and spine to be tilted downward and away from the target in a lateral (sideways) manner as far as possible from an upright and level position after both hands are assembled on a club.

The tilting of the shoulders and spine downward and away from the target in a lateral manner after both hands are gripped on a club is what will cause the forearms to rotate the elbows to a parallel alignment with the shoulders to create an on-line swing path of the clubface and the wrists to rotate the clubface to a square alignment.

The LATERAL DOWN-N-LOCK TECHNIQUE™ is compatible with all four conventional styles of grip whether that of the original Vardon overlap, modified Vardon overlap, traditional interlock or regular baseball (ten-fingers) style of grip.

How to Assemble the Lateral Down-N-Lock Technique™

First, the sole of the clubface must be grounded in the middle of the stance throughout the proceedings. It can be grounded directly behind the ball or in the near vicinity of the ball. If grounded in the near vicinity of the ball, once the proceedings are completed the sweet spot of the clubface then can be transferred and centered as near the back of the ball as possible.

Second, the shoulders should be positioned in a level and upright manner prior to gripping the club.

Third, the lead hand must be assembled on the club in a conventional (diagonal) manner and the clubface must not be allowed to rotate counterclockwise or clockwise during the gripping process.

Fourth, the trail hand then must be assembled on the club either in the form of an original Vardon overlap, modified Vardon overlap, traditional interlock or regular baseball (ten-fingers) style of grip. There can be no clubface rotation allowed during the gripping process.

The grip must be completed by locking the lifeline of the trail hand squarely and securely on the lead thumb.

Fifth, once both hands properly are gripped on the club, the shoulders and spine must be tilted downward and away from the target in a lateral manner as far as possible from an upright position.

Sixth, once the shoulders and spine are tilted laterally downward and away from the target as far as possible, the lifeline of the trail hand must be unlocked from the lead thumb by at least an inch without completely ungripping the club and then the lifeline must be relocked on the lead thumb. The shoulders then should be tilted upward and back to their original position. (Figure 34-1).

Seventh, then the SHOULDERS ONLY TEST,™ ARMS-LIFT TEST™ and STRAIGHT-UP TEST™ must be conducted to determine whether the technique has been assembled and executed correctly.

Why the Lateral Down-N-Lock Technique™ Works

This technique works because when the shoulders and spine are tilted downward and away from the target in a lateral manner as far

Figure 34-1

STEP 1: The first essential step to assemble and execute the LATERAL DOWN-N-LOCK TECHNIQUE™ is to ground the clubface in the middle of the stance and then assume a conventional style of grip on the club.

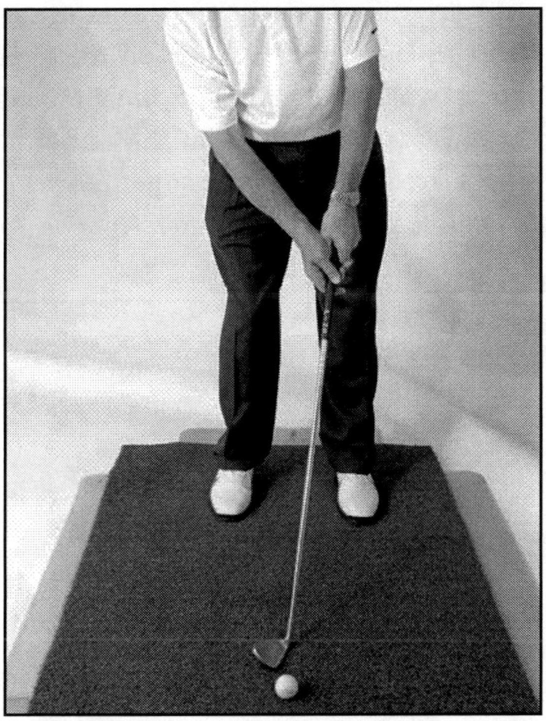

STEP 2: Then tilt the shoulders downward and away from the target in a lateral (sideways) manner as far as possible.

STEP 3: While the shoulders remain tilted downward and away from the target in a lateral manner, unlock the lifeline of the trail hand from the lead thumb by at least an inch without completely ungripping the club.

STEP 4: Then relock the lifeline of the trail hand squarely and securely on the lead thumb while the shoulders remain tilted downward and away from the target in such a lateral (sideways) manner. *(Then tilt the shoulders upward in a lateral manner to their original position.)*

as possible from a level and upright position after a conventional style of grip is formed on a club, the forearms will rotate the elbows to a parallel alignment with the shoulders to create an on-line swing path of the clubface.

When the elbows are aligned parallel with the shoulders the wrists correspondingly will rotate the clubface to a square alignment, all of which will establish a straight ball flight alignment.

Then, once the lifeline of the trail hand is unlocked from the lead thumb by at least an inch without completely ungripping the club and then relocked on the lead thumb, the straight ball flight alignment will be locked-in.

As long as you do not thereafter unlock and relock the lifeline/thumb connection, you may move the club practically anywhere you desire and the straight ball flight alignment will remain locked-in.

Disciplines Required to Assemble the Lateral Down-N-Lock Technique™

The most critical discipline when performing the LATERAL DOWN-N-LOCK TECHNIQUE™ is the proper tilting of the shoulders and spine laterally downward and away from the target after both hands have been gripped on a club in a conventional manner. The shoulders and spine must be at a level position before the hands are gripped on a club in order to provide enough room to cause the forearms to rotate the elbows to a parallel alignment with the shoulders and the wrists to rotate the clubface to a square alignment when the shoulders then are tilted downward and away from the target in a lateral manner as far as possible.

The knees may not be allowed to flex up or down during the proceedings. The arms, hands and wrists must remain inactive and passive and allowed to move only in response to the lateral tilt of the shoulders and spine downward as far as possible.

The LATERAL DOWN-N-LOCK TECHNIQUE™ requires a total of two "locks" of the lifeline/thumb connection.

The first of the two "locks" of the lifeline/thumb connection occurs when the lifeline of the trail hand is locked squarely and securely on the lead thumb to complete the grip. The second one occurs after the shoulders and spine are titled downward and away from the target in a lateral manner as far as possible when then the lifeline of the trail hand is unlocked from the lead thumb by at least an inch without completely ungripping the club and the trail lifeline then is relocked on the lead thumb.

The lifeline/thumb connection may not be unlocked and relocked thereafter. If unlocked and relocked an additional time thereafter, the forearms will rotate the wrists, clubface and elbows to establish a different ball flight alignment.

The elbows must remain disconnected from the rib cage during the proceedings. If either or both elbows are connected to the rib cage during the proceedings, the forearms will rotate the wrists, clubface and elbows to a different ball flight alignment at the completion of the proceedings.

The clubface should not be allowed to rotate except for the clockwise rotation of the clubface that is caused by tilting the shoulders and spine downward and away from the target in a lateral manner as far as possible after both hands are gripped on the club. There can be no clubface rotation allowed when the lead and trail hands respectively are gripped on the club or between the time the hands are gripped on the club.

Another discipline is the shoulders must be tilted upward in a lateral manner and returned to their original upright position at the completion of the proceedings.

The SHOULDERS ONLY TEST™, ARMS-LIFT TEST™ and STRAIGHT-UP TEST™ must be conducted at the completion of the proceedings. If during any of the three tests the clubface rotates either counterclockwise or clockwise the grip should be disassembled and the procedure repeated until there is no such clubface rotation when the three tests are conducted.

Once a straight ball flight alignment is established and locked-in, the sweet spot of the clubface must be centered as near the back of the ball as possible (if not already so centered) and the shoulders must be aligned squarely parallel with the intended target line at final address, followed by a non-manipulative golf swing if the objective is to hit the ball on a straight path in the direction of the target.

You should engage in some meaningful practice sessions before using the LATERAL DOWN-N-LOCK TECHNIQUE™ in actual play.

Recommended Practice Routines When Using the Lateral Down-N-Lock Technique™ in Combination with the Arrow Alignment Technique™

You should conduct the ARROW ALIGNMENT TECHNIQUE™ to align your shoulders parallel with your intended target line during your practice sessions as well as follow the steps below:

STEP 1: Place a ball on the surface of your practice area. Identify a very narrow

and specific target. Also identify your intended target line.

STEP 2: Ground the sole of your clubface in the middle of the stance and keep it grounded throughout the proceedings.

STEP 3: Assemble and execute the LATERAL DOWN-N-LOCK TECHNIQUE™. Remember to position your shoulders in an upright and level manner prior to gripping your club and then, once you have gripped your club, tilt your shoulders downward and away from the target in a lateral manner as far as possible.

STEP 4: Then unlock the lifeline of your trail hand from your lead thumb by at least an inch without completely ungripping your club and relock your trail lifeline on your lead thumb. Your lifeline/thumb connection may not be unlocked and relocked thereafter.

STEP 5: Once the straight ball flight alignment has been locked-in, tilt your shoulders upward in a lateral manner and allow them to return to their original upright level position.

STEP 6: Conduct the SHOULDERS ONLY TEST™, ARMS-LIFT TEST™ and STRAIGHT-UP TEST™ to determine if the procedure was assembled and executed correctly. If not, repeat the procedure until all three tests confirm such and, as a result, a straight ball flight alignment has been established and locked-in.

STEP 7: Center the sweet spot of your clubface as near the back of the ball as possible (if not already so centered) and assume a comfortable posture and stance to your ball. Align your shoulders parallel with your intended target line to the best of your ability.

STEP 8: Conduct the ARROW ALIGNMENT TECHNIQUE™ and adjust your stance, if necessary, until your alignment arrow points directly at your target when you turn your head and trail eye in the direction of your target as far as possible while immobilizing all other parts of your body.

STEP 9: Ensure the sweet spot of your clubface has remained centered as near the back of your ball as possible and then execute a non-manipulative golf swing.

Always locate a safe and relatively flat practice area.

You should begin each practice session with your most lofted club and progress through your set, using each next most lofted club thereafter in succession. With each club you should begin with a wrist swing, then with a ½ swing, on to a ¾ swing and conclude with a full swing.

SUMMARY POINTS

1. The LATERAL DOWN-N-LOCK TECHNIQUE™ requires the shoulders and spine to be tilted laterally downward and away from the target as far as possible from an upright and level position after both hands are gripped on a club in a conventional manner.

2. The LATERAL DOWN-N-LOCK TECHNIQUE™ requires the sole of the clubface to be grounded in the middle of the stance throughout the proceedings.

3. The lead hand must be formed on the club in a conventional (diagonal) manner.

4. The trail hand must be gripped on the club either in the form of an original Vardon overlap, modified Vardon overlap, traditional interlock or regular baseball (ten-fingers) style of grip.

5. The grip is completed by locking the lifeline of the trail hand squarely and securely on the lead thumb. This is the first of the two "locks" of the lifeline/thumb connection that is necessary to assemble and execute the LATERAL DOWN-N-LOCK TECHNIQUE™.

6. Once the shoulders and spine are tilted downward and away from the target in a lateral manner as far as possible from an upright and level position, the lifeline/thumb connection must then be unlocked and relocked to secure and lock-in the straight ball flight alignment. This is the second of the two

"locks" of the lifeline/thumb connection that is necessary to assemble and execute the LATERAL DOWN-N-LOCK TECHNIQUE™. The lifeline/thumb connection may not be unlocked and relocked thereafter.

7. **Once the proceedings are completed the shoulders should be tilted upward in a lateral manner to allow them to return to their original upright position.**

8. **There may not be any clubface rotation allowed during the proceedings except for that caused by the tilting of the shoulders and spine downward a lateral manner as far as possible after both hands are assembled on the club in a conventional manner.**

9. **The elbows must remain disconnected from the rib cage throughout the proceedings.**

10. **Once the proceedings are completed, the SHOULDERS ONLY TEST™, ARMS-LIFT TEST™ and STRAIGHT-UP TEST™ must be conducted. If there is any clubface rotation during the tests, the grip should be disassembled and the procedure repeated until a locked-in straight ball flight alignment has been confirmed.**

11. **The ARROW ALIGNMENT TECHNIQUE™ should be conducted to align the shoulders parallel with the intended target line when using the LATERAL DOWN-N-LOCK TECHNIQUE™.**

CHAPTER 35

INTRODUCTION OF THE LATERAL UP-N-LOCK TECHNIQUE™

The LATERAL UP-N-LOCK TECHNIQUE™ requires the shoulders to be tilted laterally upward as far as possible from a pre-tilted downward position after both hands are assembled on a club in a conventional manner.

The best way to tilt the shoulders laterally upward as far as possible after both hands are gripped on a club in a conventional manner is to pre-tilt the shoulders laterally downward as far as possible before the hands are gripped on the club. Then, once both hands are gripped on the club, simply tilt the shoulders laterally upward to their original upright level position.

How to Assemble the Lateral Up-N-Lock Technique™

First, ground the sole of your clubface in the middle of your stance and keep it grounded throughout the proceedings. It can be grounded either directly behind the ball or in the near vicinity of the ball. If grounded near the vicinity of the ball and once the proceedings are completed, the sweet spot of the clubface then can be centered behind the ball.

Second, pre-tilt your shoulders laterally downward and away from the target as far as possible.

Third, then grip your lead hand on your club in a conventional (diagonal) manner while continuing to keep your shoulders tilted downward in a lateral manner as far as possible. You must ensure there is no counterclockwise or clockwise movement or rotation during the gripping proceedings.

Fourth, then while continuing to keep your shoulders tilted downward as far as possible in a lateral manner the trail hand must be gripped on the club either in the form of an original Vardon overlap, modified Vardon overlap, traditional interlock or regular baseball (ten-fingers) style of grip. The grip should be completed by locking the lifeline of the trail hand on the lead thumb.

Fifth, once both hands are gripped on your club, simply tilt your shoulders upward in a lateral manner to an upright and level position.

Sixth, the lifeline of the trail hand then must be unlocked from the lead thumb by at least an inch without completely ungripping the club and then the trail lifeline must be relocked on the lead thumb.

Seventh, then once again the lifeline of the trail hand must be unlocked from the lead thumb by at least an inch without ungripping the club and then, once again, the lifeline of the trail hand must be relocked on the lead thumb. (Figure 35-1).

The LATERAL UP-N-LOCK TECHNIQUE™ requires a total of three "locks" of the lifeline/thumb connection.

The first of the three "locks" of the lifeline/thumb connection that is necessary to assemble and execute the LATERAL UP-N-LOCK TECHNIQUE™ occurs when the lifeline of the trail hand is locked squarely and securely on the lead thumb to complete the grip.

The second of the three "locks" of the lifeline/thumb connection occurs after the shoulders are titled upward in a lateral manner as far as possible from their pre-tilted downward position when then the lifeline of the trail hand

Figure 35-1

STEP 1: The first essential step to assemble and execute the LATERAL UP-N-LOCK TECHNIQUE™ is to pre-tilt the shoulders downward and away from the target in a lateral manner as far as possible prior to gripping the club.

STEP 2: The second essential step is to assume a conventional style of grip on the club while the shoulders are titled downward and away from the target in a lateral manner as far as possible.

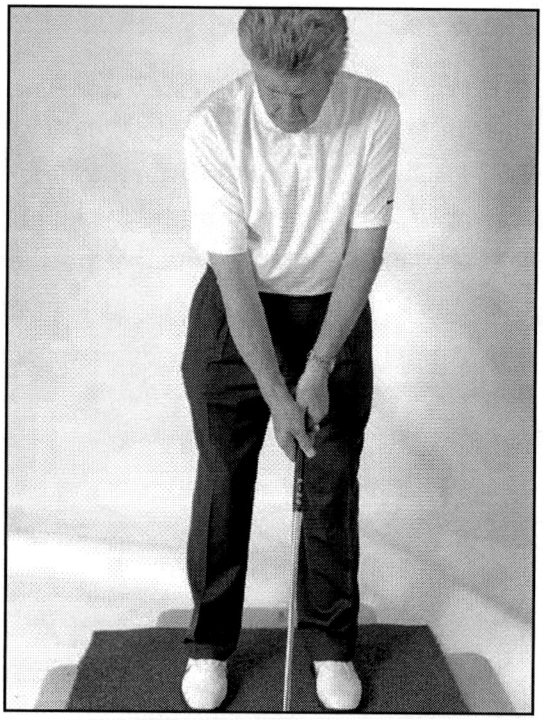

STEP 3: The next step is to then tilt the shoulders laterally upward to an upright and level position.

STEP 4: Once the shoulders are titled laterally upward to an upright and level position, the lifeline of the trail hand must be unlocked from the lead thumb by at least an inch without completely ungripping the club.

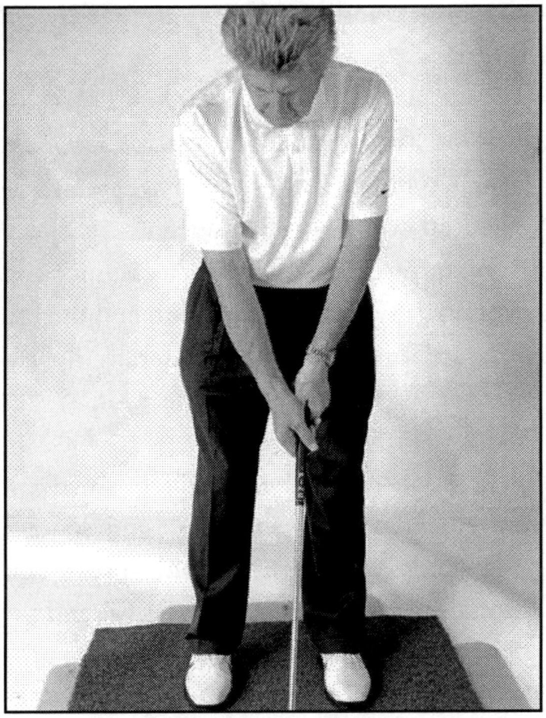

STEP 5: While the shoulders remain in an upright and level position, the lifeline of the trail hand must be relocked squarely and securely on the lead thumb. *(Then the lifeline/thumb connection must be unlocked and relocked once again.)*

is unlocked from the lead thumb by at least an inch without completely ungripping the club and then the trail lifeline is relocked on the lead thumb.

The third of the three "locks" of the lifeline/thumb connection occurs when then, once again, the lifeline of the trail hand is unlocked from the lead thumb by at least an inch without completely ungripping the club and then, once again, the lifeline of the trail hand is relocked on the lead thumb.

Eighth, once the proceedings are completed, the SHOULDERS ONLY TEST™, ARMS-LIFT TEST™ and STRAIGHT-UP TEST™ should be conducted to determine whether the technique was assembled and executed correctly and whether a straight ball flight alignment has been established and locked-in.

Why the Lateral Up-N-Lock Technique™ Works

When the shoulders are pre-tilted downward in a lateral manner as far as possible before the hands are gripped on a club and then, after the club is gripped on the club the shoulders are tilted laterally upward – back to their original pre-tilted position – the forearms will rotate the elbows to a parallel alignment with the shoulders to create an on-line swing path of the clubface.

When the elbows are aligned parallel with the shoulders the wrists correspondingly will rotate the clubface to a square alignment, all of which will establish a straight-as-an-arrow alignment.

However, the straight ball flight alignment will not be locked-in at such point. In order to lock-in the straight ball flight alignment, the lifeline/thumb connection must then be unlocked and relocked <u>twice</u> but no more thereafter.

If the lifeline/thumb connection is unlocked and relocked an additional time, the forearms will rotate the wrists, clubface and elbows to establish a different ball flight alignment.

Disciplines Required to Assemble and Execute the Lateral Up-N-Lock Technique™

The most critical discipline when performing the LATERAL UP-N-LOCK TECHNIQUE™ is to pre-tilt your shoulders downward and away from the target in a lateral manner as far as possible before gripping both hands on the club in a conventional manner. Pre-tilting the shoulders laterally downward means to tilt your shoulders sideways away from your target.

Another most important discipline is after your shoulders and spine have been pre-tilted sideways in a downward manner, away from the target, you must then assume a conventional style of grip on a club and then tilt your spine and shoulders laterally upward and back to their pre-tilted position.

When you begin the pre-tilted downward movement of your shoulders and spine in a lateral manner, you should ensure your shoulders are positioned in a level and upright manner. As a result, when you then tilt them upward in a lateral manner as far as possible, there will be sufficient room to allow the forearms to rotate the wrists, clubface and elbows to establish a straight ball flight alignment.

There may not be any connection of the elbows to the rib cage during the proceedings. If either or both elbows are connected to the rib cage during the proceedings, the forearms will not rotate the wrists, clubface and elbows to establish a straight ball flight alignment at the completion of the proceedings.

There may not be any clubface rotation during the gripping process. If the clubface rotates counterclockwise or clockwise when either the lead or trail hand is being gripped on the club or between the time the lead and trail hands are being gripped on the club, the grip should be disassembled and the procedure should begin anew.

The only clubface rotation allowed during the proceedings should be the counterclockwise rotation of the clubface when the shoulders and spine are tilted upward in a lateral manner and back to their pre-tilted and upright position.

The knees should remain inactive during the proceedings. Likewise, the arms, hands and wrists should remain passive and only move in response to the shoulders and spine being tilted upward in a lateral manner.

Another discipline is to ensure the sole of the clubface remains grounded in the middle of the stance throughout the proceedings.

A standard discipline applicable to all the LOCKED-IN TECHNIQUES™ addressed in this book is at the completion of the proceedings, the SHOULDERS ONLY TEST™, ARMS-LIFT TEST™ and STRAIGHT-UP TEST™ must be conducted to determine whether the technique was assembled and executed correctly. If not, the procedure should be repeated until a properly completed LATERAL UP-N-LOCK TECHNIQUE™ is confirmed by the three tests and, as a result, a straight ball flight alignment has been established and locked-in.

Recommended Practice Routines When Using the Lateral Up-N-Lock Technique™ in Combination with the Arrow Alignment Technique™

Once the LATERAL UP-N-LOCK TECHNIQUE™ is confirmed as properly assembled and executed and a straight ball flight has been established and locked-in, you must then center the sweet spot of your clubface as near the back of the ball as possible (if not already so centered), simultaneously align your shoulders squarely parallel with your intended target line and then execute a non-manipulative golf swing if your objective is to hit a ball on a straight path in the direction of your target.

You should use the ARROW ALIGNMENT TECHNIQUE™ to align your shoulders squarely parallel with your intended target line when practicing with the LATERAL UP-N-LOCK TECHNIQUE™.

You should locate a safe and relatively flat practice area as well as follow the steps below in each of your practice routines.

STEP 1: Place a ball on the surface of your practice area. Identify a very narrow and specific target. Also identify your intended target line.

STEP 2: Ground the sole of your clubface either directly behind your ball or in its nearby vicinity.

STEP 3: Assemble and execute the LATERAL UP-N-LOCK TECHNIQUE™ as instructed throughout this chapter. Remember to tilt your shoulders downward in a lateral manner as far as possible before assuming a conventional style of grip on your club and once your club is gripped, then tilt your shoulders upward in a lateral manner to their original upright position. Then unlock and relock your lifeline/thumb connection twice but no more thereafter.

STEP 4: Conduct the SHOULDERS ONLY TEST™, ARMS-LIFT TEST™ and STRAIGHT-UP TEST™ at the completion of your proceedings. If the clubface rotates counterclockwise or clockwise during any of the three tests, you should disassemble your grip and repeat the procedure until a properly assembled and executed LATERAL UP-N-LOCK TECHNIQUE™ is confirmed.

STEP 5: Center the sweet spot of your clubface as near the back of the ball as possible (if not already so centered) and assume a comfortable posture and stance to your ball. Align your shoulders parallel with your intended target line to the best of your ability.

STEP 6: Conduct the ARROW ALIGNMENT TECHNIQUE™ and adjust your stance, if necessary, until your alignment arrow points directly at your target when you turn your head and trail eye in the direction of your target as far as possible while immobilizing all other parts of your body.

STEP 7: Ensure the sweet spot of your clubface has remained centered as near the back of your ball as possible and execute a non-manipulative golf swing.

You should begin each practice session with your most lofted club and then with each next most lofted club in succession thereafter.

With each club you should begin with a wrist swing, then with a ½ swing, on to a ¾ swing and conclude with a full swing.

SUMMARY POINTS

1. The LATERAL UP-N-LOCK TECHNIQUE™ requires the shoulders and spine to be tilted downward in a lateral manner and away from the target as far as possible before a conventional style of grip is formed on a club.

2. The shoulders and spine then must be tilted upward in a lateral manner back to their pre-tilted position after both hands are gripped on the club.

3. The sole of the clubface should be grounded in the middle of the stance throughout the proceedings.

4. The LATERAL UP-N-LOCK TECHNIQUE™ is compatible with all four conventional golf grips, whether that of an original Vardon overlap, modified Vardon overlap, traditional interlock or regular baseball (ten-fingers) style of grip.

5. The lead hand must be gripped on the club in a conventional (diagonal) manner and must not be allowed to rotate during the gripping process.

6. The trail hand then must be assembled on the club in a conventional manner and the grip completed by locking the lifeline of the trail hand firmly on the lead thumb.

7. Once both hands are gripped on a club in a conventional manner, the shoulders and spine then must be tilted upward in a lateral manner to their original upright position.

8. **The lifeline of the trail hand then must be unlocked from the lead hand by at least an inch without completely ungripping the club and then relocked on the lead thumb to complete the proceedings.**

9. **The lifeline of the trail hand then, once again, must be unlocked from the lead thumb by at least an inch and then, once again, the lifeline of the trail hand must be relocked on the lead thumb. The lifeline/thumb connection may not be unlocked and relocked thereafter.**

10. **The SHOULDERS ONLY TEST™, ARMS-LIFT TEST™ and the STRAIGHT-UP TEST™ must be conducted at the completion of the proceedings. If the clubface rotates counterclockwise during any of the three tests, the grip should be disassembled and the procedure repeated until there is no such clubface rotation during the tests.**

11. **The ARROW ALIGNMENT TECHNIQUE™ should be conducted to align the shoulders parallel with the intended target line when using the LATERAL UP-N-LOCK TECHNIQUE™.**

CHAPTER 36

WHY THE NON-MANIPULATIVE SWING WORKS BEST

Most of what I have discussed so far in this book has been about the pre-swing proceedings. However, you could create a perfect setup in having established a straight ball alignment, ideal ball position and shoulder-to-target alignment and yet mis-hit the golf shot if a non-manipulative golf swing then is not executed.

Once any of the thirty-two techniques discussed in this book establish and lock-in a straight ball flight alignment, swinging the clubface to the outside or to the inside of its established swing path during the backswing will not rotate it to another ball flight alignment, as mentioned previously. If a non-manipulative downswing is then executed, the ball will fly on a straight path parallel with the shoulders. If the shoulders are aligned squarely parallel with the intended target line and the sweet spot of the clubface is centered as near the back of the ball as possible at final address, the ball also will fly on a straight path in the direction of the target as well as on a straight path that parallels the shoulders.

However, even though an established and locked-in straight ball flight alignment at final address will remain in tact during a backswing when the clubface is swung either to the inside or to the outside of the shoulder line, it will not remain in tact if the clubface is swung to the inside or to the outside of the shoulder line during the downswing.

Any attempt to "steer" the clubface to the inside or to the outside during the downswing, even though a straight ball flight alignment may have been established at final address, will change both the "ball position" and the shoulder alignment and cause the clubface to contact the ball with either an open or closed clubface on either an inside or outside path across the shoulder line at impact. A mis-hit golf shot will result.

Therefore, a non-manipulative golf swing must be executed both during the backswing and the downswing. If a straight ball flight alignment has been established and locked-in at the completion of the pre-swing proceedings, a manipulative backswing will not destroy the straight ball flight alignment but a manipulative downswing will.

The Reason Why It Is So Easy to Execute a Non-Manipulative Golf Swing When Using the Thirty-Two Locked-In Techniques™

The reason why it is so easy to execute a non-manipulative golf swing when using the thirty-two techniques discussed in this book is a straight ball flight alignment is both established and locked-in during the pre-swing proceedings. As a result, there must be some forced muscle-movement to swing the clubface out of its established alignment and swing path during the downswing.

This means when a straight ball flight alignment has established and locked-in, the sweet spot of the clubface has been centered as near the back of the ball as possible and the shoulders have been aligned squarely parallel with the shoulders at final address , the clubface will remain true to its alignment and swing path unless there is some intentional or inadvertent force to re-route the clubface to a different alignment and swing path during the downswing.

However, if the forearms, wrists, clubface and elbows are not locked-in to a straight ball flight alignment at final address, they easily can rotate either to the inside or to the outside of the established swing path during the golf swing and produce an errant golf shot.

A non-manipulative golf swing is one in which the forearm bones, wrists bones and elbow bones are swung in keeping with their pre-shot alignments without any intentional or inadvertent force exerted during the swing to change such alignments.

The Best Way to Execute a Non-Manipulative Golf Swing Is to Maintain a Steady Head and Planted Feet During Your Backswing

In deference to Ben Hogan and other legendary golfers who have suggested the golf shot is ninety percent completed before it even begins, such suggestions are accurate only if related to the techniques that have been addressed in the previous chapters, the thirty techniques introduced and discussed in HOW TO HIT A GOLF BALL AS STRAIGHT-AS-AN-ARROW and the twenty-eight techniques introduced and addressed in HOW GOLF WORKS.

When using any of these techniques and once the pre-shot proceedings are completed, if you merely swing the club while keeping your head steady and your feet planted during your backswing and allow your club, reflexively, to return to the ball during your downswing without any effort to re-route it, you will execute a perfect non-manipulative golf swing. However, if you have not established and locked-in a straight ball flight alignment at the completion of your pre-shot routine, you will be inclined to manipulate the clubface in some way during your golf swing in an attempt to re-route your clubface to a square alignment and on-line swing path by the time your clubface contacts your ball.

As a consequence, I am not a proponent of the "two axis" swing theory in which the center of your swing is shifted to your trail side on your backswing, then shifted back to your center and then to your lead side during your downswing. Such shifting not only requires superb tempo, timing, rhythm and balance, it also involves too much head movement to produce consistency in shot making for the average recreational and weekend golfer.

I much prefer what great players such as Jack Nicklaus and Arnold Palmer have always stressed: keep a steady head position.

This does not mean the head should not rotate somewhat during the golf swing. Jack Nicklaus purposely rotated his head before even beginning his golf swing. He however did not move his head up or down or. sideways, during his golf swing.

I do not subscribe to a habit of lifting the lead heel during the golf swing. Even though some of the greatest golfers do just that, superb tempo, timing, rhythm and balance are required so the lead heel will return precisely to its original position during the downswing, a skill that far surpasses that of the average recreational and weekend golfer.

If the Shoulders Are Not Aligned Squarely Parallel with the Intended Target Line or, if the Clubface Is Not Centered as Near the Back of the Ball as Possible at Final Address, the Natural Tendency Will Be to Manipulate the Golf Swing

As expressed numerous times throughout this book, if your shoulders are aligned squarely parallel with your intended target line and, simultaneously, the sweet spot of your clubface is centered as near the back of the ball as possible after having established and locked-in a straight ball flight alignment, a non-manipulative golf swing will produce a straight ball flight in the direction of your target as well as on a straight path parallel with your shoulder line. All you have to do is swing the golf club naturally and in a non-manipulative manner without engaging any "muscle-memory." Simply allow your muscles to move your bones in their established pre-swing alignments instead of engaging your muscles to force your bones out of their established alignments during the golf swing.

However, if you do not align your shoulders squarely parallel with your intended target line and do not have the sweet spot of your clubface centered as near the back of the ball as possible after establishing and locking-in a straight ball flight alignment at the completion of your pre-shot routine, you will tend to swing the clubface along the intended target line during the takeaway phase of your backswing. Then during the downswing, you will tend to steer the clubface down the target line which will change the "ball position" and shoulders-to-target alignment and cause the clubface to contact the ball at an oblique angle.

This is why you have been encouraged throughout the book to learn how to conduct the ARROW ALIGNMENT TECHNIQUE™ and to use it each and every time in your pre-shot routine. You should find it to be the most reliable means to align your shoulders squarely parallel with your intended target line during your pre-shot routine.

Posture Is a Product of Ball Position and Stance Instead of Ball Position and Stance Being a Product of Posture When the Locked-In Techniques™ Are Used

How far you stand from your ball, how wide your stance and the position of your ball in relation to your stance will determine your posture rather than, vice-versa, assuming you have established and locked-in a straight ball flight alignment at the completion of your pre-shot routine.

Certainly, you may flex your knees up or down more or less or incline your spine up or down more or less, all of which will influence your posture in relation to your ball to some extent.

Notwithstanding, what most influences and determines your posture when using the thirty-two LOCKED-IN TECHNIQUES™ addressed in this book is the width of your stance, angle of your stance and how far you stand from the ball when you center your clubface as near the back of the ball as possible at the completion of you pre-swing routine.

Whether you then want your knees flexed up or down more or less or your spine (shoulders) inclined up or down more or less is your own personal choice.

As long as you have established and locked-in a straight ball flight alignment, centered the sweet spot of your clubface as near the back of the ball as possible and, simultaneously, aligned your shoulders parallel with your intended target line at final address, followed by a non-manipulative golf swing, your posture should not affect the direction of your ball flight to any significant extent, although it could influence the trajectory of your ball in flight. This proposition however does not apply unless a straight ball flight alignment is established and locked-in at final address.

Unless your forearms have rotated your wrists, clubface and elbows to establish a straight ball flight alignment and then such alignment is locked-in at the completion of the pre-shot proceedings, practically any body movement thereafter will rotate your forearms, wrists, clubface and elbows to some extent and most likely to a different ball flight alignment during the pre-shot proceedings.

As a general proposition, the less your spine is inclined downward, the taller you stand to the ball which, in turn, creates a steeper swing path. In contrast, the more your spine is inclined downward, the shorter you stand to the ball which, in turn, creates a shallower swing path.

Likewise, the farther you stand from the ball, the shorter you stand to the ball which also creates a shallower swing path. In contrast, the nearer you stand to the ball, the taller you stand to the ball which, in turn, creates a steeper swing path.

These are all personal choices, depending on your comfort level and also how high or low you wish to hit your ball. It also depends on the lie angle of your club.

There are many factors that influence the trajectory (height) of the ball, such as club selection, clubhead speed, ball position, how high on the clubface the ball is struck but, also, how far you stand from the ball, the width of your stance, angle of your stance and the angle of your feet in relation to your target and target line.

These are all part of golf course management.

The purpose of this book, however, is devoted to overcoming the "Vardon Curse." Its objective has been to teach you thirty-two different techniques to establish and lock-in a straight ball flight alignment, then to center your clubface as near the back of the ball as possible and simultaneously align your shoulders squarely parallel with your intended target line at the completion of your pre-shot routine so that a non-manipulative golf swing will flight your ball on a straight path in the direction of your target.

Club selection, stance width, how far to stand from the ball, posture, and so on, will be dictated by the type of golf shot you will need to produce. Your first priority, however, is to forever rid yourself of the "Vardon Curse." Then all other such matters will take care of themselves.

Variety Is the "Spice of Life" in Terms of the Thirty-Two Locked-In Techniques™ Addressed in This Book

I do not expect you to spend an equal amount of time in learning and mastering each of the thirty-two LOCKED-IN TECHNIQUES™ discussed in this book. Nonetheless, they are your's for the taking.

I predict you will have as much enjoyment in experimenting with each of them as you will have in choosing the one you eventually will come to prefer.

I may have created less anxiety and frustration on your part had I chosen only one of the thirty-two techniques and addressed it alone in this book. Had I done so, however, I would not have provided you with the choices you now have.

Frankly, I would have suffered a certain amount of anxiety and frustration of my own had I been forced to address only one of the thirty-two LOCKED-IN TECHNIQUES™ in this book. How could I possibly pre-judge and predict the one that you eventually will come to prefer.

That is why I have made all thirty-two available to you.

Your enjoyment now will derive from experimenting with all thirty-two as well as selecting the one you eventually will come to prefer.

ABOUT THE AUTHOR

Gordon Jackson is a lifelong student of golf and is the author of six instructional books about the game, including

- **HOW TO HIT A GOLF BALL AS STRAIGHT-AS-AN-ARROW**
- **HOW GOLF WORKS**
- **THE JACKSON GOLF METHOD**
- **HOW TO SHAPE GOLF SHOTS**
- **HOW TO LOCK-IN A PERFECT PUTT**
- **HOW TO LOCK-IN A PERFECT GOLF SWING**

After thousands of experiments, he was the first to discover the fundamental flaw of golf which he characterizes as the "Vardon Curse." That is, the instant a conventional style of grip is formed on a golf club – whether that of an original Vardon overlap, modified Vardon overlap, traditional interlock or a regular baseball (ten-fingers) – the forearms will rotate the wrists and elbows to create a slice alignment of the clubface and its swing path.

Since such discovery, he has developed more than 150 techniques to convert a slice alignment to a square alignment and, in turn, to establish, lock-in and produce straight golf shots. Thirty-two of these techniques are addressed in this book. In addition, he has developed a new and revolutionary technique to align the shoulders squarely parallel with the target line, an essential requirement if the objective is to flight a ball on a straight path to the intended target. The Arrow Alignment Technique™ likewise is addressed in this book.

He also has developed three innovative tests to determine whether a square clubface and an on-line swing path are established and locked-in at final address.

The Shoulders Only Test™, Arms-Life Test™ and Straight-Up Test™ also are addressed in this book.

He currently is working on his seventh instructional book, HOW TO MASTER THE LOCKED-IN SHORT GAME, all of which books are designed to transform golf from a "GAME OF GUESS TO A GAME OF SUCCESS."